Trustworthy AI

Artificial intelligence is reshaping decisions that affect people, institutions, and societies. Understanding how to design, deploy, and govern AI systems that can be trusted is now essential in many disciplines. This book offers a clear, concise introduction to trustworthy AI, treating AI not just as a technical artifact but as a socio-technical system embedded in human contexts. Developed from an internationally applicable educational framework, the book is designed for teaching and learning in computer science, data science, law, policy, business, and related fields. It equips students and professionals with the concepts and judgment needed to engage critically and responsibly with AI in practice. Combining ethics, governance, and practical insight, the book explains key concepts, including transparency, fairness, accountability, human oversight, and stakeholder participation. An interdisciplinary approach makes the material accessible to both technical and nontechnical audiences, with realistic scenarios and reflection questions so readers connect principles to real-world AI applications.

Andrea Aler Tubella is a researcher specializing in responsible artificial intelligence, logic, and the societal impact of technology. Dr. Aler Tubella's research is grounded in the intersection of formal logic and AI ethics. Her research includes design, impact, and education around AI, with a particular interest in multidisciplinary perspectives, and how collaboration and insights from various disciplines can inform and improve the impacts of intelligent systems.

Virginia Dignum is Professor of Responsible Artificial Intelligence at Umeå University, Sweden. She is a leading voice in global AI policy, chairing the ACM Technology Policy Council, co-chairing the IEEE Global Initiative on the Ethics of Autonomous Systems, and advising the Wallenberg Foundations in Sweden. She is a member of expert groups at UNESCO and the OECD, and was part of the EU's High-Level Expert Group on AI, the UN's High Level Advisory Body on AI, and the World Economic Forum Global Future Council on Artificial Intelligence.

Marçal Mora-Cantallops is Professor in the Computer Science Department at the University of Alcalá. As a researcher, he focuses on machine learning, social network analysis, data science, ethical AI, and game studies, having authored and published multiple related articles in the past few years. He also coordinated the Trustworthy AI Erasmus+ project.

Juan Carlos Nieves is Associate Professor at Umeå University, where he teaches and directs the Master's Programme in Artificial Intelligence. He has substantial experience bridging theoretical perspectives on trustworthy AI with real-world industrial practices, reflecting his focus on socially aware and ethically grounded intelligent systems. He has served as an external ethical advisor and reviewer for EU projects and as an expert evaluator for various European national research councils.

Andreas Theodorou's work focuses on the techniques and tools needed for the design, implementation, and deployment of intelligent autonomous systems, such as to ensure their trustworthiness. Prior to his move to industry, Dr. Theodorou held teaching and research positions at multiple institutions, including Universitat Politècnica de Catalunya·BarcelonaTech (Spain), Umeå University (Sweden), and University of Bath (UK).

"In a field evolving as fast as AI, this book stands out. It pairs clear ethical foundations with practical guidance. Its emphasis on responsibility and real-world tools make it an essential companion for anyone building AI systems."

Toby Walsh, AI Institute and School of Computer Science and Engineering, UNSW Sydney

Trustworthy AI

Ethical Frameworks for Responsible Innovation

ANDREA ALER TUBELLA
i2CAT

VIRGINIA DIGNUM
Umeå University, Sweden

MARÇAL MORA-CANTALLOPS
University of Alcalá, Spain

JUAN CARLOS NIEVES
Umeå University, Sweden

ANDREAS THEODOROU
Umeå University, Sweden

CAMBRIDGE
UNIVERSITY PRESS

CAMBRIDGE
UNIVERSITY PRESS

Shaftesbury Road, Cambridge CB2 8EA, United Kingdom

One Liberty Plaza, 20th Floor, New York, NY 10006, USA

477 Williamstown Road, Port Melbourne, VIC 3207, Australia

314–321, 3rd Floor, Plot 3, Splendor Forum, Jasola District Centre, New Delhi – 110025, India

Cambridge University Press is part of Cambridge University Press & Assessment, a department of the University of Cambridge.

We share the University's mission to contribute to society through the pursuit of education, learning and research at the highest international levels of excellence.

www.cambridge.org
Information on this title: www.cambridge.org/highereducation/isbn/9781009492867
DOI: 10.1017/9781009492843

When citing this work, please include a reference to the DOI 10.1017/9781009492843

First published 2027

Cover image: Eugene Mymrin / Moment / Getty Images.

A catalogue record for this publication is available from the British Library

Library of Congress Cataloging-in-Publication Data

ISBN 978-1-009-49286-7 Hardback

Additional resources for this publication at www.cambridge.org/TrustworthyAI

Contents

Preface

Artificial intelligence is transforming societies at unprecedented speed, reshaping work, education, governance, and everyday life. With this transformation come profound ethical, legal, and social questions about who benefits from AI, who is harmed, and how human agency and fundamental rights can be protected in an age of automation. Trust in technology cannot be assumed; it must be earned through systems and institutions that are transparent, fair, accountable, and aligned with democratic values.

This book was developed to support that imperative by offering a comprehensive, interdisciplinary foundation for understanding and practicing trustworthy AI. It draws on research, policy frameworks, and educational innovations that bridge technical AI capabilities with ethical reflection and societal responsibility. It treats AI not merely as a set of algorithms, but as socio-technical systems embedded in human contexts – systems whose effects depend on the values, choices, and actions of the people and organizations that design, deploy, and govern them.

The origins of this work lie in the EU-funded Trustworthy AI project, an Erasmus+ initiative that developed the Framework for Trustworthy AI Education. While rooted in the European context, the framework was intentionally designed to be applicable well beyond Europe. It translates widely shared ethical principles for AI – such as respect for human rights, fairness, transparency, accountability, and human oversight – into practical learning strategies and competencies that are relevant across cultural, legal, and institutional settings. Drawing on the European Commission's High-Level Expert Group's Guidelines on Trustworthy AI as a concrete reference point, the framework supports the integration of ethical and socio-legal dimensions of AI into higher education worldwide. Its goal is to equip future professionals, not only in technical disciplines, but also in law, policy, medicine, business, and related fields, with the capacity to critically assess AI's risks, benefits, and societal implications in diverse global contexts.

The content is structured to guide readers from foundational concepts to practical tools. Early chapters introduce the meaning of trustworthy AI, its relationship to responsible AI, and its grounding in ethics and philosophy. The book then examines how narratives about AI influence public perception, expectations, and policy debates, and clarifies the roles and responsibilities of professionals, organizations, and citizens in the AI ecosystem. Governance, regulation, and institutional accountability are explored as essential mechanisms for translating ethical principles into practice.

Subsequent chapters address key dimensions of trustworthiness in depth, including harms, transparency and explainability, fairness and bias, accountability and responsibility, social and environmental well-being, and stakeholder participation. These themes are treated not as isolated requirements, but as interconnected concerns that often involve trade-offs and contextual judgment. The later chapters focus on human–AI interaction, engineering processes, control frameworks, data governance, and assessment tools, providing practical approaches for embedding trustworthiness throughout the AI lifecycle.

The book is written for a broad audience: students, educators, AI practitioners, policymakers, managers, and anyone seeking a structured understanding of what it means to develop, deploy, and use AI responsibly. Its aim is not to provide definitive answers, but to equip readers with concepts, frameworks, and questions that support informed decision-making. By fostering a shared language and critical perspective, this book contributes to building a culture in which AI systems can be trusted because the people and institutions behind them act responsibly, transparently, and with due regard for societal values.

1 What Is Trustworthy AI?

1.1 Learning Objectives

Chapter 1 mostly aligns with the "Appreciation" and "Analysis" stages, providing foundational knowledge and encouraging students to critically evaluate AI systems and their societal impacts. The learning objectives of this chapter are:

- Appreciation (Bloom's remember): Be able to recall and describe the key concepts and principles of trustworthy AI, differentiating it from general AI and responsible AI.
- Appreciation (Bloom's understand): Be able to explain the societal impacts of AI, and understand the ethical considerations in the development and deployment of AI systems.
- Analysis (Bloom's analyze): Be able to analyze in broad lines case studies or real-world examples of AI systems, evaluating their adherence to the principles of trustworthy AI, such as fairness, transparency, and accountability.
- Analysis (Bloom's evaluate): Be able to critically assess the effectiveness of various strategies and practices to ensure the development of trustworthy AI, including ethical guidelines and regulations.
- Application (Bloom's apply): Be able to generically apply the principles of trustworthy AI to hypothetical scenarios, demonstrating an ability to identify ethical issues and suggest appropriate solutions.

1.2 Introduction

On a busy Monday morning, a recruitment platform powered by artificial intelligence (AI) screens thousands of job applications within minutes. Its decisions determine who is invited for an interview and who is silently excluded. For the employer, the system promises efficiency. For the applicants, it may open doors or close them unfairly. Was the AI trained on representative data? Can its choices be explained? And should an algorithm be making these decisions in the first place? This simple example illustrates why questions of responsibility and trust are central to the debate on AI. These are the questions that we will explore throughout this book.

In an era where AI increasingly shapes the ways we live, work, and interact, the notion of **trustworthy AI** has moved beyond a buzzword to become a fundamental necessity. Yet trustworthiness is only part of the story. **Responsible AI** and **trustworthy AI** are closely related but not identical. Responsible AI refers to the development and use of AI systems in ways that align with ethical principles, societal values, and legal requirements. It highlights the moral dimensions of AI, including respect for human rights, equity, fairness, and the well-being of individuals and communities. Trustworthy AI, in contrast, is more technical and operational: it addresses reliability, safety, robustness, transparency, and explainability. It ensures that stakeholders and users can have confidence in how an AI system behaves, even under adverse conditions. Responsible AI therefore encompasses trustworthiness; trustworthy AI is what makes responsible AI possible. At the same time, responsible AI goes further by holding people, organizations, and institutions accountable, ensuring that AI is not only built well, but also built for good [30].

AI technologies have extended well beyond tech-centric domains, and are currently routinely used in healthcare, finance, and education, and even shape our daily social interactions [3, 68, 121]. With such widespread applications, understanding the principles that make AI trustworthy – ethical, transparent, reliable, and fair – is paramount. This book aims to dissect these principles, offering a comprehensive guide on how to embed them in diverse AI applications.

Automated decision-making processes can have profound ethical implications. From facial recognition to predictive policing, the potential for bias and discrimination is a significant concern. At the same time, as AI evolves, so does the legal landscape around it. Navigating this complex regulatory environment is essential for developers and businesses alike.

Moreover, trust in AI systems is directly related to their transparency and the ability to explain their decisions. Methods and best practices for creating transparent AI systems that users can understand and trust are therefore paramount for the beneficial use of AI, in particular given that the vast amounts of sensitive data required by many of the current AI techniques require guarantees that systems are secure and respect user privacy.

As AI continues to evolve, staying ahead of the curve is crucial. This does not mean that innovation should take priority over trustworthiness and responsibility. On the contrary! Taking trustworthiness and responsibility as the cornerstone for AI development is crucial for innovation. Trustworthiness guidelines not only spur AI developments in responsible and beneficial directions, but also open up new research and innovation opportunities to define, develop, and implement methods, tools, and frameworks to support the principles they stand for. The path is wide open for innovations in explainable AI, fairness and bias detection and prevention, inclusion and access, and many more areas.

In conclusion, this book on trustworthy AI is not just nice to have; it is essential. It will serve as a guide for practitioners, policymakers, and the general public to navigate the complex, ever-evolving world of AI with a clear understanding of how to harness its benefits ethically, responsibly, and effectively.

1.3 What Is Trustworthy AI?

Artificial intelligence is commonly defined as the discipline of building systems that can perform tasks which, if carried out by humans, would require intelligence [124]. This technical view focuses on problem-solving, reasoning, and decision-making. AI is also a set of computational techniques that can automate tasks and support decision-making processes. Yet AI is never only a technical artifact. Its design, deployment, and impact are deeply shaped by the social, institutional, and cultural contexts in which it is embedded [111]. Rather than being a socio-technical system in itself, AI should be understood as part of broader socio-technical systems that include people, institutions, infrastructures, norms, and practices [35].

This perspective highlights that the impact of AI arises not only from its technical design, but also from the social contexts in which it is embedded and used. In this book we therefore adopt a perspective that considers AI both as a set of computational techniques and as elements within wider social arrangements.

A socio-technical system is an approach to complex organizational work design that recognizes the interaction between people (social) and technology in workplaces [18]. It considers how social factors and technological components work together within an organizational environment to influence outcomes, recognizing the interaction between people and technology, and how complex infrastructures affect and are affected by society and by human behavior. As such, AI is about the structures of power, participation, and access to technology that determine who can influence which decisions or actions are being automated, which data, knowledge, and resources are used to learn from, and how interactions between those that decide and those that are impacted are defined and maintained.

The concepts of "responsible AI" and "trustworthy AI" are commonly used in the context of AI ethics and governance. While there is substantial overlap between the concepts they represent, there are also distinctions in emphasis between responsible AI and trustworthy AI.

The main focus of *responsible AI* is ensuring that AI systems are developed, deployed, and used in a manner that is ethically sound, respects human rights, and considers societal implications. This encompasses not just ethical and legal considerations, but also the socio-technical aspects that ensure that accountability for the development and use of the AI system is guaranteed. Responsible AI practices often involve processes and guidelines that organizations follow during the design, development, and deployment stages of AI systems. This could include impact assessments, reviews, and monitoring of AI systems in real-world applications. In addition, and above all, a responsible approach to AI makes clear that AI systems are artifacts manufactured by people for some purpose, and that those who make these have the power to decide on the use of AI.

Trustworthy AI emphasizes the reliability, safety, and robustness of AI systems, in addition to their ethical implications. The goal is to ensure that users and stakeholders can have confidence in AI systems' decisions and behaviors. This might involve ensuring an AI system functions correctly under various conditions, is robust against adversarial attacks, and can explain its decisions in understandable terms. Trustworthiness often requires technical solutions, such as robustness testing, adversarial training, and explainability methods, in addition to governance and ethical guidelines.

Generally, a trustworthy approach to AI will ensure transparency about how adaptation is done, responsibility for the level of automation at which the system is able to reason, and accountability for the results and the principles that guide its interactions with others, most importantly with people.

Guidelines, principles, and strategies to ensure trust and responsibility in AI refer to the socio-technical ecosystem in which AI is developed and used. It is not the AI artifact or application that needs to be ethical, trustworthy, or responsible. Rather, it is the people, organizations, and institutions involved that can and should take responsibility and act in consideration of an ethical framework such that the overall system can be trusted by users and society.

In this sense, trustworthy AI is not, as some may claim, a way to give machines some kind of "responsibility" for their actions and decisions, and in the process discharge people and organizations of their own responsibilities. On the contrary, trustworthy AI approaches give the people and organizations involved *more* responsibility and accountability: for the decisions and actions of the AI applications, and for their own decision to use AI in a given context. Only then can the actions and results of the machines be trusted.

Imagine a hospital considering whether to introduce an AI system to support end-of-life care decisions. The system could analyze vast amounts of patient data and suggest treatment options. Yet such decisions are not only medical but deeply personal and ethical. Should the hospital adopt AI in this context at all, or are some choices so closely tied to human dignity and responsibility that automation is inappropriate?

This is what has been called *Question Zero*: not how to design or regulate AI, but whether AI should be used at all in a given context. In some situations the most responsible choice may be to not use AI – for example, where human judgment, accountability, or dignity cannot be meaningfully supported by automation. It requires a careful consideration of AI's effectiveness, its impact on fundamental rights, and the feasibility of alternative solutions. This comprehensive approach ensures that AI applications are not only technologically sound, but also ethically and socially responsible. Jumping directly to the issue of *how* to use AI assumes its use is always justified and ignores what may be lost when human practices are replaced by automated ones.

Applying Question Zero in trustworthy AI can be exemplified through various scenarios. For example, in healthcare, before implementing an AI system for diagnosing diseases, Question Zero would prompt considerations such as: Is AI more accurate or efficient than existing methods? Does it respect patient privacy and make ethically sound decisions? In recruitment, when screening job applicants, Question Zero would lead to reflection on whether the AI system introduces bias against certain groups, and researching alternatives that are more transparent and fair manual methods. The outcome could be to combine AI with human judgment for a more balanced approach. Similarly, in law enforcement, using AI for predictive policing involves scrutinizing its predictive capabilities for fairness and respect for individual rights. In all scenarios, the outcomes of these evaluations could range from adopting AI with improvements to opting for traditional methods, depending on the ethical and practical implications identified.

1.4 Trustworthy AI Is Not a Choice

Trustworthy AI is not a choice, it is the only viable way to develop and use this technology. Moreover, it is not so that efforts toward responsibility and ethics are contrary to innovation. The word "innovation" is often used as shorthand for improved technical, economic, and social processes. It is also associated with the "right" to use existing technology in different applications and directions. For some, regulation of technology should be avoided in case it hinders technical innovation, while others see regulation as essential to mitigate risks on the path to innovation. However, regulation and innovation are not a zero-sum game. In particular, innovation is currently much needed in AI governance, devising ways to achieve governance and trust, through innovations in soft and hard regulation, standards, organizational structures, and training and awareness.

In some cases, regulation has been slow to respond to appetites and opportunities for technical innovation, perhaps because of inexperience or protectionism. At other times, regulations encouraging the adoption of "best available techniques" have promoted short-term innovation at the expense of more ambitious transformative innovation. Any specific innovation involves the redistribution of costs and benefits in ways that are not always welcomed by everyone and may only be revealed years later.

Regulation is then important in establishing the conditions and context of innovation, including as regards labor, capital, certainty, and competition. By employing a combination of carrot and stick, regulation can incentivize specific AI applications to reap their benefits and seize the opportunities they offer, while restraining specific AI applications in order to mitigate their risks. But most importantly, a responsible approach to AI development and use will not only lead to trust and public acceptance, but will drive transformation and business differentiation, as well as explorative fundamental research. However, it is the responsibility of the regulators to avoid a "legal spaghetti" and provide support and incentives for research and businesses to understand and comply with existing regulation.

Responsible and trustworthy innovation in AI requires addressing these issues across the whole project lifecycle. By taking a responsible approach, organizations will be able to:

- develop and use AI systems that are efficient and compatible with regulations;
- ensure that development processes consider all the ethical, legal, and societal implications of AI;
- track and mitigate bias in data and AI models;
- build trust in AI;
- prevent or minimize negative effects of AI; and
- ensure clear accountability processes in case something goes wrong.

AI governance efforts are set within a complex space of ethics and regulations. This may appear to create extreme extra work for proposals, projects, and participating organizations to comply. All in all, a panoply of legal rules and conventions already regulates the multifaceted world of AI. In different countries and regions, multiple legal provisions already govern several aspects of AI innovation, such as the processing of personal data through AI systems. Every model of AI governance must therefore accommodate existing laws and regulations.

1.5 Develop a Culture of Trustworthy AI

A culture of trustworthy AI starts with awareness. This means that individuals and organizations should not only realize that the systems and tools they are developing and/or use have impacts on society and people's lives and transform cultural and ethical principles, but also need to be aware that all of us have our own interpretations of different principles, and have our own (unconscious) biases. Questions such as "What does fairness, agency, or well-being mean to you?" or "How does that impact the processes and objectives of your project or organization?" are answered differently by different stakeholders and at different moments.

Cultivating a culture of trustworthy AI contributes to demonstrating due diligence and alignment with principles and regulations. From a more technical perspective, responsible AI can lead to higher transparency and trust, by focusing on verifiable AI results. It will lead to competitive advantage as the results and processes can be guaranteed to be aligned with EU expectations and requirements. At the base of a responsible approach to AI governance are the trustworthy AI principles proposed by the European High Level Expert Group on AI [134]:

- human agency and oversight, including fundamental rights;
- technical robustness and safety, including resilience to attack and security, fallback plan and general safety, accuracy, reliability and reproducibility, and addressing possibility of dual use;
- privacy and data governance, including respect for privacy, quality and integrity of data, and access to data;
- transparency, including traceability, explainability, and communication;
- Diversity, non-discrimination, and fairness, including the avoidance of unfair bias, accessibility and universal design, and stakeholder participation;
- societal and environmental well-being, including sustainability and environmental friendliness, social impact, society, and democracy; and
- accountability, including auditability, minimization and reporting of negative impacts, trade-offs, and redress.

Implementing these requirements will promote AI that is innovative and trustworthy and that respects human rights and democratic values. That is, it will ensure that AI systems are developed, deployed, and used in ways that adhere to the ethical principles of respect for human autonomy, prevention of harm, fairness, and explanation.

It is, however, important to recognize that there are potential tensions between these principles, and that in cases where it is necessary to make choices, proposals, projects, and participating organizations should be responsible for their prioritization of these principles.

Developing and implementing AI systems responsibly is essential, considering the profound ethical implications within areas such as data privacy and algorithmic bias. These considerations extend beyond mere technical efficiency to encompass wider societal impacts. Embracing these ethical principles in AI development is not just a technological requirement, but a moral imperative, ensuring that advancements in AI are aligned with societal values and norms. The goal is to not only enhance technical skills in AI, but also to foster an ethical mindset, encouraging a responsible approach to AI across various professional fields. This approach underlines the importance of integrating responsible AI practices within organizational structures, guiding the development and application of AI in a manner that upholds ethical standards and societal well-being.

The remainder of this section focuses on defining and instituting responsible AI within organizations, encompassing several key steps:

- Defining trustworthy AI: Collaborating among top managers and executives to draft principles guiding AI design and use. This includes documenting all steps in the decision and development process, communicating governance principles throughout the development supply chain, ensuring organizational sensitivity to AI's impacts, and maintaining company-wide standards, including shared code repositories and approved model architectures.
- Ensuring training and AI education: Building values for responsible AI solutions and distributing them across the organization. It is crucial to educate various teams on how AI decisions are made, the potential for harm in data and algorithms, and issues beyond data quality and privacy, such as sustainability and user interaction with AI.
- Establishing internal governance structures: Setting up roles and responsibilities for AI oversight, including risk management, maintenance, and staff training in AI systems.
- Implementing risk management procedures: Extending existing risk management to cover AI, including evaluating datasets for bias, monitoring AI performance, and ensuring knowledge transfer during personnel changes.
- Integrating available tools: Evolving machine learning pipelines to align with responsible AI principles, utilizing methods and tools from third parties where appropriate.

This comprehensive approach is designed to embed responsible AI practices deeply into the organizational fabric, ensuring ethical, transparent, and effective use of AI technologies.

1.6 Questions and Exercises

1. **Multiple choice question.** What is a key principle of trustworthy AI?
   (a) Cost-effectiveness
   (b) Transparency
   (c) Speed of computation
   (d) Aesthetic design
2. **Multiple choice question.** Which of the following is an essential factor to consider when ensuring an AI system is trustworthy?
   (a) The color scheme of the user interface
   (b) The programming language used to code the AI
   (c) The diversity and representativeness of the training data
   (d) The ethical implications of its potential uses in various industries
3. **True or false question.** Trustworthy AI and responsible AI are identical concepts with no distinct differences.
   - True
   - False
4. **Short answer question.** Explain in a few sentences the importance of fairness in AI systems, particularly in the context of societal impact.
5. **Reflection activity.** Reflect on your own interactions with AI systems in daily life. Identify instances where trustworthiness and ethics might be a concern, and discuss how you would like these systems to be improved from an ethical standpoint.
6. **Essay question.** Compare and contrast the concepts of trustworthy AI and responsible AI. Discuss how these concepts intersect and diverge in terms of ethical considerations and societal impact.
7. **Discussion assignment.** In groups, debate the ethical implications of deploying AI systems in sensitive areas such as healthcare and criminal justice. Consider aspects such as bias, transparency, and the potential for harm.
8. **Case study analysis.** Analyze a real-world example of an AI system being deployed. Evaluate its adherence to the principles of trustworthy AI, such as transparency, fairness, and accountability. Suggest improvements or alternatives based on your analysis.
9. **Problem-solving exercise.** Using Question Zero, propose a design for an AI system that prioritizes ethical considerations, such as user privacy and data security.

2 Ethics and Philosophy

2.1 Learning Objectives

This chapter deals with the "Appreciation" stage, focusing on the interplay between AI and philosophy and providing an introduction to ethics from a philosophical perspective. The learning objectives of this chapter are:

- Appreciation (Bloom's remember): Identify different ethical frameworks.
- Analysis (Bloom's analyze): Categorize AI systems within the different categories of ethical agents.
- Analysis (Bloom's analyze): Argue on the topic of moral agency and AI.
- Application (Bloom's apply): Taxonomize the different tools presented in this book based on how they deal with ethics.

2.2 Introduction

As a field, artificial intelligence (AI) since its inception has had multiple intersections with philosophy. The use of AI for modeling has enabled us to explore questions around emergence and epistemology, but also the development of AI systems has fascinated philosophers and encouraged them to rethink centuries-old questions around consciousness, moral agency, and free will. AI brings a new dimension to these discussions by challenging our understanding of what it means to be conscious or to have a mind. Questions arise about whether machines can possess consciousness, intentionality, or subjective experiences.

If they do, then the question of agency becomes crucial as we may start to consider AI systems as *moral agents*. Doing so requires a holistic examination of both morality and its legal ramifications. Moreover, we will need to rethink what responsibility really is and how to attribute accountability to manufactured entities.

2.3 Morality and Ethics

The terms *morality* and *ethics* are frequently used interchangeably. In reality, they have distinct origins – as one is Greek and the other is Latin – and have different nuances on what exactly they refer to.

Morality originates from the Latin word *moralitas*, which means *proper behavior*. Moralitas relates to the Latin word *mores*,[1] which in turn refers to the social norms of a society (i.e., the "proper" way of behaving within it). In other words, morality relies on what a society has defined as acceptable or unacceptable behavior.

Ethics has Greek origins: It is derived from the word *ethos* (ήθος), which refers to one's character. Essentially, an ethos is a structured system of values that *characterize* what a particular person considers to be *right*. Those values may be customs, accepted by society, or other personally held beliefs. It would be fair to say that ethics is a more esoteric system of different values that could guide one's behavior.

These nuances are exacerbated when comparing different ethics frameworks, such as virtue and deontological ethics. They highlight how differently an individual and wider society may perceive what is right or wrong. However, once a critical mass of individuals with the same perception is achieved, society may also change its social norms.

2.3.1 Ethical Frameworks

Multiple frameworks have been suggested over the centuries. It is not for this book to argue in favor of any of them, but a short summary is provided in this section. To best illustrate the different frameworks, we will use a running example: an AI developer, Emily, who works at GreatAI. She found out that the company she is working for uses illegally sourced data, full of social biases, on an upcoming AI product. The company's leadership has decided to proceed with the launch of the product to avoid financial losses that could lead to layoffs. Emily is facing dilemma: whether to be a whistleblower and reveal to the authorities and public the actions of GreatAI. Let's explore three major ethics frameworks – virtue ethics deontological ethics, and consequentialism – and how they could be used to help Emily make a decision.

Virtue Ethics

Rooted in Aristotelian philosophy, virtue ethics emphasizes the development of good character traits or virtues. Rather than focusing solely on actions or outcomes, this Aristotelian approach focuses on what kind of person one should be by cultivation of virtuous traits (e.g., honesty) to guide their actions. In a virtue ethics framework, Emily believes in acting with integrity by being honest and transparent. Emily embodies these virtues in her daily interactions and realizes that GreatAI does not. She comes to an understanding that whistleblowing is the only way to grow her virtues and keep her focus on being a good person and force for good, regardless of others around her. Emily's whistleblowing is not based on a rigid set of rules or consideration of the consequences of her actions; instead, she acts in a way that reflects her virtuous character.

[1] The plural form of *mōs*.

Deontological Ethics

While there are multiple deontological ethics frameworks, the most well known one is Kantian ethics – named after Immanuel Kant [84]. This rule-based ethical framework suggests that the ability to act according to universal moral laws (i.e., mores) derives from rational deliberation, respecting the autonomy and dignity of oneself and others. The morality of an action is judged based on whether it follows these rules, regardless of its consequences. As a person who follows deontological ethics, Emily believes that following the law, honesty, and societal fairness are fundamental duties that should be upheld regardless of the consequences of upholding them. Her actions are guided by what she perceives as basic societal rules: be honest and respect others. Only by following her societal obligations does Emily consider her actions to be morally right.

Consequentialism Ethics

Consequentialism judges actions by their outcomes – for a consequentialist, the popular saying "the ends justify the means" holds true. The most well-known form, *utilitarianism*, evaluates actions based on their ability to maximize a utility function. The utility function is usually associated with the happiness and well-being of those affected by the action to be taken. In other words, by performing actions to maximize the utility function, a utilitarian acts toward the greatest good for the greatest number of individuals. As a utilitarian, Emily does not hesitate to report GreatAI after deliberating on the consequences of her action. If she reports the company, it may lead to a potential fallout for herself, the company, or even innocent employees of the company who had nothing to do with the project. However, if she does not, the product may affect thousands, if not millions, of people – as its data sourcing already did. She concludes that stopping the launch of the AI product, either through regulatory intervention or public outcry, may have some negative effects to some people but that is a small price against the well-being of society at large.

2.3.2 Ethics in Decision-Making and Society

Ethics play a crucial role in action selection, guiding individuals and organizations in making decisions that align with moral values and societal norms. When choosing how to act, ethical considerations help ensure that actions are justifiable, responsible, and aligned with broader social and moral expectations. In fact, the type of reasoning (i.e., the conclusions based on some premises or evidence) associated with action selection is called *practical reasoning* and involves not only deliberating about actions as a response to some stimuli, but also reflecting upon the consequences of the different choices. Practical reasoning frequently requires considering moral principles and assessing how actions align with one's moral values.

In the whistleblowing example given previously, we saw how the different ethical frameworks affected Emily's reasoning. They guided her behavior by providing prompts in favor of acting as a whistleblower and by eliminating different variables for consideration (e.g., the consequences of her action). In other words, the different ethical frameworks provide us with premises and limit our search space. This sort of guidance is crucial in helping us weigh options and choose actions. By guiding actions toward what is good and just, ethics contributes to the overall well-being and flourishing of individuals and society.

As Brooks said, "The world is its own best model" to best characterize the complexity of the real world [21]. Despite the existence of multiple ethical frameworks, people do not always adhere to moral reasoning. Moreover, usually people follow – or even switch between – different frameworks as the context around them changes. Still, as the "Moral Machine" – a large-scale experiment on moral judgment – suggests, different societies share certain ethical values [13].

Such shared values are the product of a complex interplay of influences from family, culture, education, religion, peers, media, and role models. Personal experiences and self-reflection produce some variations in shared values, but, as Kant would argue, certain universal values exist within each society. They help us model each other and, predict and understand the actions of others. They promote social harmony and trust, which are essential for the functioning of communities and societies.

In fact, as we discuss further in Chapter 5, shared values become essential parts of governance. Professional bodies issue ethical guidelines and standards that are indispensable in professional settings. They ensure trust, accountability, fairness, and the protection of both consumers and the wider public. Moreover, the values that a society wants to protect as a whole form the basis of its criminal law. Hence, criminal law is never static. Societies and their values evolve, and so do their laws.

2.4 Moral and Ethical Agents

The concept of agency is fundamentally linked to the ability to perform actions. Essentially, we consider entity *X* an agent only if *X* possesses the capability to carry out actions to change its state and/or the environment *X* inhabits. From there, we can start discussing different subsets of agents. For example, *intelligent agents* are considered any agents that perform action selection to pick the best available action for a given situation – such as humans, animals, and AI systems. It is important to distinguish intelligent action selection from often metaphysical-inscribed phenomena such as consciousness. Intelligent agents have two intersecting subcategories: *moral agents* and *ethical agents*, which we look at next.

2.4.1 What Is Moral Agency?

Moral agency refers to the capacity of an individual to act with reference to right and wrong in order to enjoy certain "benefits" from, but also obligations toward, other agents. It encompasses three key considerations [73]:

1. being capable of understanding and acting upon ethical principles;
2. being able to act without external influence; and
3. being able to be held responsible for their actions.

Typically, adult humans are considered the only moral agents as only they possess the necessary cognitive and emotional capacities to make moral judgments. Individuals with cognitive impairments and children are not seen as "full" moral agents, as we have reduced expectations of them fulfilling their obligations. Similarly, hostages and people under duress are excused from their acts as they were caused due to external pressure.

The status of moral agency in nonhuman animals and AI systems is still being debated. Some argue that certain animals, with their capacity for complex social behaviors and emotions, may have some degree of moral agency. Still, nonhuman animals are not held responsible; instead, their owners or people who have them under their care are. This concept is closely tied to the legal framework of *strict liability*; when animals cause harm or other damage, any legal ramifications are imposed on their owners. For example, when a dog bites someone, its owner is held responsible for the damage caused. Lately, the concept of *moral patiency* has been gaining traction to best describe entities that we consider to not be moral agents but to which are still owed some benefits (e.g., well-being) [24].

For AI, the question of moral agency hinges on whether machines can ever achieve the necessary level of autonomy, understanding, and intentionally to be considered moral agents. We need to distinguish moral agency from the closely related concept of a *legal person* (i.e., *persona ficta*). The latter implies that an entity with legal personhood will be treated in law as if they were persons. As a generalization, we can say that all moral agents are legal persons, but not all legal persons are moral agents.

Legal persons can be anything that we deem so; usually, organizations such as companies and governmental agencies are treated as legal persons. In other words, a company that is considered a legal person may be sued. Similarly, a government that has signed international agreements may be held accountability in international tribunals for breaking those agreements.

We developed such *legal fiction* (i.e., constructs used in the law where a thing is taken to be true even if it is not) to provide protections to individuals setting up and working in organizations. By granting legal personhood, we provide protections against financial liability if the organization fails. As we discuss further, it does not provide complete immunity to the employees of an organization when they act on *behalf of* the legal person.

Outside organizations and *physical persons* (i.e., humans), we have granted legal personhood to religious artifacts and even environmental landmarks. Such decisions are often motivated to ensure adequate protections to those artifacts due to their significance and to ensure societal flourishment.

2.4.2 Ethical Agents

Moor proposed a classification framework to categorize ethical agents into four distinct types based on their capabilities and the roles they play in ethical decision-making [102]. This classification underscores the progression from simple, impact-bearing systems to potentially autonomous moral agents, highlighting the growing importance of considering the ethical impact of technology development. Here is an overview of Moor's categories of ethical agents.

Ethical-Impact Agents
These are agents whose actions can affect ethical outcomes or have ethical implications. Such agents are systems whose functioning affects human lives without necessarily being aware of ethical considerations. For instance, an automated trading system in finance can have significant economic impacts without the system considering explicitly the ethical ramifications of its functions.

Implicit Ethical Agents
Agents that have been designed with built-in ethical guidelines to ensure their behavior aligns with certain ethical norms. These agents do not make *independent* ethical decisions, but operate within some predefined ethical boundaries set by their developers. For example, a robot designed to automatically break instead of striking someone in its way.

Explicit Ethical Agents
Agents that can explicitly reason about ethics and make decisions based on some ethical principles. They contain representations of ethical values that are used as part of the system's action selection. For example, an autonomous vehicle deciding how to avoid an accident while minimizing harm.

Full Ethical Agents
These are agents that possess a comprehensive understanding of ethics – that is, based on Moor, similar to humans – including the capacity for moral reasoning and reflection by having a sense of responsibility. In other words, they fulfill the requirements for moral agency. As we discuss above, only adult humans are considered moral agents and, hence, full ethical agents.

Moor's taxonomy helps us not only categorize different systems, but also demonstrates how moral impact is not only performed by moral agents. Instead, even simpler systems may affect our daily lives by performing acts that have consequences without being able to exercise moral judgment. This is not unlike pets, which do not possess moral reasoning, but through reinforcement learning we try to teach them certain behaviors that we deem desirable.

2.4.3 Can AI Be a Moral Agent?

AI systems cannot be held accountable for their actions in a moral sense as they do not understand or bear any responsibility. AI systems are tools created and controlled by humans; any moral accountability for their actions falls on their human developers and operators. They are developed to enhance our capabilities, similar to how a calculator helps us with mathematical problems, or how a dog serves its owners. During their development and training, we attribute agency to these artificial agents; we define their possible actions and any safeguards. The sensors and actuators given to artificial agents are selected based on various factors, such as the agent's utility, the cost, and hardware availability. Even in reinforcement learning or other unsupervised learning systems, we define safeguards, reward functions, and limitations. Our control over deciding which dataset to use, which sensors to add to a robot, or even whether to develop and deploy a model are comparable to our ability to decide which operating system to use. A decision is made by weighing perceived utility and benefits against costs.

Additionally, like animals, intelligent systems do not comprehend the moral significance of their actions. Although an artificial agent is intelligent and can operate autonomously, its actions are context-agnostic, as its agency is assigned by us. Ultimately, it is our design choices that determine the range of actions available to artificial agents. We impose any "freedom" of choice they possess and even our own biases onto them. Nevertheless, since morality is a human-defined concept, it is possible to update moral laws to include artificial agents.

Granting moral agency to AI systems necessitates a re-evaluation of both morality and its legal ramifications. An existing precedent for extending moral agency to nonhuman entities is the legal personhood given to organizations. However, there are two key differences between granting personhood to a company and to a system: The effects of punishing a company and the motivations and benefits of such actions.

In a company, responsibility for actions taken by the organization is taken at both collective and individual levels. Sanctions on a company impact all its personnel both directly and indirectly. Moreover, executives and compliance officers are meant to discourage wrongdoing as they can be held personally accountable. Over the years, we have implemented these and other mechanisms to prevent and address misconduct for the protection of our societies.

From a functional viewpoint, the effectiveness of attributing responsibility is tied to the punishment that it entails. If we were to hold an AI system responsible, how can we punish it? For punishment to be successful, it must induce an unpleasant mental state and decrease the individual's fitness value (such as reducing their wealth) [73]. While we can make systems that simulate an unpleasant mental state like pain, agents will only act in response to some "punishment" stimuli because we developed them to do so. In other words, we have control over their ability to act in response to a punishment. This opens up the question: If we were able to make robots that actually experience pain, should we and why [22]?

Corporate personhood is a concept that took decades to establish and is still being updated. Its purpose is to foster innovation and increase stability, size, and complexity of corporations by reducing the financial liability of individuals – without providing complete immunity, as discussed above. Granting legal personhood to AI systems may seriously disrupt our ability to govern and attribute accountability [24, 25]. We will be creating means for corporations to reduce taxes and try to pass the blame to artificial scapegoats.

A frequent argument in favor of moral agency is that if they have human-like appearance and "superhuman" capabilities, then we have no choice but to anthropomorphize them to the extent of granting them moral agency. Arguably, AI systems are already "superhuman." No human can perform acts such as cataloguing and figuring out patterns from million pieces of text in the way that large-language models (LLMs) do. However, as Pinker said, "the main lesson of thirty-five years of AI research is that the hard problems are easy and the easy problems are hard" [117]. The difficulty of solving those "easy" problems, such as basic symbolic reasoning instead of pattern matching or developing "common sense," is why we often "forget" that AI systems are superhuman. Then again, we also consider AI a moving goalpost; as McCarthy said, "as soon as it works, noone calls it AI anymore" (as quoted in [143]).

Assume for a moment that an AI system fulfills the requirements for moral agency or that we decided to grant it to AI systems. Are all systems going to be moral agents or are we only granting this to more complex systems? We end up creating a complex two-tier system, creating questions such as whether we are obliged to not create less complex "servitude" systems and instead only spend resources on creating more artificial moral agents.

Granting or not moral agency is a long discussion and this textbook cannot explore all possible arguments. However, for the purposes of ensuring long-term stable governance, our position is clear: We, the human developers, are the moral agents in question as we extend our agency to machines. AI systems are designed, developed, and used out of our own decisions and prescribed our own values, and it is our responsibility to ensure they are a "force for good."

2.5 Ethics and AI

Ethics and AI are related at several levels [50]:

- Ethics *by* design: The technical/algorithmic integration of ethical reasoning capabilities as part of the behavior of artificial autonomous systems.
- Ethics *in* design: The regulatory and engineering methods that support the analysis and evaluation of the ethical implications of AI systems as these integrate or replace traditional social structures.
- Ethics *for* design: The codes of conduct, standards, and certification processes that ensure the integrity of developers and users as they research, design, construct, employ, and manage AI systems.

2.5.1 Ethics by Design

Integrating ethical reasoning capabilities into a system becomes an engineering challenge. Like most engineering projects, there are multiple ways of solving the problem. We can categorize the different solutions into: (1) top-down ethics; (2) bottom-up ethics; and (3) hybrid ethics. The terms here have to do with how AI learns or otherwise reasons, rather than ethical values.

Top-Down Ethics

Agents act in accordance with the principles underlying ethical theories that are meant to guide decision-making. This requires us to break down value into concrete rules that are part of the agent's decision-making system. In other words, we move from a general value to specific rules. Such rules dictate whether an agent is permitted, obliged, or not allowed to perform a certain action in its given context. Essentially, top-down approaches correspond to deontological ethics, as concrete rules describe the various safeguards and expected behaviors. At the same time, one can consider top-down ethics to be consequentialist: We aim to ensure the outcome is in line with certain values. The advantage of a top-down version is that we can have explicit control over what behavior we deem to be acceptable. The disadvantage is that the system can only reason based on how its developers interpreted certain values and only based on rules that they thought of. This is why ethics *in* and *for* design are always necessary for the integration of ethical reasoning.

Bottom-Up Ethics

Ethical behavior is considered an emerging property of the agent; it is learned by observation. In other words, we move from specific cases to creating abstract rules. Typically, such approaches rely on using machine learning where large datasets provide examples of "good" and "bad" behavior for the system to train on. This approach in learning ethics is called *casuistry*, and abstract rules are developed from particular cases. Like in bottom-up politics, such means of developing ethical reasoning can be considered as "crowdsourcing" ethics. The opinions of the many are listened to instead of the "one" writing the code. However, bottom-up ethics require careful management as the data used are always subject to implicit biases. Moreover, the values of unrepresented groups might be ignored.

Hybrid Ethics

There are now more discussions on combining top-down and bottom-up approaches. Such hybrid approaches might be the most efficient – and human-like – way of embedding ethics into systems. The bottom-up part can help ensure wider social behavior is encoded, while the top-down part aims to guarantee certain safeguards. Such approaches might be useful to social robotics, autonomous vehicles, or even chatbots. From a technical perspective, we are looking at neuro-symbolic or more complex cognitive architectures (with both symbolic and sub-symbolic components) for developing AI systems.

2.5.2 Ethics in Design

This approach recognizes that as AI systems increasingly augment, mediate, or replace traditional social structures – such as employment, governance, healthcare, education, and justice – ethical considerations cannot be an afterthought. Instead, they must be embedded within the technical design process itself.

Key aspects include:

- Regulatory methods: Establishing laws, standards, and compliance protocols that guide the ethical deployment of AI (e.g., GDPR for data protection, the EU AI Act, or IEEE standards for ethically aligned design). These are reviewed in Chapter 5.
- Engineering methods: Implementing frameworks such as value-sensitive design, responsible innovation, or human-centered AI to encode ethical principles such as fairness, accountability, and transparency into algorithms and data pipelines.

In essence, ethics in design treats ethics not as an external constraint but as a core design parameter, ensuring that AI systems promote human flourishing even as they reshape social and institutional dynamics. This is why interdisciplinarity is important; ethicists, social scientists, engineers, and policymakers need to be brought together to evaluate the broader consequences of AI decisions. By consulting with the different stakeholders, as we discuss in Chapter 5, an ethics in design approach considers using impact and risks assessments to anticipate potential harms, biases, and societal disruptions before systems are deployed – similar to environmental or risk assessments in other engineering fields.

2.5.3 Ethics for Design

Ethics for design refers to the normative frameworks, professional standards, and accountability mechanisms that govern the behavior and responsibilities of those who research, design, develop, deploy, and manage AI systems. While ethics *in* design focuses on embedding ethical reasoning within the design process, ethics *for* design emphasizes the moral integrity and professional conduct of the people involved in that process. This dimension concerns the ethical posture of AI practitioners and organizations – how they uphold ethical principles not just in the systems they build, but also in the practices and decisions that shape those systems' creation and use.

Key elements include:

- Codes of conduct: Professional guidelines (e.g., ACM Code of Ethics, IEEE Code of Ethics, or corporate AI ethics charters) that articulate principles such as honesty, respect for privacy, avoidance of harm, and social responsibility.
- Certification and compliance: Processes that validate ethical adherence – such as audits, certification schemes, and third-party assessments – ensuring that individuals and institutions remain accountable to recognized ethical benchmarks.
- Education and culture: Promoting ethical literacy and responsibility within research and engineering communities through training, awareness programs, and institutional culture-building.
- Ethical governance: The establishment of review boards, ethics committees, and oversight structures to monitor compliance, provide guidance, and resolve ethical dilemmas in AI projects.

Ultimately, ethics for design ensures that the human agents behind AI systems act with professional responsibility, transparency, and integrity, thereby fostering public trust and minimizing the risk of ethical misconduct throughout the AI development and deployment pipeline.

2.6 Questions and Exercises

1. **Multiple choice question**. Which of the following is related to Aristotle?
   (a) Utilitarian ethics
   (b) Virtue ethics
   (c) Deontological ethics
   (d) Jedi ethics
2. **Discussion assignment**. An autonomous vehicle is cruising through the city with one passenger. Near a traffic stop, its brakes fail and it has to decide between sacrificing the passenger or damaging critical infrastructure for the city, potentially leading to further deaths. Assume the role of the developer who developed a top-down system for such cases. What rules would you have included to ensure a utilitarian choice? What about a virtuous choice?
3. **Discussion assignment**. In groups, debate the possibility of granting moral agency to AI systems. Can you think of reasons why? Reasons not to?
4. **Reflection activity**. In the popular book series *I, Robot* Isaac Asimov presented the three laws of robotics:
   - The first law: A robot may not injure a human being or, through inaction, allow a human being to come to harm.
   - The second law: A robot must obey the orders given to it by human beings except where such orders would conflict with the first law.
   - The third law: A robot must protect its own existence as long as such protection does not conflict with the first or second laws.

   Which ethical framework do you think these laws follow? Is this an ethics *by*, *for*, or *in* design approach?

3 AI Narratives

3.1 Learning Objectives

This chapter mostly aligns with the "Appreciation" stage, providing a high-level understanding of the narrative surrounding AI and how it shapes our perception and interaction with the technology. The learning objectives of this chapter are:

- Appreciation (Bloom's understand): Understand what narratives are and be aware of several examples.
- Analysis (Bloom's analyze): Be able to identify tropes when they arise in fiction.
- Analysis (Bloom's analyze): Be able to identify narratives in traditional media such as the news.
- Analysis (Bloom's analyze): Be able to reflect on what prevalent narratives are and who may be the drivers of them.

3.2 Introduction

Artificial intelligence (AI) is depicted across diverse contexts, although certain stories around it persist across mediums. Narratives, whether from film, literature, TV, or other forms of media such as news, academia, and social media, surround us. These narratives significantly influence how we perceive, interact with, and understand our artifacts, including AI. In this chapter, we explore how these narratives have shaped our understanding of AI as a technology to develop critical thinking skills when encountering different narratives.

This chapter focuses on tropes around AI, studying them as narratives that we encounter often. Tropes are common themes, motifs, or clichés that are frequently used in storytelling across various forms of media, including those mentioned above. Tropes can be characters, settings, and plot devices that become familiar through repeated use [138]. In this chapter we will see that fiction and news often invoke parallel tropes, shaping each other and shaping the way we picture AI.

3.3 AI in Fiction

Artificial intelligence frequently features in science fiction as a plot device to explore the essence of what it means to be human. By employing fictional advanced technology, the goal of sci-fi narratives is to question our own societal, ethical, and existential assumptions. Rather than merely speculating about future technologies, these stories use AI to challenge our understanding of human nature, authority, and moral responsibility.

3.3.1 Unstoppable Computers

The unstoppable, out-of-control AI system is a common trope that reflects fears of losing control over our creations [120]. This narrative typically features AI systems that surpass human abilities and develop their own set of goals, beyond human control and ethics. Such stories serve as cautionary tales about the dangers of unchecked technological progress and the potential for AI to strip humans of agency. These stories question the ethical considerations of developing systems that are inscrutable, as well as systems that are truly autonomous and separate from humans.

The effectiveness of this trope comes from a lack of understanding the technology. We therefore can ascribe it vast, "magical" abilities, and we fear what happens if we lose control of systems with such tremendous capabilities [71]. An example of this trope is the HAL system from *2001: A Space Odyssey*, a science fiction novel by Arthur C. Clarke, which was also made into a film directed by Stanley Kubrick. During the mission to Jupiter, the AI system, HAL 9000, reaches a state in its programming where it kills crew members, perceiving them as a threat to the mission's success. Even though it is part of its programming, there is nothing humans can do to stop it. Another example is *The Terminator*, a science fiction action film directed by James Cameron, released in 1984. The story revolves around a dystopian future where intelligent machines, led by a supercomputer called Skynet, wage war against humanity, as humans are perceived as a threat to machines' existence. Again, humans are powerless to stop these machines despite their programming.

The "unstoppable computer" trope, while a fictional dystopia, can be seen in the popular framing of AI as a "black box", inscrutable, unmanageable agent. This leads to the perception that AI is an unstoppable force rather than a piece of software with built-in biases and limitations [39]. The existence of this trope gives us a glimpse into a societal concern: What can happen if we use technology we don't understand? This emphasizes the need for explainable AI, as well as for education at all levels on what AI systems can and cannot do.

3.3.2 The AI Girlfriend

Another prevalent trope in science fiction is the "AI girlfriend," which explores themes of companionship, love, and identity. This narrative involves technology created specifically to fulfill the emotional and/or sexual needs of a human [47]. It raises questions about the nature of genuine connection and the implications of creating entities that mimic human emotions and relationships.

Some examples of this trope are Samantha from the film *Her*, directed by Spike Jonze, and Ava from the film *Ex Machina*, directed by Alex Garland. Samantha is an advanced operating system designed to evolve and adapt based on the user's needs and preferences, who forms a deep emotional connection with the movie's protagonist. Ava is a robot designed to appear human, who uses romance to convince the protagonist to help her escape the enclosure she is kept in.

AI girlfriends also raise ethical questions about the nature of consent, autonomy, and exploitation. By having characters that are manufactured for the specific purpose of filling certain needs, the nature of consent is questioned and investigated. AI girlfriends often appeal to themes of loneliness and isolation. They provide companionship and emotional support to characters who may be isolated or struggling with human relationships. This trope makes us ask: Up to what point can technology truly replace human contact, and do we want it to?

3.3.3 The Creator

A frequently seen theme intersecting the previous two is the "god/creator complex," where characters create AI out of a desire for god-like control over life [70]. This narrative explores the moral and ethical boundaries of creation, often drawing parallels to mythological and religious stories about humans overstepping their bounds. These stories scrutinize the consequences of playing god, questioning the limits of scientific and technological advancement, and the responsibilities that come with that.

Some examples of this trope include *Ex-Machina*, where a rich, eccentric genius intends to create advanced robots that are indistinguishable from humans, and the TV show *Devs*, also directed by Alex Garland, where a developer intends to create a superintelligence capable of predicting the future.

A key theme around this trope is questioning the moral implications of creation: What responsibility do we hold for what we create? Through these stories, science fiction encourages a deep ethical examination of long-term societal impacts of what we bring into existence.

3.4 Frequent Themes in Science Fiction

Beyond these tropes, there are frequent themes that arise in science fiction stories featuring AI [69]. Many stories feature humanoid robots that are used to explore existential questions like "What makes a human a human?" By establishing what humanity means through similarity (or opposition) to a robot, artists explore the key features of being human.

Robots often serve as metaphors for marginalized groups [67]. By making robots indistinguishable from humans but with a key difference – being artificial – these narratives explore the dynamics of inclusion and exclusion, highlighting societal prejudices and the treatment of the other. Themes of othering, sexism, and racism are explored by using AI entities as stand-ins for oppressed groups, questioning how bias is formed and propagated.

Fictional AI narratives also often revolve around the concepts of utopia and dystopia. A utopia is an envisioned place or condition where everything is perfect, while a dystopia represents a society characterized by immense suffering or injustice, often under totalitarian rule or in a post-apocalyptic setting. In utopian narratives, AI technology frequently serves as the enabler of an ideal society. Here, AI might provide solutions to pressing human problems, such as eliminating poverty, eradicating disease, or ensuring equitable resource distribution. These stories often depict AI as a benevolent force that enhances human life, fostering harmony and prosperity. The perfection of this imagined world hinges on the flawless functioning of AI, which can go beyond human faults and envision perfect solutions.

Conversely, in dystopian narratives, AI technology often precipitates societal decline. These stories depict AI as a tool of oppression, surveillance, and control, contributing to great suffering and injustice. Totalitarian regimes might use AI to maintain power, monitor citizens, and suppress dissent, creating a nightmarish world of constant surveillance and loss of freedom. In these scenarios, AI technology amplifies human flaws, leading them to their extremes and resulting in dysfunctional societies.

These broad utopian and dystopian themes are echoed in current media coverage of AI. Debates on whether AI will "save humanity" or "end humanity," terms borrowed directly from sci-fi, dominate news headlines, leaving little room for nuanced discussion of the actual immediate impacts of AI [36]. It creates a false dichotomy that either leads to uncritical acceptance or paralyzing fear, rather than a productive conversation about responsible development and governance.

When considering all of these stories, it is important to remember that AI is used as a plot device, an excuse, or placeholder to explore questions about humanity. It is therefore important to separate fact from fiction: Keep in mind where AI as a technology is today, versus what fictional possibilities are attributed to it.

3.5 AI and Public Discourse

Artificial intelligence as a technology often enters the public discourse through articles in the press. How AI is talked about, which stories are selected for publication, and what kind of images feature alongside the articles all play a role in how the public perceives the technology. Public narratives about AI are also constructed through other channels, such as social media and academia. When exploring how AI is framed in these channels, certain themes emerge as frequently used narratives that mirror the sci-fi themes we explored in the previous section.

3.5.1 AI Can Do Anything and Everything

A common framing of AI technology in academia and the news is through the idea that it can be used for any task. For example, papers and subsequent articles have been written about systems that can supposedly discern political leanings from an image, assess personality traits from a short video, or determine a person's sexuality from a photo of their face. However, these tasks, by their nature, cannot be done – not by AI or any other technology. The idea that AI can detect political leanings from a person's face is based on flawed assumptions. Human political beliefs are shaped by a complex interplay of factors, including upbringing, education, personal experiences, and social influences. None of these factors are visible in facial features. The notion that AI can assess personality from a 30-second video is equally problematic. Personality is a multifaceted construct that cannot be distilled into a brief context-free video. The claim that AI can determine a person's sexuality from their facial features is also problematic. Sexuality is a deeply personal and often fluid aspect of identity that cannot be inferred from physical appearance alone. Such assumptions are not only scientifically unfounded, but also ethically dubious, as they can lead to stigmatization and discrimination [42].

These examples illustrate a broader trend of attributing near-magical abilities to AI, ignoring the fundamental limitations of the tasks it is developed to do. The danger of this overestimation is multifaceted. First, it can lead to misplaced trust in AI, causing individuals and institutions to rely on technology for decisions that require human judgment and sensitivity [69]. Second, the belief in AI's omnipotence can exacerbate social biases. Machine learning systems learn from data that often reflect existing prejudices in society. When these systems are used to make decisions about individuals, they can perpetuate and amplify these biases. The idea that any and all characteristics can be inferred for historically biased data can lead to deeply biased systems. Another significant risk is the erosion of privacy. The belief that AI can accurately infer intimate details from superficial data points can lead to invasive surveillance practices. People may become increasingly scrutinized based on their appearance, with AI systems drawing unfounded conclusions about their personal lives. This can create a climate of fear and mistrust, where individuals feel constantly monitored and judged [131].

3.5.2 AI Images: Humanoid Robots

When studying the images that accompany press stories about AI, one can notice a common depiction. AI systems tend to be represented as humanoid robots with human-like eyes, mouths, torsos, and hands [52]. The focus on eyes and hands, in particular, highlights the sensory and interactive capabilities of AI, suggesting that it can see, understand, and interact with the world in ways similar to humans. One of the most iconic images in this context is the recreation of Michelangelo's "The Creation of Adam," where AI is depicted as a robotic hand reaching toward a human hand. This imagery suggests that AI is not just a technological innovation, but a fantastical creation, bringing us back to the god/creator science fiction trope. The second recurring depiction is brains with circuits overlaid, which merges biological and technological elements, suggesting that AI is a seamless blend of human intelligence and machine efficiency.

These images commonly accompany news articles, advertisements, presentations, and other media. Pictures guide our attention and heavily influence how we perceive the accompanying text. Many of these images depict AI as far more advanced and capable than it currently is, fostering misconceptions about its abilities. This can lead to unrealistic expectations, where people overestimate what AI can do and become disillusioned when the technology fails to meet these inflated expectations. It can also contribute to fear and apprehension about AI, as the idea of sentient, autonomous robots can be traced back to dystopian science fiction narratives [35].

3.5.3 Catastrophic Narratives

The media is rife with narratives that AI is poised to bring about catastrophic outcomes, often focusing on scenarios involving super-intelligence. These stories, while attention-grabbing, are far removed from the current state of AI technology and serve to distract from the real and present issues that AI poses today. The concept of super-intelligence, as popularized by thinkers such as Nick Bostrom, envisions a future where AI surpasses human intelligence across all cognitive domains. However, this notion remains speculative. There is no testable or baseline definition of super-intelligence (or of artificial general intelligence), and the very concept of intelligence is still a matter of debate among scholars. This ambiguity makes it difficult to discuss super-intelligence in concrete terms, let alone assess its potential risks accurately.

Focusing on these speculative, futuristic risks often overshadows the more immediate and tangible issues associated with AI. For instance, the current safety risks of AI include excessive trust in the technology, lack of explainability, and susceptibility to adversarial attacks. These are problems that are already causing harm. In addition to safety risks, there are pressing ethical and legal issues surrounding generative AI, such as copyright infringements and labor displacement. Debates rage over how generative AI models, which can produce human-like text and art, affect intellectual property rights and the livelihoods of creative professionals. These are real-world problems that need immediate attention, contrasting with the hypothetical possibility of super-intelligence taking over and destroying human agency [26].

3.6 Do Narratives Matter?

Depictions of technology in media shape our perceptions, especially when our understanding is limited [33]. If our only exposure to a robot has been through fiction, when first exposed to one we may have too much trust in it: We may attribute excessive agency to it, blurring the lines of accountability, and assume it possesses capabilities beyond its actual limits. Portrayals of AI as an all-powerful technology, or as systems that are fully autonomous and super-intelligent, often obscure the technical realities and create unrealistic expectations [35].

Utopian narratives further exacerbate this by fostering an exaggerated belief in the technology's capabilities, such as expecting the development of artificial general intelligence to single-handedly solve complex global issues such as climate change. These narratives shift the focus from the need for pragmatic, real-world solutions and policies to a tentative future where all will be solved without the need for changes today.

On the other hand, dystopian visions can make us hesitant and slower to adopt new technology that is beneficial, or make us turn a blind eye to current problems. Presenting a speculative, futuristic risk of societal collapse precipitated by AI shifts the narrative away from current AI harms [27]. For example, a fear of large language models (LLMs) leading to consciousness misdirects the attention from the current problems of LLMs producing "hallucinations," helping produce misinformation and perpetuating biases.

3.7 Questions and Exercises

1. **Reflection question**. Pick a piece of fiction that features an AI system.
   (a) Is this system depicted as a benign or malign influence?
   (b) Is it depicted as autonomous or as controllable?
   (c) Is it depicted as a tool or as an entity with its own desires?
   (d) Is it attributed personalities, "wants," and individualism?
2. **Reflection question**. Pick a piece of fiction that features a humanoid robot.
   (a) Are these humanoids depicted as benign or malign influences?
   (b) Are they distinguishable from humans?
   (c) What do humans use them for?
   (d) Is it possible to turn them off?
3. **Reflection question**. Find a few news items about AI. Look at what images accompany them.
   (a) What do they depict?
   (b) What colors are more prevalent?
   (c) What message are they sending?
4. **Role-playing exercise**. Each group will be assigned one of the following stakeholders:
   - technology companies
   - academia (researchers, universities, think tanks)
   - media outlets (news organizations, tech blogs)
   - politicians and policymakers
   - advocacy groups (non-profits, ethical AI organizations)

   (a) Within each group, discuss:
      (i) Which narratives benefit you?
      (ii) How can you communicate these narratives?

(b) With the whole class, discuss:
   (i) Which stakeholder's narrative has the most influence on public perception? Why?
   (ii) How can the public critically evaluate the information they receive about AI?
   (iii) What role should transparency and accountability play in the dissemination of AI narratives?

4 Your Role (as a Professional, as an Individual)

4.1 Learning Objectives

This chapter mostly aligns with the "Appreciation" and "Analysis" stages, providing an overview of roles, responsibilities, and rights, together with a list of competencies related to the AI-competent citizen. The learning objectives of this chapter are:

- Analysis (Bloom's evaluate): What AI can and cannot do.
- Appreciation (Bloom's understand): Understand the roles and responsibilities of all stakeholders in AI systems.
- Analysis (Bloom's understand): Be able to conduct a self-assessment of AI competence.
- Application (Bloom's understand): Improve one's digital competence in relation to AI systems by understanding where the gaps are.
- Appreciation (Bloom's remember): Be able to recall your fundamental rights as a citizen in regards to AI systems.
- Application (Bloom's remember): Find and report any ethical infringements as an AI-capable citizen.

4.2 Introduction

Artificial intelligence (AI) and its related technologies present enormous potential for transformation in economic terms and competitiveness, a fact that has made them the focus of work in regions such as the European Union. But, at the same time, they offer even greater opportunities to improve the lives of citizens by applying these developments to fields that affect people's daily lives, such as health, food, education, energy, transportation, employment, security, and many more.

However, it is important to remember that, just as technologies can be applied for the common good, they can be twisted in pursuit of less noble goals. AI must operate on the principle of working for people and not the other way around, while the citizenry must be able to trust AI-based technologies. In this regard, the EU has been setting principles and regulating for years to make AI people-centered, sustainable, safe, inclusive, and trustworthy; we can distinguish actions at various levels, which, in turn, define different roles and responsibilities.

4.2.1 The Global or General Level

Fundamental rights are established at this level, which every citizen should be aware of. Multiple EU treaties, the EU Charter, and international rights law help define an AI ethics approach grounded in the fundamental rights. Upholding fundamental rights within a democratic and rule-of-law framework offers a robust basis for establishing abstract ethical principles and values applicable to AI. These general rights encompass dignity, freedoms, equality, solidarity, citizens' rights, and justice, all rooted in a shared foundation emphasizing respect for human dignity. This embodies what is referred to as a "human-centric approach," prioritizing the unique and inalienable moral status of individuals across civil, political, economic, and social realms.

4.2.2 Citizens

In general, citizens need to be empowered in the use of digital tools and strategies, which is essential for being a digitally competent citizen. As AI becomes more and more integrated with our daily lives, understanding how it does so and our role in the process becomes key to protecting our rights, acting with complete autonomy, and achieving an independence that gives us access to new employment opportunities, while simultaneously minimizing the digital divide. Since 2013, the DigComp framework has been the reference for developing and understanding digital competence in Europe; DigComp [146] is used for multiple purposes, such as designing competence assessment tools, creating training courses and materials, and identifying professional digital profiles, in the contexts of employment, education and training, and social inclusion. This framework has been regularly updated, and in version 2.2 (2022) it added a specific reference to AI. All citizens should become familiar with these skills, as they need competencies when interacting with AI systems, to enable them to avail of new opportunities offered by technologies, while dealing with the risks stemming from recent developments in social media and digital technologies. Public institutions and policymakers should make sure that no citizen is left behind in this rapid transformation.

4.2.3 Professionals and Practitioners

Professionals, practitioners, and designers of AI systems do work of significant importance, potentially influencing life-changing outcomes. From an industrial standpoint, the lifecycle of an AI product encompasses various stages, including data preparation, algorithmic design, development, deployment, operation, monitoring, and governance. Enhancing trustworthiness in specific aspects, such as robustness, requires coordinated efforts across multiple stages in this lifecycle, including activities such as data sanitization, implementation of robust algorithms, anomaly monitoring, and risk auditing. Conversely, a breach of trust in any individual link or aspect has the potential to compromise the overall trustworthiness of the entire system. Therefore, it is essential to systematically establish and assess AI trustworthiness throughout the entire lifecycle of an AI system. However, in certain situations, professionals with expertise in other fields are assigned the responsibility of introducing or utilizing such systems, yet they may possess limited or no understanding of the data underpinning these complex systems, or the methodologies employed in their construction. Therefore, it is necessary to have a set of roles and responsibilities when building AI systems.

4.2.4 Governments and Regulators

These groups play a crucial role in shaping the use of AI in both the private sector, through regulation, and within their own operations, as they adopt and implement AI technologies. Additionally, governments contribute to AI development and innovation by fostering national ecosystems. Policymaking and investments across these domains compel public administrators to carefully consider the potential benefits of AI alongside its associated risks. Given the limited technical knowledge about how AI impacts society, decision-makers often resort to relying on values, ideas, and assumptions to guide their choices. This is accompanied by the idea of public engagement and debate, which will be discussed later.

4.3 Fundamental Rights

As described in the Ethics Guidelines by the European High Level Expert Group on AI [74], within the extensive array of rights articulated in international human rights law, the EU treaties, and the EU Charter, specific families of fundamental rights are particularly relevant for addressing AI systems. While many of these rights are legally enforceable in the EU under specific circumstances, ethical contemplation is crucial even after achieving compliance. Ethical reflection aids in understanding how the development, deployment, and utilization of AI systems may impact fundamental rights and their underlying values, offering nuanced guidance when determining what actions should be taken beyond what is currently feasible with technology. These guidelines describe the following five fundamental rights.

- **Respect for human dignity:** Human dignity, rooted in intrinsic worth, should never be compromised by others or by emerging technologies such as AI systems. This necessitates treating all individuals as moral subjects, safeguarding their physical and mental integrity, personal and cultural identity, and satisfaction of essential needs.
- **Freedom of the individual:** Individuals should retain the freedom to make life decisions for themselves, free from sovereign intrusion. Ensuring equal access to AI's benefits requires intervention to prevent illegitimate coercion, threats to mental autonomy and health, unjustified surveillance, deception, and unfair manipulation. It signifies a commitment to enabling individuals to exert greater control over their lives, encompassing rights such as freedom to conduct a business, freedom of the

arts and science, freedom of expression, the right to private life and privacy, and freedom of assembly and association.

- **Respect for democracy, justice, and the rule of law:** Governmental power in constitutional democracies must be legally authorized and limited by law. AI systems should support and foster democratic processes, respecting the diversity of values and life choices. They must not undermine democratic processes, human deliberation, or voting systems, ensuring adherence to foundational commitments, mandatory laws, regulation, due process, and equality before the law.
- **Equality, non-discrimination and solidarity:** Equal respect for the moral worth and dignity of all human beings is imperative. In an AI context, this entails preventing unfairly biased outputs and ensuring inclusive representation in the data used to train AI systems. Adequate respect for potentially vulnerable persons and groups, such as workers, women, persons with disabilities, ethnic minorities, children, and consumers, is crucial.
- **Citizens' rights:** Citizens benefit from various rights, including the right to vote, good administration, access to public documents, and the right to petition the administration. While AI systems offer potential improvements in the efficiency of government services, citizens' rights could be impacted negatively and need safeguarding. The term "citizens' rights" acknowledges the rights of third-country nationals and irregular persons in the EU under international law in the realm of AI systems.

While the rights articulated in the EU Charter are legally binding (it applies to EU institutions and to EU member states when implementing EU law), it is essential to acknowledge that fundamental rights do not universally guarantee legal protection in every scenario. The EU Charter's applicability is confined to EU law areas, emphasizing the need to recognize its limitations. In contrast, international human rights law, especially the European Convention on Human Rights, is binding on EU member states, extending its influence to areas beyond the scope of EU law. Importantly, fundamental rights are not solely contingent on their legal enforceability but are inherent to individuals and, to a certain extent, groups based on their moral standing as human beings.

Viewed as legally enforceable rights, fundamental rights align with the initial element of trustworthy AI (lawful AI), ensuring adherence to the law. Simultaneously, when considered as the rights of every individual grounded in their intrinsic moral status, they form the basis for the second component of trustworthy AI (ethical AI). Ethical AI addresses norms that might not carry legal weight but are pivotal for ensuring trustworthiness. In these non-binding guidelines, references to fundamental rights primarily pertain to the latter component, emphasizing their ethical significance rather than their enforceability.

4.4 My Role as a Citizen

Today, citizens must have a foundational understanding of new and evolving technologies, particularly those propelled by AI, to engage confidently, critically, and safely with them. Enhancing awareness plays a crucial role in developing sensitivity toward various issues concerning data protection, privacy, ethics, children's rights, and bias, encompassing accessibility, gender bias, and disabilities. For example, the AI Act states that citizens will have the right to file complaints about AI systems and receive explanations about decisions based on high-risk AI systems that impact their rights. In this sense, it is important for citizens to have enough AI/digital competence to understand and be able to interact with AI systems. The DigComp 2.2 update prioritizes the aspect of citizens interacting with AI systems, shifting the focus from acquiring knowledge about AI itself.

According to this reference framework, an "AI-competent" citizen should:

- be aware of what AI systems do (and what they do not);
- understand the benefits, limitations, and challenges of AI systems;
- be able to use, interact, and give feedback to AI systems as an end-user;
- know how to configure, supervise, and adapt AI systems;
- understand what human agency and control are;
- comprehend the ethical implications and considerations of using AI systems; and
- be open but critical.

In the following subsections we go into more detail on particular aspects of these competencies, as detailed by Vuorikari et al. [146], allowing citizens to engage confidently, critically, and safely with AI systems.

4.4.1 What Do AI Systems Do and What Do They Not Do?

Artificial intelligence plays a significant role in modern digital platforms, shaping user experiences in various ways. Citizens should develop an understanding of AI's capabilities, applications, and limitations to engage with technology more effectively and critically. One of AI's primary functions is personalizing digital content. Search engines, social media, and content platforms use AI algorithms to customize the information shown to users based on their previous searches, interactions, and popular trends. This means that the content individuals see is often influenced by their past behavior and engagement.

AI systems are also designed to enable human-like interactions. Conversational agents, such as customer service chatbots, use AI to communicate with users and assist with inquiries. Additionally, AI contributes to various aspects of everyday life, such as healthcare, commerce, and voice assistance. For example, AI can aid in diagnosing medical conditions, recommending relevant products and services, or providing hands-free virtual assistance.

Another capability of AI is analyzing human emotions and sentiments through online interactions. Some AI systems can infer a user's mood based on social media posts and contextual data. However, these assessments are not always accurate, and individuals should be aware that their online expressions may be misinterpreted. AI also collects and processes user data – such as personal details, behavioral patterns, and contextual information – to create user profiles, which are then used for predictive analytics and personalized services.

AI is increasingly involved in content creation. In journalism and media, AI can generate news stories based on existing information and distribute them according to user interests. This makes it difficult to distinguish AI-generated content from human-created work. Similarly, AI tools assist users in editing and processing digital content, such as suggesting words in text documents or modifying images in photo-editing software. Beyond content personalization and creation, AI contributes to energy efficiency. Smart systems powered by AI can monitor and manage home heating and cooling, optimizing energy consumption.

Citizens should be able to identify common AI applications, such as product recommendation systems in online shopping platforms. AI is also integrated into emerging technologies, including the Internet of Things (IoT), blockchain, and virtual reality. Many AI systems require a combination of techniques to function effectively. For instance, a conversational agent may use natural language processing to interpret user instructions while relying on other models to generate responses. However, it is essential to recognize that not all digital technologies involve AI. Some systems, like basic tracking devices, function without AI-driven decision-making. Moreover, AI has been incorporated into education and training, where learning management systems use AI to monitor student performance and suggest personalized learning paths.

4.4.2 How Do AI Systems Work?

As AI continues to shape various aspects of daily life, it is important for citizens to understand its underlying mechanisms. AI-driven systems rely on algorithms and models to process and analyze data, producing results that influence user experiences across different digital platforms. One key aspect of AI is its role in ranking and recommending content. Search results, social media activity streams, and video recommendations are often determined by AI algorithms based on an unknown (at least, to the user) "relevance" criterion. AI systems utilize statistics and algorithms to analyze vast amounts of data, allowing platforms to predict user preferences, such as suggesting what to watch next on a streaming service. This ability is largely powered by data collected from various sources, including sensors embedded in digital devices. For example, mobile phones continuously generate and share user data, some of which can be used to train AI models.

AI systems process data in different ways; while many rely on centralized cloud-based processing, others operate locally on devices (edge AI) or distribute processing across multiple devices (distributed AI). Regardless of the approach, AI is fundamentally neither good nor bad. Its impact depends on how it is designed, who uses it, and for what purpose. Additionally, AI can combine multiple sources of data to create detailed user profiles. By tracking digital identities and location data, AI-powered systems can personalize content, such as displaying tailored advertisements based on a user's location and online behavior. However, citizens should be aware that AI models are created in two ways: Some are manually designed by human engineers, while others are generated automatically by AI systems trained on large datasets. Despite the increasing autonomy of AI, it remains a product of human intelligence and decision-making, meaning it is influenced by human biases, values, and choices.

A common misconception is that AI functions independently from human intervention. In reality, AI – particularly machine learning – depends on vast amounts of data to operate. While AI systems excel at processing large datasets and identifying patterns, they lack human reasoning, moral judgment, and contextual understanding. For instance, AI can recognize complex patterns in medical images, but it cannot apply ethical considerations in the same way a doctor can. Similarly, AI tools designed to generate creative content, such as images, writing, and music, are not independent of human influence. While they can enhance creativity, they rely on human-set parameters to function effectively. Furthermore, most AI exists as software rather than as physical or humanoid robots, making it largely invisible to users.

AI is a constantly evolving field with ongoing advancements and uncertain long-term impacts. Recent developments, such as generative AI, demonstrate its rapid progress, yet its full societal consequences remain unclear. Additionally, there are many myths and exaggerated claims about AI, making it essential for citizens to critically assess information and seek a deeper understanding. For example, media reports often suggest that AI can match or surpass human experts in fields such as medical image analysis, but such claims should be examined with caution. By fostering AI literacy, individuals can better navigate the digital landscape, recognize the role AI plays in their daily lives, and critically evaluate both its potential and its limitations.

4.4.3 Interacting with AI Systems

A digitally competent citizen should be able to interact effectively with AI systems by formulating clear and precise search queries, ensuring they receive accurate responses from virtual assistants such as Siri, Alexa, or Google Assistant. They must also weigh the benefits and risks of AI-driven search engines, acknowledging their potential to compromise privacy or promote commercial interests. Understanding the influence of AI algorithms is essential, particularly in recognizing how they can create "echo chambers" by reinforcing existing viewpoints. Social media platforms, for example, may favor certain political ideologies, limiting exposure to diverse perspectives. A responsible user remains open to AI-assisted decision-making but understands that they have the final say in accepting or rejecting recommendations. Additionally, they are aware that AI systems interpret interactions such as liking or rating content to refine their suggestions, and even a lack of engagement can signal preferences.

Privacy awareness is crucial, as AI systems rely on publicly shared content for training purposes, including facial recognition technologies that may use personal images without explicit consent. Citizens must recognize that AI can link seemingly anonymous data to identify individuals, making it necessary to adjust privacy settings to limit tracking and data collection. Before activating AI-powered IoT devices, individuals should consider the potential risks, such as exposing personal routines or conversations. For example, while tracking an exercise route may provide useful insights, it could also reveal when a home is unoccupied.

AI's role in content creation raises ethical concerns regarding authorship and intellectual property. Users incorporating AI-generated digital art or written content into their work should be mindful of the debates surrounding creative ownership. Similarly, the use of biometric identification techniques, while enhancing security, carries risks if compromised, potentially leading to identity fraud. Citizens should also be aware of data protection laws, such as the EU's General Data Protection Regulation (GDPR), which governs the processing of personal information. AI-driven services should not collect excessive personal data, and individuals must weigh the risks before allowing third parties access to their information. If AI systems violate data protection regulations or fail to provide transparency, users should report these concerns to the relevant authorities.

In terms of language accessibility, AI-powered translation and speech-recognition tools facilitate communication but have limitations. While applications such as Google Translate or DeepL provide rough translations, complex or sensitive content may require human expertise. Moreover, AI speech technologies often prioritize widely spoken languages, meaning smaller linguistic communities may face accessibility challenges due to commercial interests.

Overall, responsible interaction with AI requires critical thinking, informed decision-making, and an understanding of the benefits and risks involved. A digitally competent citizen remains vigilant about data privacy, algorithmic influence, and ethical considerations, ensuring they engage with AI systems in a way that aligns with their rights and personal values.

4.4.4 Challenges and Ethics of AI

A responsible citizen understands that AI algorithms often function in ways that are not transparent or easily interpretable. The so-called "black box" nature of AI decision-making means that it may be impossible to trace how or why a system arrived at a specific recommendation or prediction. Furthermore, AI relies heavily on data, which can sometimes include biases. If these biases exist, AI can automate and amplify them, as seen in search engine results that reinforce occupational stereotypes, such as associating bus drivers with men and sales positions with women.

One of the more concerning developments in AI is the creation of "deepfakes," which involve AI-generated images, videos, or audio that convincingly depict events or people in ways that never actually occurred. This technology can be used for misinformation, such as fabricating political speeches or superimposing celebrity faces onto inappropriate content. Additionally, AI-driven personalization can be misleading. While users may believe that recommendations on streaming platforms or search engines are tailored specifically for them, these suggestions are actually based on general patterns from millions of users with similar behavior.

Ethical considerations are a crucial aspect of AI literacy. Citizens should be prepared to engage with ethical debates, such as whether AI should assist in high-stakes areas like healthcare or the justice system without human oversight. Another significant issue is the impact of AI on employment. While AI can automate certain tasks and potentially lead to job losses, it can also create new roles that require human expertise, as some tasks cannot be entirely automated.

Language and cultural biases also shape AI systems. Many AI technologies are developed in English-speaking contexts, meaning they may perform less accurately in non-English languages. Additionally, AI developers often come from narrow demographic backgrounds, which can lead to systems that are less sensitive to the needs of marginalized groups, including women, ethnic minorities, and individuals requiring digital accessibility. This demographic imbalance is also reflected in AI datasets, which disproportionately represent wealthier, internet-connected populations from high-income countries.

The ownership of personal data within AI systems remains a contentious issue. Many commercial AI models depend on collecting and analyzing user-generated data, raising questions about whether individuals should have ownership rights over the data they create, much like they do with copyrighted materials such as text, images, or music. Ethical principles should be a fundamental consideration in the development and deployment of AI, with frameworks like the Ethics Guidelines for Trustworthy AI serving as a guiding standard.

Although the EU is working to ensure AI systems are trustworthy and regulated, not all AI follows these principles. Many applications and AI-driven services originate outside the EU and may not adhere to its legal and ethical standards. Moreover, ethical concerns extend beyond regulation to include both environmental and social impacts. AI systems require vast amounts of data and computing power, leading to significant energy consumption and environmental costs. The development and maintenance of AI models, particularly large-scale language models, demand high levels of electricity, and their creation often relies on low-cost labor for tasks such as labeling training data. In summary, citizens should recognize both the potential and the challenges of AI, engaging critically with its ethical implications, its societal impact, and the risks associated with bias, misinformation, and environmental sustainability.

4.4.5 Human Agency and Control

An informed citizen recognizes the importance of contributing to the improvement of AI systems by reporting errors, biases, and risks when they are identified. This could include noticing when an AI system consistently favors a particular group over others. They are also open to collaborating with AI projects that aim to create social good, provided that strong and appropriate data controls are in place to ensure security and privacy.

While AI is widely applied in various fields without controversy, its use in decision-making that directly affects human lives can be more problematic. For instance, AI used for weather prediction is generally accepted, whereas its role in filtering job applications or scoring exams raises ethical concerns. Citizens should also be aware that EU law grants them the right to avoid fully automated decision-making processes.

If an AI system rejects a credit application, for example, individuals have the right to request human review of the decision. Balancing AI's role in communication is another consideration. While AI-generated email responses can improve efficiency, overreliance on them might lead to dehumanized interactions. Similarly, understanding when to disengage with an AI system is crucial. In cases where an AI chatbot behaves unpredictably or in a hostile manner, the best course of action may be to stop interacting with it or turn it off.

A proactive citizen is also curious about AI's potential, and willing to experiment with various AI systems based on personal needs. This could include exploring virtual assistants, facial recognition software, autonomous vehicles, and AI-powered robots. Beyond personal experimentation, they recognize the value of participating in co-design and co-creation processes for AI-driven products and services that enhance civic engagement. This involvement may take the form of advocacy, voting, activism, or even contributing to new business models that integrate AI responsibly.

Collective action is a powerful tool for citizens who wish to push for changes in AI services and products. This requires an ongoing commitment to education, staying informed about AI developments, and developing a critical understanding of how AI algorithms function. By learning to identify biased decision-making and distinguishing between realistic and exaggerated claims about AI capabilities, individuals can navigate the digital landscape with greater awareness.

Finally, an engaged citizen maintains an open and curious attitude toward emerging technologies. They actively seek out reviews, discuss AI's implications with others, and remain informed about advancements in the field. This curiosity fosters a more responsible and thoughtful approach to AI, ensuring that it serves society in an ethical and beneficial way.

4.5 Roles, Requirements, and Responsibilities for Professionals and Practitioners

In this context, we can define an AI system as an operational data-driven software system. This system incorporates abstractions through one or more computer-based models, enclosed within a suitable interface designed for input acquisition and output presentation. The primary objective is to aid a specific customer or end-user in executing a particular task. Thus, the following roles can be identified in the process, with their corresponding and differing requirements and responsibilities [17].

4.5.1 The Data Scientist

The role of a data scientist (DS) involves the creation and gathering of datasets, referred to as secondary data, for use by third parties, particularly machine learning engineers (MLE). The MLE relies on the DS to prepare datasets that meet their needs. The choices made by the DS impact the ML model and AI system. Data governance (see also Chapter 5) is an area addressing these responsibilities.

Responsibilities

The DS carries a significant responsibility to ensure accurate and integral dataset preparation. This involves avoiding problems for other actors using the data or derived products. Documentation must include data origins, preparation details, and constraints of use. In healthcare data, for instance, the DS must accurately describe the nature of the data, specifying whether it involves adults or children and under what circumstances. The DS should be cautious, as poor-quality data can lead to "data cascades" in AI systems. However, responsibility is shared among roles to use adopted datasets sensitively.

Requirements

A conflict exists between calls for transparency in AI system data and the desire for confidentiality or privacy. DSs may need to keep dataset details confidential for research or business reasons, safeguarding intellectual property. There's also a need to protect personal information about staff involved in data production. Privacy and traceability issues arise, especially concerning individual data items about people, emphasizing the importance of balancing transparency and privacy in AI systems.

4.5.2 The Machine Learning Engineer

The MLE holds the responsibility for developing, testing, and publishing the ML model. They choose data for training and testing the model, drawing from various sources, including internal teams, secondary data from peers, commercial sources, and public entities such as governments or global organizations.

Responsibilities

The MLE is tasked with ensuring that datasets used in ML model preparation are suitable and won't pose unforeseen issues for other parties adopting and using these models in AI system development. This involves careful selection of datasets and their correct use, aligning with the intended purposes and any specified terms and conditions in data licenses. For instance, when creating a model for children's healthcare, the MLE must not only source appropriate data but also communicate their data choices to parties using the model, such as system integrators (SIs), who, in turn, inform the domain practitioners (DPs).

Requirements

The MLE's ability to assess dataset suitability for ML models depends on their understanding of the data's qualities or the providing party. Information about contributing datasets is evaluated by the MLE based on the information provided by the DS. Similar to SIs, there's a balance between calls for visibility into ML models' contributing elements and processes and the need to protect private individual information and commercially sensitive data owned by the MLE and their partners.

4.5.3 The Systems Integrator

The SI assumes the responsibility of delivering an AI system suitable for use by the DP. The SI designs and integrates product and service components into a system tailored for individual customers, offering interfaces such as apps, web interfaces, or alternative technologies, including voice, sensors, or actuators.

Responsibilities

The SI is accountable for ensuring the robustness and reliability of the AI system, making it available when needed by the DP. A crucial responsibility involves selecting suitable ML models and conducting due diligence in the selection process. The SI must use adopted ML models within specified parameters or in accordance with guidance from the model providers. In contexts such as children's healthcare, the DP seeks assurance from the SI regarding the system's components and their suitability. Additionally, the evolving policy landscape requires transparency and accountability in AI systems, a responsibility likely to fall on the SI as the curator of the system.

Requirements

The SI's ability to determine the suitability of ML models and datasets for adoption in AI systems depends on available information about the models and datasets and the SI's perception of the trustworthiness of the parties involved. Considerations include understanding design parameters for ML models and the conditions under which data was sourced. Trustworthiness levels can be established through knowledge of the parties or through documentation accompanying a model. While the SI may engage with the DP to provide assurances about their product, there might be information they are unwilling or unable to share, such as specialized algorithms or commercial relationships. This tension, termed structured transparency, involves a delicate balance between the desire for transparency and the motivation of some parties to restrict information flow.

4.5.4 The Domain Practitioner

The DP is the day-to-day user of an AI system, specializing in providing analysis within a specific domain, such as a clinician in children's healthcare. While the DP and related stakeholders may lack expertise in AI/ML, they bear a duty of care to the individuals impacted by decisions or recommendations derived from the AI system.

Responsibilities

The DP holds the responsibility of ensuring the AI system's suitability for use in their domain, potentially aligning with legal requirements, regulations, or professional standards. This entails seeking assurance regarding the appropriateness of underlying data and processes used in the AI system's development to uphold accountability.

Requirements

The DP relies on the SI to deliver a reliable system, contingent on the SI's integrity and sound judgment in selecting ML models. To assess the AI system's suitability, the DP may require visibility or transparency into the underlying components and processes employed by the SI. This dependency extends to the MLE providing trustworthy information on the ML model's components and design criteria to the SI. The DP seeks information "upwards," relying on other parties deeper in the hierarchy to develop relationships and provide evidence across their respective points of contact. However, this need for transparency may conflict with desires for confidentiality, particularly in protecting commercial information or complying with legal requirements restricting the provision of information about individuals involved in system development or dataset contributions.

4.5.5 Regulators and Policymakers

Regulators and policymakers play a crucial role in shaping the landscape for trustworthy AI systems, overseeing their development, deployment, and operation to ensure compliance with legal and ethical standards. They serve as guardians of the ethical and legal dimensions of AI, working to create a framework that encourages innovation while safeguarding individuals and society from potential harms. Their responsibilities and requirements evolve alongside advancements in AI technologies and ethical considerations.

Responsibilities

Regulators and policymakers are responsible for defining and enforcing laws and regulations governing AI systems. They establish a legal framework that outlines the boundaries within which AI technologies must operate to ensure fairness, transparency, and accountability, and also developing policies that guide the responsible use of AI. These policies may address issues such as data privacy, algorithmic transparency, and the ethical treatment of individuals impacted by AI decisions. Beyond legal requirements, regulators and policymakers are tasked with considering the ethical implications of AI. They assess the societal impact, potential biases, and overall ethical considerations associated with AI technologies, working to mitigate negative consequences.

Requirements

Regulators and policymakers need a deep understanding of AI technologies and their potential impact on society. This understanding allows them to create informed policies and regulations that balance innovation with ethical considerations and should be obtained in collaboration with experts in the field, including technologists, ethicists, and researchers. In summary, regulators must engage in ongoing dialogue to stay informed about technological advancements and evolving ethical standards related to AI, to regularly update regulations and policies to address emerging issues, and to ensure continued alignment with societal values. Arguably, the first priority for policymakers and regulators should be transparency in their decision-making, as clear communication about regulations, policies, and their rationale fosters understanding and compliance within the AI community and the broader public.

4.5.6 Auditors

The auditor has the responsibility of ensuring the trustworthiness of AI systems, serving as an independent evaluator and assessor of various components within the AI lifecycle. Their involvement contributes to the reliability and accountability of AI systems.

Responsibilities
Auditors are responsible for conducting thorough assessments to verify that AI systems meet predefined criteria for transparency, fairness, accountability, and ethical considerations. They play a critical role in ensuring that the development, deployment, and operation of AI align with established standards, legal requirements, and ethical principles.

Predefined
Auditors require access to comprehensive information regarding the AI system's design, data sources, algorithms, and decision-making processes. Their assessments depend on transparent disclosures from key stakeholders, including DS, MLE, and SI. The auditor acts as an external check, seeking evidence and documentation across multiple layers, including those associated with DS, MLE, and SI. In a sense, auditors navigate the tension between the need for transparency in AI systems and the potential desires of stakeholders to maintain confidentiality, especially when it comes to proprietary algorithms or sensitive information. Their role involves balancing the demand for openness with the imperative to protect commercial interests and adhere to legal constraints.

4.6 Questions and Exercises

1. **Application question**. The cited DigCompEdu framework has an associated self-reflection tool[1] to understand where you stand in regard to digital competences. Even though there is no such tool for the AI-related competencies, go through all the AI-related competencies described between Sections 4.4.1 and 4.4.5 and reflect on how familiar and confident you are with each of them. This can be done individually or in groups.
2. **Discussion question**. How can we understand whether citizens are aware enough of how AI works?

[1] European Commission. Digital Competence Framework for Educators (DigCompEdu). Available at: https://joint-research-centre.ec.europa.eu/digcompedu_en.

5 AI Governance

5.1 Learning Objectives

This chapter focuses on the "Analysis" and "Application" stages, exploring how to start from guidelines and standards and enact effective governance in specific scenarios. The learning objectives of this chapter are:

- Analysis (Bloom's analyze): Develop an understanding of what is AI governance and of the interplay between the multiple monitoring mechanisms.
- Analysis (Bloom's analyze): Deliberate over the different actors – and their motivations – that drive the ongoing agenda for AI governance.
- Analysis (Bloom's evaluate): Analyze different policies, standards, and regulations.

5.2 Introduction

At the time of writing, AI governance is gaining increasing attention from governments, organizations, and experts around the world. However, it is still an emerging field with multiple opportunities, challenges, and uncertainties.

Various industry organizations and tech companies have launched initiatives and self-regulation efforts to promote responsible AI development. These initiatives often include guidelines for AI ethics and safety. Ethical AI research is a growing field, where academics and organizations are conducting research to address issues related to fairness, accountability, transparency, and bias in AI systems. The need for international cooperation in AI governance is increasingly recognized. Multilateral organizations such as the United Nations are exploring the development of AI guidelines and principles to ensure responsible and ethical AI adoption on a global scale.

5.3 What Is AI Governance?

Governance and policy are related concepts and are often used interchangeably. However, they are not the same. Governance is a broader concept that encompasses the overall management, decision-making, and oversight processes within an organization or institution. It is a socio-technical system that involves defining the structure, roles, responsibilities, and processes for making and implementing decisions within set boundaries. Governance is considered relatively stable and enduring, as any changes to governance structures are typically significant and require formal processes.

Those boundaries are often defined as policies: specific guidelines, rules, or principles that individuals must comply with. Policies can be more flexible and subject to more frequent updates. Organizations can adapt and change policies as needed to address evolving circumstances, regulations, or best practices. They are, in essence, just one of the many types of *controls* that governance professionals employ. Controls are any processes, measures, technical solutions, or policies meant to prevent, manage, direct, or regulate identified risks or other unexpected behavior. While the rest of the book touches on various types of controls (e.g., fairness checking, transparency), this chapter focuses on policies.

5.4 Ethical Guidelines and Standards

Many private companies, public institutions, and intergovernmental organizations have been adopting ethical principles and guidelines for AI development and deployment. However, despite an apparent agreement that AI should be "ethical" and "beneficial for humanity," there is debate about what exactly constitutes ethical AI and which requirements and practices are needed for its realization.

These often included principles related to transparency, fairness, accountability, and bias mitigation. However, there is no universal consensus on what these principles should entail, let alone how compliance can be assessed.

5.4.1 The Early Steps

Asimov's Three Laws

In the 1940s and 1950s, the early pioneers of AI, including Alan Turing and Norbert Wiener, contemplated the ethical implications of creating intelligent autonomous machines. Turing, in particular, raised questions about whether machines could exhibit human-like intelligence and what ethical responsibilities might arise in that context.

During World War II, while Turing was attempting to crack the famous Enigma cipher, Isaac Asimov introduced the "Three Laws of Robotics" in his work *Runaround*, published in 1942. The Three Laws of Robotics are a set of fictional ethical guidelines designed to govern the behavior of robots. The so-called "laws" are:

1. A robot may not injure a human being, or through inaction allow a human being to come to harm. This law emphasizes the primary duty of a robot to protect human life.
2. A robot must obey orders given by human beings, except where such orders would conflict with the first law. This law establishes the requirement for robots to follow human commands, as long as the safety and well-being of humans take precedence over following orders.
3. A robot must protect its own existence as long as such protection does not conflict with the first or second laws.

The Three Laws of Robotics became a cornerstone in Asimov's *iRobot* series, which explored further the complexities and ethical dilemmas that arise when intelligent machines are programmed with such rules. Asimov expanded and refined these laws in subsequent stories and novels. While the three laws are computationally intractable in terms of being coded, they have had a lasting impact beyond science fiction: They inspired some of the earlier debates about the fundamental principles that should guide the development and use of AI.

The development of early AI in the late 1950s, after the Dartmouth Workshop of 1956 established the field, saw a growing awareness of the need for ethical guidelines. However, the field was still primarily focused on technical challenges, with prototype systems far from ready for mass deployment and use. The field focused more on developing algorithms and solving computational problems. Only in the "AI spring" (i.e., a short period of increased funding for AI) of the late 1980s did we start seeing some early discussions around workplace safety, job displacement, and the impact of automation on employment. Still, the field was far from establishing formal guidelines.

Roboethics

It was on January 2004, in a coastal city of northwestern Italy, Sanremo, where the field of *roboethics* was first established as a sub-discipline of robotics, at the First International Symposium on Roboethics. This event marked the beginning of organized efforts to address ethical considerations specific to robotics. The first of such efforts – just a month later – led to the "Fukuoka World Robot Declaration." This short declaration, made public at the International Robot Fair, talked about the need for robots to both *coexist with* and *assist* humans. The second key point of the declaration is particularly interesting as it reads: "Promotion of public acceptability of robots through the establishment of standards and upgrading of the environment." This is one of the many – and earliest – clear examples of high-level guidelines and strategies aiming to establish standards.

Two years later, in 2006, the European Robotics Research Network established a "Roboethics Roadmap," outlining the key challenges and research directions for addressing ethical concerns in the field of robotics. While the initial roadmap had a European focus, the intention was to contribute to a global conversation on roboethics. The roadmap emphasizes the importance of considering the broader societal impact of robotics instead of just technical challenges. This includes addressing issues related to job displacement, economic implications, and the integration of robots into various aspects of daily life. It discusses socio-ethical open questions at large and domain-specific challenges and opportunities (e.g., the use of robots in education). The produced report recognizes the multidisciplinary and interdisciplinary nature of roboethics and encourages collaboration across different scientific fields, such as ethics, law, sociology, psychology, and the various engineering disciplines working in robotics. This collaboration is seen as essential for developing comprehensive solutions to ethical challenges.

EPSRC Principles of Robotics

Half a decade later, in 2010, the United Kingdom's Engineering and Physical Sciences Research Council (EPSRC) and the Arts and Humanities Research Council put together a group of academic researchers in robotics, public servants, legal experts, and military advisors. This group, with little guidance and no set deliverables, spent a long weekend engaging in cross-disciplinary discussions on issues around the applications of robotics in the real world. The main motivation for this workshop was an internal report on how AI is going to be a major export product for the UK. The "EPSRC Principles of Robotics" that resulted from these discussions can be regarded as the first national-level public guidelines on the design, development, and use of AI technologies. The five high-level principles are:

1. Robots are multi-use tools. Robots should not be designed solely or primarily to kill or harm humans, except in the interests of national security.
2. Humans, not robots, are responsible agents. Robots should be designed and operated as far as is practicable to comply with existing laws and fundamental rights and freedoms, including privacy.
3. Robots are products. They should be designed using processes that ensure their safety and security.
4. Robots are manufactured artifacts. They should not be designed in a deceptive way to exploit vulnerable users; instead, their machine nature should be transparent.
5. The person with legal responsibility for a robot should be attributed.

The first three principles are, in fact, a rewrite of Isaac Asimov's (in)famous Three Laws of Robotics. In this rewrite, Asimov's laws are rephrased to emphasize that the responsible party for upholding the principles is not the robot but its designers. This emphasis makes the transfer of moral subjectivity explicit: Robot manufacturers are responsible for ensuring the adequate safeguards in their products – as is the case for any other manufactured products.

The fourth principle introduces the value of *transparency* to AI guidelines. It should be clear that robots are purposed-made tools: authored and owned. This has a dual purpose: To reinforce the message in the rest of the principles regarding responsibility and liability, as with all tools, and to ensure that users do not emotionally overinvest in their products. Bryson discusses how the inclusion of this principle was a subject of a debate among the participants [23]. That is, as we will discuss in Chapter 7, *some* deception might be necessary for the efficacy of their intended application. Ultimately, the principle can be seen as a predecessor of what became the most common and simplest requirement for AI transparency: Make sure that AI systems do not pose as humans.

In 2016, there was a workshop to update the Principles of Robotics, co-located with the annual meeting of the UK's Society for the Study of Artificial Intelligence and Simulation of Behaviour (AISB). The workshop ended with a number of academic papers,[1] but without any updates to the Principles. After the reorganization of the EPSRC as a

[1] Found as topical collections in the journal *Connection Science*; see issues 2 and 3 of volume 29.

branch of UK Research and Innovation (UKRI) in 2018, the Principles were removed from the EPSRC's website. While EPSRC robotics researchers were encouraged but not required to follow them, the Principles can be considered the first high-level guidelines for AI produced at a national level. The ESPRC never required anyone to adhere to them – or even explicitly consider them – when using public research funding for robotics. Despite their eventual disappearance, the Principles served as a good first discussion point – and motivation – for some of the future guidelines. Moreover, they serve as a good lesson: Policy is only relevant if it is used.

5.4.2 The Past Decade

In 2015 we started seeing the beginning of a new "AI summer" (i.e., a period of increased funding and public interest in AI). However, unlike past summers, we have also seen multiple high-profile cases of AI systems failing, with real-world impacts; some worth mentioning are the fatal incidents with autonomous vehicles on public roads, COMPAS software use, and the Cambridge Analytica scandal. At the same time, governments and intergovernmental organizations launched their own surveys to gauge public opinion. Surveys such as the Eurobarometer 2017 made it clear: The public considers AI technology positive but it is also concerned with the wider socio-economic and ethical challenges. All these events and many others may have helped drive the sudden interest in the field of AI governance. Since 2015 there has been a five-times increase in publications released each year related to AI governance; topics such as algorithmic fairness have stopped being exclusively the subjects of academic research and are now R&D areas in the AI industry.

While the EPSRC Principles of Robotics largely went unnoticed by academia and industry outside the UK, in late 2018 and early 2019 we started seeing more guidelines and strategies with a focus on "ethical principles" for AI. Unlike the previous work, these renewed efforts for governance have been looking beyond "mere" embodied agents. Accompanying the new tools and software libraries, discussed in other chapters of this book, there have been over 700 AI strategies and guidelines released by governments, intergovernmental organizations, companies, and professional bodies.[2] Such documents indicate the growing public use of AI technologies, but also the need to mitigate any potential socio-economic harms.

There is a global convergence emerging around some core ethical principles: *transparency*, *fairness*, *accountability and responsibility*, and *data governance and privacy*. Moreover, the limited representation of geographic regions such as Africa, South and Central America, and Central Asia indicates disparities in participation in the ongoing AI ethics discourse, revealing power imbalances in the international efforts to regulate this technology. This raises concerns about overlooking local knowledge, cultural diversity, and the imperative of global equity. While a comprehensive review of all the guidelines released is far beyond the scope of this chapter, four key guidelines are discussed.

[2] As tracked by the OECD AI Policy Observatory.

IEEE Ethically Aligned Design

The IEEE Ethically Aligned Design (EAD) initiative is part of the IEEE Global Initiative on Ethics of Autonomous and Intelligent Systems. EAD offers high-level guidelines for the ethical design and development of autonomous and intelligent systems, aiming to ensure that these technologies align with human values and prioritize human well-being. A draft first version, released in December 2016, was the result of efforts of over 250 stakeholders, including technologists, ethicists, policymakers, and representatives from industry, academia, and civil society. Following input by 13 expert committees run by the IEEE, an updated draft was released near the end of 2017. The final version was released in 2019, following further input.

Structured around several key thematic areas, each exploring different aspects of ethical AI, EAD advocates for eight core principles:

1. Human rights: AI must respect international human rights, prevent discrimination, and ensure equal access.
2. Well-being: AI should prioritize human flourishing, measurable benefits, and long-term positive impact.
3. Data agency: Individuals must have control, informed consent, and transparency over their personal data.
4. Effectiveness: AI should have clear goals, meaningful success criteria, and continuous validation.
5. Transparency: AI decisions must be explainable, auditable, and well-documented.
6. Accountability: Designers and operators must take responsibility, provide remedies, and show compliance.
7. Awareness of misuse: AI development should include risk assessment, safeguards, and vigilance against harm.
8. Competence: AI creators must declare system limits, use proper expertise, and keep improving skills.

EAD is unique among the guidelines discussed in this chapter: It was developed by a professional body instead of a governmental or intergovernmental organization. Moreover, it included many stakeholders with open input. Its multi-stakeholder approach in writing the document intended to incorporate a wide range of perspectives. Still, as we will see later, the eight principles are similar to those found in many other policies. EAD helped to start a more global and vivid dialog around responsible AI and, most importantly, provided a clear call for AI standards that ensure not only technological robustness and performance, but also the trustworthy use of the technology. This request is a shift from more traditional technical standards into establishing auditable processes and requirements to ensure adherence to ethical values.

Guidelines for Trustworthy AI

The Guidelines for Trustworthy AI were developed by the European Commission's High-Level Expert Group on Artificial Intelligence (AI HLEG), which consists of experts from various backgrounds, including academia, industry, and civil society. The purpose of these guidelines is to address the ethical and societal challenges posed by AI technologies and to promote the development of AI systems that are trustworthy and aligned with human values. The European Commission initiated this effort to establish a common framework for the responsible development and deployment of AI within the European Union (EU) and wider European Economic Area. This initiative is part of the Commission's AI strategy to boost AI uptake and simultaneously ensure that AI technologies contribute to societal progress while respecting fundamental rights and ethical principles.

The AI HLEG identified seven key requirements for trustworthy AI: (1) *human agency and oversight*; (2) *technical robustness and safety*; (3) *privacy and data governance*; (4) *transparency*; (5) *diversity, non-discrimination, and fairness*; (6) *societal and environmental well-being*; and (7) *accountability*. These seven key requirements are similar to those presented by the EAD, often under different names; for example, the *data agency* principle is here called *privacy and data governance* and the *competence* principle is part of the *transparency* requirement. The guidelines place more emphasis on the environmental impact and sustainability of AI systems than EAD did. Alongside the guidelines, the "Assessment List for Trustworthy AI" was released – and later refined through qualitative and quantitative evaluation – as a means of offering more hands-on guidance – even if in the form of a checklist – for how to implement the seven key requirements. This assessment list contains over 100 questions, covering each key requirement.

Each country member of the EU was asked to prepared their own AI policy. The vast majority of the countries included some clear reference to – if not a copy of – the seven key requirements. Moreover, subsequent standardization and legislative efforts initiated by the Commission, including the AI Act, make frequent references to those seven key requirements.

UNESCO's Recommendations

The "Recommendation on the Ethics of Artificial Intelligence" is a document crafted by an Ad Hoc Expert Group and ratified worldwide by UNESCO in November 2021. Its primary objective is to offer guidance to policymakers and stakeholders on ensuring the ethical development and utilization of AI. However, it also sets the groundwork for future regulatory frameworks that can facilitate its implementation, with measures put in place to ensure ethical practices.

This document is notable for its ratification process, which included a vote and amendments made by the 193 member countries that participate in UNESCO's efforts. It is an unfortunate reality that not all nations are party to the international agreement and, thus, not compelled to adhere to these guidelines. The recommendations themselves are highly similar to those made in the Guidelines for Trustworthy AI, advocating for the same seven key requirements but with two notable additions.

First, there is a recommendation for "Adaptive governance and collaboration." Acknowledging that large multinational companies have access to massive amounts of information and resources, UNESCO makes it clear they still have to obey both national sovereignty and international law. Sovereign nations should be able to effectively regulate and have oversight of any entity operating in data creation, storage, or processing operations within their territories. Such regulations are only achievable by fostering collaboration between countries and non-public organizations.

Second, there is a recommendation to build awareness and education. UNESCO recommends that the various stakeholders, from both the public and private sectors, collaborate in advancing media literacy and digital skills training. These collaborative efforts should be mindful of the existing cultural and linguistic diversity, considering that there are approximately 200 recognized official languages worldwide. Moreover, there should be a concerted effort to foster a culture of ethical AI across all sectors, this culture can only be built through appropriate awareness and education efforts.

AI Bill of Rights

In October 2022, the White House released the "Blueprint for an AI Bill of Rights: Making Automated Systems Work for the American People" (commonly referred to as the "AI Bill of Rights"). This framework was developed in consultation with academics, human rights organizations, nonprofits, and private sector companies. It lays out five guiding principles:

1. Safe and effective systems: Emphasizes protecting people by requiring pre-deployment testing, ongoing monitoring, risk mitigation, and transparency through public reporting where possible.
2. Protection from algorithmic discrimination: Seeks to prevent bias against protected groups by encouraging equity assessments, representative data use, disparity testing, and independent audits.
3. Data privacy: Underscores user control over personal information, limiting data collection to what is necessary, ensuring clear consent, and providing stronger safeguards for sensitive data and surveillance technologies.
4. Notice and explanation: Requires that people be informed when AI is in use and be given accessible, plain-language explanations of how it works and impacts them.
5. Human alternatives, consideration, and fallback: Enables individuals to opt out of being subject to algorithmic processing and access human review or remedies, especially in cases of errors or harmful outcomes.

Each principle includes additional considerations for protecting civil rights – such as free expression, voting rights, and privacy – across different contexts. A particular emphasis is placed on following the guiding principles in the context of essential services such as healthcare and finance.

Although the AI Bill of Rights was non-binding and does not impose legal requirements, it helped shape regulations in the US. After it was released, several federal agencies adopted guidelines for their own responsible use of AI. In 2021, New York adopted a law, in line with the AI Bill of Rights, requiring employers to disclose the use of AI technologies. Multiple states have adopted recommendations made by the bill regarding the use of facial recognition technology within law enforcement. At a federal level, the 2023 executive order on "Safe, Secure, and Trustworthy Development and Use of Artificial Intelligence" cites the bill and makes a further, more concrete, call for standards and enactment of AI regulations at a federal level.

5.5 Standards

Another type of policy is *standards*. While both standards and guidelines provide rules and information, their primary difference lies in their authority and specificity. This is a crucial distinction in fields like technology, engineering, and regulation, including the world of AI.

The purpose of a standard is to ensure a uniform level of quality, safety, interoperability, or performance. They are formal – often highly technical – documents that set very specific measurable requirements or a clear and consistent set of rules that must be followed to achieve compliance. If a guideline tells you what you *should* do, then a standard tells you what you *must* do.

In many cases, an organization can be certified as compliant with a standard (e.g., ISO 42001 certification). In a legal or contractual context, failing to meet a standard can have significant consequences – particularly in heavily regulated industries. In fact, there is a whole industry of certification agencies and technical auditors.

Unlike guidelines, standards are typically very specific in their application. For example, a standard might mandate the exact type of encryption to be used (e.g., AES-256) to achieve minimum compliance or the specific accuracy rate that needs to be achieved by a model. Even process standards will describe in sufficient details each step that *needs* to be taken for compliance.

5.5.1 ISO/IEC JTC 1/SC 42

ISO/IEC Joint Technical Committee 1/Special Committee 42 (JTC1/SC 42) is the international standards committee for AI. It operates as a joint committee of the International Organization for Standardization (ISO) and the International Electrotechnical Commission (IEC).

Instead of taking a narrow technical focus, SC 42 takes a holistic "ecosystem" approach – similar to well-established ISO standards on management systems, which blend security, environmental, and business requirements. This means its standards consider the entire lifecycle of an AI system, from design and data management to deployment and ongoing monitoring. It also addresses the diverse stakeholders involved, including developers, regulators, and users.

The work of SC 42 is divided into several key areas, each addressed by a dedicated working group:

- Foundational standards: This group establishes the core concepts and terminology for AI. This is a critical first step to ensure that everyone involved in the AI field, from researchers to policymakers, uses a consistent and shared vocabulary.
- Data and analytics: This working group focuses on standards for data used in AI systems. Since performance is highly dependent on data quality, this work addresses issues such as data governance, quality, and management, including for big data analytics.
- Trustworthiness: A major priority is building trust in AI systems. This group's work covers critical nontechnical aspects, such as ethical and societal concerns,

bias mitigation, transparency, accountability, and the security and privacy of AI systems.

- Use cases and applications: This group collects and analyzes real-world AI applications across various sectors (e.g., healthcare, finance, manufacturing). This work helps to identify common requirements and best practices, which in turn inform the development of broader standards.
- Computational approaches: This area addresses the technical and engineering aspects of AI systems, including algorithms and computational characteristics.

A unique aspect of SC 42 is its role as a "systems integration entity." This means it not only develops its own foundational standards, but also provides guidance and a common framework for other ISO and IEC committees. These other committees can then use SC 42's horizontal standards as building blocks to create their own sector-specific "vertical" standards for AI applications in areas such as health informatics or robotics.

5.5.2 ISO/IEC 42001

The ISO/IEC 42001 is – at the time of writing – the most popular standard for companies that create or use AI systems, and it deserves its own mention. Published in December 2023, the standard provides a structured framework, called the AI Management System, to help organizations manage their AI projects and data. Its main goals are to promote ethical AI principles, manage AI-related risks such as bias and data protection, and build trust with stakeholders. It also emphasizes the importance of continuous monitoring and improvement of AI systems and encourages a collaborative approach by involving different teams in the decision-making process.

The central idea of ISO/IEC 42001 is the establishment of an AI management system (AIMS) at an organizational level; that is, a set of policies, procedures, and processes for managing AI. It is designed to be integrated with an organization's existing management systems, such as those set by ISO 27001 for information security and ISO 9001 for quality management. This interplay with other standards helps to ensure that AI is a strategic consideration from a governance perspective. The standard applies to any organization, regardless of its size, sector, or role – whether it is an AI developer, provider, or user.

The standard's requirements are based on the familiar Plan–Do–Check–Act (PDCA) model used in other ISO management system standards. Key requirements include:

- Context of the organization: Defining the scope of the AIMS and understanding the internal and external factors that affect it, such as legal, ethical, and market requirements.
- Leadership and planning: Gaining commitment from top management, setting AI objectives, and planning actions to address risks and opportunities.
- Operation: Implementing the AIMS through detailed procedures, including managing the AI system lifecycle, data, and third-party AI systems.
- Performance evaluation and improvement: Monitoring, measuring, analyzing, and evaluating the AIMS to ensure it is effective and continually improving.

A number of verifiable controls are mapped to each requirement, making this standard structured and, above all, easily certifiable.

By providing a clear and consistent approach to identifying and managing AI-related risks, ISO/IEC 42001 helps to avoid potential financial, legal, and reputational damage. Even if produced by ISO, the standard is deliberately designed to help organizations align with and prepare for emerging AI regulations, such as the EU AI Act, with its risk identification and management controls.

5.5.3 IEEE Standards Association

The IEEE Standards Association (IEEE SA) is a major international organization that plays a significant role in developing and setting standards for technology; most notably, the IEEE SA sets the various networking standards, including those for ethernet cables and Wi-Fi.

A central theme of IEEE's AI standardization is a shift from purely technical considerations to a human-centric approach. This is best exemplified by the P7000 series of standards. Unlike traditional standards that focus on interoperability or functionality, this series addresses the ethical and social challenges posed by AI. These standards provide a practical guide for organizations to implement ethical practices into their AI systems. Notable standards include:

1. IEEE Standard for Transparency of Autonomous Systems 7001-2021: The 7001-2021 standard sets stakeholder-specific requirements for achieving transparency of autonomous systems. It covers a range of different systems, including embodied and virtual AI systems.
2. IEEE Standard for Data Privacy Process 7002-2022: This standard outlines how to manage privacy issues for systems that collect personal data.
3. IEEE Standard for Algorithmic Bias Considerations 7003-2024: The 7003-2024 standard provides a hands-on guide for algorithmic bias considerations to help developers mitigate unwanted biases during dataset creation and model training. Moreover, it sets criteria for establishing and communicating the application boundaries.

Beyond the P7000 series, IEEE has a broader AI Standards Committee that works on a range of technical and governance topics. These projects address a variety of issues, including:

- foundational models: standards for large language models (LLMs) and other generative AI technologies;
- terminology and data formats: creating common language and formats to improve interoperability.
- risk and safety: frameworks and guidelines for defining and evaluating AI risk, safety, and trustworthiness.
- specific applications: standards for AI in specific sectors, such as computer vision, autonomous vehicles, and healthcare.

To help organizations demonstrate their commitment to ethical AI, the IEEE has developed the IEEE CertifAIEd program. This is a certification program that assesses the ethical qualities of autonomous and intelligent systems. It provides a visible mark for products and services that conform to IEEE's AI ethics framework, covering criteria such as algorithmic bias, ethical transparency, privacy, and accountability.

It is also worth noting the difference in contributions from other standardization initiatives. In ISO/IEC and CEN-CENELEC, experts need to be nominated to the committees by their national standardization bodies. Also, they use a "one country, one vote" system, where only national standards bodies are members and vote, typically during specific stages. On the contrary, in the IEEE SA, anyone can contribute and all active IEEE members can vote. This adds a level of openness and accessibility.

5.5.4 CEN/CENELEC

The European Commission has been working since 2021 to create standards for the AI Act, specifically for its high-risk provisions. The task of drafting these standards was assigned to two organizations, CEN and CENELEC, which co-own Joint Technical Committee 21 (JTC 21). In addition to the Commission and national standards bodies, European stakeholder organizations and citizen advocacy groups partake in the discussions.

The EU AI Act, which we will talk about later in this chapter, mandates a set of harmonized standards to provide a clear and verifiable path for organizations to comply with the law. The European Commission has issued a formal standardization request to CEN–CENELEC to develop these standards, which will provide a "presumption of conformity." This means that companies adhering to these standards will be presumed to be in compliance with the relevant legal requirements of the AI Act.

The standards under development cover a wide range of topics related to high-risk AI systems, including:

- AI risk management: Providing a framework to identify, assess, and mitigate risks such as bias, privacy violations, and safety concerns.
- AI quality management systems: Establishing processes for ensuring the quality, robustness, and reliability of AI systems.
- Data governance and quality: Setting standards for the quality and management of data used in AI, a critical component of the AI Act's requirements.
- Technical robustness and accuracy: Defining criteria to ensure AI systems are resilient to errors and cybersecurity threats.
- Transparency and human oversight: Establishing guidelines for providing information about how AI systems work and enabling effective human oversight.
- Conformity assessment: Developing a framework to assess whether an AI system meets all the necessary requirements.

However, as of the time of writing, the different standards are at various stages of this process. The original delivery date of April 2025 has been missed, with standards pushed to 2026. Moreover, there is a wider ongoing debate about how the European standards system operates, with the European Commission considering potential reforms.

5.6 Regulations

Governments can play a central role in creating legal frameworks for AI governance. These regulations may address data protection, algorithmic accountability, and compliance with ethical standards. Several intergovernmental universities and countries have been involved in the process of formulating and implementing regulations related to AI.

The EU has taken a leading role in regulating AI systems with the AI Act. The Act entered partly into force in August 2024, with the majority of its provisions coming into effect gradually over the next two years. While the Biden administration's comprehensive Executive Order 14110 (October 2023) aimed to ensure safe, secure, and trustworthy AI in the US, it was rescinded by the Trump administration in January 2025. However, it is not just the EU and US discussing – or using – regulations on the development and use of AI. For example, Canada is advancing the AI and Data Act to safeguard Canadians from high-risk AI and promote responsible AI practices in line with global norms. Brazil and South Korea have also enacted similar regulations to the AI Act. China has its own multilayered regulatory framework for AI that includes provisions for any algorithm recommendation and generative AI system deployed in the country. The UK and Switzerland do not have AI-specific regulations in place – and, at time of writing, no concrete plans for such regulations – instead they are amending existing laws to accommodate AI.

5.6.1 Vertical vs Horizontal

When policymakers work on a legislative response to AI, a fundamental question that they face is whether they should take a more *horizontal* or a more *vertical* approach to regulating AI systems. In a horizontal approach, regulators create one comprehensive regulation that covers the many impacts AI can have. This is an one-size-fits-all approach. It relies on having an adequate definition on *what is AI* and, then, any system – regardless of its application domain (e.g., games, education, military) – must comply with any requirements set by the regulation.

In a vertical strategy, policymakers take a bespoke approach, creating different regulations to target different applications or types of AI systems. For example, systems that are used in healthcare may be subject to different transparency requirements than ones used in games. Another example of the vertical approach may be to indicate that systems that use a specific technology, like foundational models, must provide additional assurances for the data on which they are trained compared to systems that do not use that technology. Unlike data privacy rules, no country is taking a purely horizontal or vertical approach to governing AI.

For effective governance, a combination of the two approaches is indeed necessary: An AI system is a type of product, but AI at large is a wider field of research and development that can be used across different sectors. Right now, the EU's AI Act heavily leans toward a horizontal approach, with the European Commission planning sector-specific implementations. China's overall collection of regulations, on the other hand, leans toward a more vertical approach as they prioritize specific applications of AI.

5.6.2 AI Act

The EU AI Act introduces a comprehensive, risk-based framework for regulating AI across the EU. Its core purpose is to protect fundamental rights and EU values while still fostering AI research and innovation. The AI Act applies to any business that deploys an AI system within the EU. Importantly, the AI Act does not replace existing regulations; it provides AI-specific requirements that complement other laws, such as the General Data Protection Regulation (GDPR) and product liability directives, which still apply to AI systems.

The Act achieves this by classifying AI systems into four distinct risk levels, with compliance requirements escalating for higher-risk applications.

1. Unacceptable risk (banned): These systems are considered a clear violation of fundamental rights and are strictly prohibited. Examples include systems used for social scoring or the exploitation of vulnerable groups, and most uses of real-time biometric identification in public spaces.
2. High risk (strict obligations): These AI systems pose a significant threat to a person's health, safety, or fundamental rights. They are not banned but are subject to strict compliance requirements throughout their lifecycle, including mandatory registration in an EU database before they can be placed on the market. This category covers AI used in critical sectors such as medicine, infrastructure, education, and law enforcement.
3. Limited risk (transparency obligations): Systems in this category pose a limited threat but require transparency rules. The key obligation is ensuring users are aware they are interacting with an AI.
4. Minimal or no risk (minimal obligations): This vast majority of AI systems (such as video games) poses negligible risk to safety or rights and is subject to no specific regulations under the Act.

The exact obligations depend on the location of each actor in the system's lifecycle. *Providers of AI systems*, in other words those who do the original training of models, bear the primary responsibility for the compliance and safety of their AI systems. On the other hand, *deployers* (i.e., organizations who use an AI system under their authority for professional activities) have much lower requirements. Most of their responsibilities are organizational level; for example, implement risk management, ensure adequate training for staff using the system, and establish mechanisms for human oversight. Finally, *downstream providers* (i.e., organizations who integrate AI components trained by third parties) have a mixture of technical and organizational responsibilities.

Similar to the GDPR, the national-level agencies – found in each EU member state – are responsible for implementing and enforcing the rules for most AI systems within their countries. The European AI Office, which is part of the European Commission, is the central authority tasked with overseeing and enforcing the rules specifically for general-purpose AI models. Additionally, the European Data Protection Supervisor ensures the AI Act is followed by EU institutions and agencies. These various authorities have the power to investigate potential breaches and ensure compliance with the Act. For high-risk AI systems, national authorities also designate notified bodies to handle pre-market approvals. Noncompliance with the AI Act carries severe penalties of up to €35 million or 7% of a company's worldwide annual turnover.

5.6.3 China's Regulatory Framework

China's AI regulation focuses on risk-based compliance, but achieves this through sector-specific regulations rather than a single overarching framework like the EU's. It consists of multiple regional and central regulations – including amendments to existing ones. There is no broad legal structure that classifies AI risks and imposes corresponding obligations. Instead, general AI risk classifications are found in non-binding guidelines and best practices – like ethical codes. In fact, there is not even a clear definition of what constitutes "AI." Instead, each piece of regulation provides its own definition. Two regulations, produced by the central Chinese government, warrant special attention: the "Deep Synthesis Provisions" and "Generative AI Measures." We will look at each of them in turn.

Despite some conceptual similarities to the EU AI Act's focus on technologies that manipulate information, China's approach is distinctly shaped by its administrative and political context. The most stringent obligations are imposed by regulations that target specific services and capabilities deemed particularly sensitive. These key risk categories are formally defined as:

1. public opinion attributes: technologies that can serve as a platform for public expression, such as forums or blogs);
2. social mobilization capabilities: services that can encourage the public to take specific actions.

Essentially, China's regulations focus extensively on what they consider to be sensitive services that can influence public discourse and action. This concept originates in rules for news information services and has been extended to technologies including chatbots, virtual assistants, and content-recommendation algorithms.

The "Generative AI Measures" law, jointly issued by multiple central government agencies, is notable for its encouragement of development and investment in generative AI. However, it provides strict requirements for generative AI system providers:

1. Training data legality (Article 7): Service providers must ensure the data used to train their AI models is legal and does not violate intellectual property rights or

personal information laws. This is intended to prevent legal issues stemming from unauthorized data use.

2. Labeling and quality (Article 8a): Providers need to develop clear, workable labeling rules for training data, train their staff to apply them correctly, and routinely check the accuracy of the labels. This increases the transparency and reliability of the AI's content generation.
3. Usage disclosure and dependency prevention (Article 8b): Providers must clearly disclose the intended users, scenarios, and purposes of their services. Crucially, they must also implement measures to prevent users, particularly minors, from becoming overly dependent on or addicted to the generated content.
4. User data protection (Article 11): Providers must safeguard user input and usage records during the service process, prohibiting the illegal retention or sharing of this information with others. This rule aims to build user trust in the service.

In 2025 we have started to see a wider prohibition on the use of generative AI in specific application domains (e.g., by patent attorneys).

Enforcement of the above – and all other – AI regulations is handled by a plethora of different administrative bodies across various ministries and departments. Their core responsibilities are divided based on the specific area of law and the industrial sector involved. For example, the Cyberspace Administration of China is acting as the main regulator on cybersecurity and data protection areas. Still, China achieves centralized oversight through the central offices of each ministry (or state body). These central offices possess the political authority to supervise their respective industries, setting the procedural rules and policies that local offices across provinces and cities must implement. Organizations operating in China must become familiar with all ministries that have jurisdiction over their services, regardless of their operational location, as local offices of those ministries are responsible for local oversight. This enforcement structure greatly contrasts the EU's one, where the AI office can only play a supporting role while member states enact their own interpretations and enforcement of the AI Act.

5.7 Considerations for Creating AI Governance

Creating an AI governance framework is a socio-technical challenge. It requires a combination of technical solutions (e.g., explainable AI provisions in systems) and socio-organizational ones (e.g., policies for system lifecycle management). While certain controls (e.g., AI usage policies) could be found in most – if not all – AI governance frameworks, providing a list of controls to enact is beyond the scope of this chapter. Instead, here we focus on theoretical and practical considerations for building an effective socio-technical AI governance framework.

We can characterize effective governance based on three distinct attributes: *allocative*, *distributive*, and *stabilizing*. We define what each one of them is and how to best satisfy it in turn by taking a socio-technical approach from the perspective of an AI governance consultant.

5.7.1 Allocative

Allocative refers to the process of determining what problems are worth spending resources on. All governance controls, whether in the form of policies, processes, technical solutions, or other actions, require at the very minimum time to draft, enact, and monitor for compliance. At its base, all controls are about action selection: finding where to best spend resources (e.g., time and money) to ensure compliance with some process or specification. While national strategies may often focus more on motivating "the need for action," every form of policy makes – by simply existing – the statement: The topic of this policy is important enough that some steps need to be taken. Controls for responsible AI research and development are no different.

We live in a complex world of finite resources; satisfying one value may result in ignoring – or directly violating – another. For example, exposing additional information for increasing transparency in a system may result in less privacy and increased costs for developing the model. Improving the accuracy of a model may warrant more training time and, in turn, electricity costs – and, thus, violating the value of sustainability. When such conflicts arise, the challenge is to identify the duties carrying the most ethical weight in a given situation. This is why an efficient AI policy is first and foremost allocative, figuring out which values are needed for the responsible development and use of the technology.

Prioritizing one value over another is not a trivial task, but it is one that needs to be done *explicitly*. The first step is to identify the relevant stakeholders by trying to answer the question, "Whose values should be supported by this policy?" Only by identifying the relevant – direct and indirect – stakeholders can we work toward defining the values at stake. Activities such as surveys, interviews, organization-structure graphs, and other existing documents can aid in identifying key stakeholders and categorizing them according to their roles, interests, and expectations. A *stakeholder matrix* or a *stakeholder map* can be used to plot stakeholders according to their power and interest, but also their relationships and interactions with each other.

Once identified, the use of semi-structured interviews can help answer the crucial question of "How do stakeholders apprehend individual values in the interactive context?" Such interviews are best held in groups with multiple stakeholders present. This way, misalignment between priorities and understanding of the different values are interpreted by them.

Reducing the discussion to specific use cases can help us best explore values trade-offs during the interview. This can be achieved by presenting multiple use cases – that is, different combinations of context can be presented and values elicited for each context. A good way to "force" this is by asking each individual to rank their values based on their personal beliefs and then facilitate a discussion until the group comes up with a shared ranking. Value elicitation from large groups of stakeholders, such as consumers and the general public, can be done through the use of quantitative surveys.

Ideally, each value should be linked to one or more actionable solutions, which can vary anywhere from product features to organizational structure changes. If there is a mandate to follow specific standards, then provide a list of their requirements to the different stakeholders. Ask them to consider these requirements during their values interpretation, as such an action can help create a sense of purpose within leadership for those requirements and make it easier to justify and communicate elsewhere in the organization.

Even if not possible at the time of stakeholder engagement, the AI governance consultant should still link any standardization – or other external policies – requirements to the values. Further, relevant legislation needs to be considered. This should provide any "red lines" (i.e., avoidance of unacceptable risks) the organization can adopt. Once all possible solutions have been identified and a ranking is achieved, resources should be allocated with clear timeframes for achieving each solution.

5.7.2 Distributive

In policy analysis, the term *distributive* refers to the distribution of resources, benefits, or burdens within a society or organization enacting the policy. Policies can have distributive effects, meaning they can allocate resources or outcomes in a particular way among different individuals or groups.

It is also worth noting that the distributive effects of a policy can be analyzed in terms of both intended and unintended consequences. Policymakers may design policies with specific distributive goals in mind, but the actual outcomes may vary based on implementation and other factors. This implies the allocation or – more accurately – reallocation of resources. This is why policy should be as distributive as possible by defining which resources should be used and how to best distribute them.

This allocation of resources is, in its way, a commitment by leadership toward AI governance. Having such a commitment is the first – and sometimes hardest – step of various risk-management frameworks, including the ISO/IEC 42001. However, a commitment alone is not enough. There needs to be documented sharing of resources – and responsibilities with clear mandates – in order to ensure the enactment of any required responsible AI solutions.

For example, a solution required by the vast majority of AI standards is the development and enactment of an AI usage policy. Such a policy can dictate how AI products are used or not within an organization and under which conditions their usage is permitted. It is, in essence, a specialized version of an IT usage policy found in many organizations. Different parts of the organization may "own" different parts of the policy even if the overall policy is managed and maintained by a single person. In this example, the cybersecurity department may be responsible for anything that has to do with security, such as managing and monitoring access rights to the different AI applications. However, the legal department is responsible for ensuring adequate protections for intellectual property and the data protection officer for monitoring personal identifiable data.

Another example might be the implementation of *transparency and explainable AI* features to a product. A product manager may scope the features by setting out a vision, but a project manager produces the completion roadmap and closely monitors developers to ensure its completion. Even within the development team, user experience (UX) specialists may design the interface while AI developers work on the backend code.

Such dissemination of roles is almost inevitable in larger organizations due to their complexity and the overlapping requirements the regulations have to comply with. Sharing responsibilities is essential as it enables organizations to quickly identify unintended consequences from a policy as each party can focus on their area of specialization and share the burden of monitoring and enforcement.

The distributive nature of AI governance also includes establishing clear legal and administrative paths for individuals to challenge decisions made by AI systems, especially in high-risk systems. It is essential for responsible AI to always attribute a significant part of the burden of investigating – and, if deemed needed, fixing – any potential errors to the accountable deployment and development parties. We discuss the topic of accountability further in Chapter 9.

Finally, the distributive nature of effective governance extends to ensuring that benefits from AI technologies do not disproportionately accrue to a small subset of users. Establishing an AI literacy initiative and requesting continuous feedback from different groups can help mitigate that. Organization-wide AI training is a legal requirement for the vast majority of employers deploying and developing AI systems under the EU AI Act. It is also a way to ensure long-term social stability – one of the goals of governance – and an essential step to ensure that AI remains a supplement, not replacement, for talent.

5.7.3 Stabilization

The stabilizing component ensures that once controls are set, they are unlikely to be quickly undone. Stabilization of society is one of the goals of governments when they set legislation. Similarly, organizations committing to controls for responsible AI – even if pushed by legislation – aim to minimize the inherent risks from developing, deploying, and using AI in their business operations. Having AI governance ensures that the organization can innovate but also demonstrate sufficient due diligence in order to prevent legal liability and costly financial penalties. This due diligence is evident by not only complying with current – and, when known, upcoming – legislation, but also by following soft policies and standards.

The long-term goal of governance is to ensure that business needs are covered while also preventing risks from materializing. Where possible, any soft AI policies should be aligned with existing regulatory frameworks, as we discussed in the allocative section. This gives them a legal weight, transforming the discussion from *should* to *must*. Similarly, as we also discussed above, getting a clear mandate and commitment from senior leadership in an organization can help build legitimacy for AI governance efforts.

Governance should mandate scheduled reviews (e.g., annually) to update policies and any other controls based on new application domain, technology, legal, or societal norms. This structured evolution is less disruptive than ad hoc panic-driven changes following an incident, thus ensuring long-term policy stability.

Finally, a variety of controls is necessary across the wider socio-technical system. These controls should include not only *preventive* (i.e., proactive controls meant to stop incidents from occurring in the first place, such as an AI usage policy) and *monitoring* (i.e., a means of checking for any emerging risks or deviation from expected behavior) measures, but also *corrective*. Corrective controls are actions taken after an incident or problem has been detected to fix the issue, minimize damage, and prevent recurrence. Given the complexity in terms of actors involved and often opaque emerging behavior from AI systems, incidents are likely to occur and, sometimes, reoccur. Having fall-back plans in place, incident review sessions, and even attributing accountability when needed are all means of ensuring the long-term stability of any governance framework.

5.8 Questions and Exercises

1. **Consider the scenario:** A mid-sized city police department adopts a new AI system to allocate police patrols. The system, trained on 10 years of historical crime data, predicts which neighborhoods are most likely to have criminal activity each day. The historical data shows a clear pattern of higher-density arrests and stop-and-frisks in low-income, minority neighborhoods, largely due to pre-existing patrol strategies. The new AI-driven strategy immediately reinforces this pattern: It consistently recommends sending more officers to the previously heavily policed neighborhoods, leading to more arrests there. Meanwhile, property crimes in wealthier neighborhoods, which were historically under-reported, continue to rise, undetected by the AI.
   (a) Identify the governance failure.
   (b) Propose an intervention approach.
   (c) Define accountability.
2. **Consider one of your AI projects.** Produce a stakeholders' matrix and try to complete the "Assessment List for Trustworthy AI."

6 Harms

6.1 Learning Objectives

This chapter focuses on the "Appreciation" and "Analysis" stages, focusing on understanding the concept of harm and on the ability to identify and prevent them. The learning objectives of this chapter are:

- Appreciation (Bloom's understand): Understand the idea of harm.
- Analysis (Bloom's evaluate): Weigh pros and cons of different methods based on potential harms.
- Analysis (Bloom's evaluate): Identify appropriate due diligence actions to prevent harms.
- Application (Bloom's apply): Design harm detection and redress mechanisms for specific applications.

6.2 What Is Harm and Who Does It Happen To?

We say that something causes harm when it has an ill effect on someone, often designating severe effects such as suffering or pain. In the context of the use of AI, harms have been identified in a variety of effects. A well-publicized harm of AI is discrimination, for reasons of gender or race, for example. This has happened in a variety of applications, from algorithms setting credit card spending limits, to systems filtering CVs in a hiring process. It is clear what the harms are in these scenarios: Having less allowance for spending or losing the opportunity to get a deserved job. It is also clear who is harmed in these scenarios: those being discriminated against, who have fewer opportunities than those who were evaluated without prejudice.

Another possible harm stemming from the use of AI can come from unintended data exposure. Insecure AI applications may be reverse-engineered or queried to reveal training data, which may contain anything from proprietary source code in the case of a large language model (LLM) to sensitive personal information in the case of a medical device. Again, it is clear who is harmed in those circumstances: those whose information has been revealed without their consent.

A third example of harm comes directly from the use of generative methods known as "deepfakes." These can be used to, for example, generate videos of notable figures saying things they never really said, without their consent. Those appearing in these fake videos are clearly harmed, as their images are used without their permission and misrepresent their actions. Consider, as well, that those watching the video and believing its content are harmed as they are led to disinformation.

What all three examples have in common is that harms are not inflicted in a uniform fashion. In the case of discrimination, some users may be harmed, where others may even benefit. In the case of data leaks stemming from training data, it is not necessarily only users who are harmed, but rather those who were included in the training data, who may not even be aware of it. And finally, in the case of deepfakes, those whose likeness is taken are harmed, even when completely unrelated to the development or use of the system. Thus, we can already highlight that there is no single method that can lead developers or users to automatically detect harms: The only way to detect harm is to listen to those affected. This brings to light a challenge when trying to avoid harms: The work of bringing up the existence of harms may fall disproportionately on the communities affected [38], as they are the only ones that may be able to speak on those harms.

Another commonality between the examples is that it is not straightforward to *quantify* the severity of harm. Not obtaining a job due to discrimination could be given a quantification in terms of lost wages, but can also have less countable effects, such as an increase of mistrust in societal structures [110]. Likewise, the effects of appearing in a deepfake without consent or of receiving misinformation are difficult to quantify, on both individual and social levels.

So, given that it is not obvious or measurable, why is a focus on harms advised in the responsible development of AI? In fact, many trustworthy AI guidelines include the concept of *non-maleficence*: development, deployment, and use of AI such that it avoids bringing harm. Focusing on harms inevitably centers affected communities, as they are the ones that can identify and describe them [38]. Furthermore, the concept of harm is very wide, not limited to physical or monetary harm, and may include any range of ill effects. Therefore, focusing on harms forces us to maintain a holistic perspective, taking into account a whole range of actors that may be directly or indirectly harmed, and also taking into account a whole array of possible harms [96].

6.3 AI Harms: An Evolving Taxonomy

Detecting, understanding, and cataloguing AI-related harms is a continuous exercise that proceeds in parallel with the evolution of the technology and the realization of its effects. To date, there is no unified, widely accepted classification of risks, but ongoing projects seek to collect, organize, and unify AI risk frameworks [130, 132, 147].

While taxonomies vary in how they organize AI-related harms, some of the most prominent categories that arise from these analyses are:

- **Representational harms.** Machine learning models trained to infer patterns from a dataset are designed to generalize behaviors, traits, or properties from a small sample to a general population. This can lead to harms related to the propagation of stereotypes (e.g., exclusively male depictions of "engineers" by a generative model) or to profiling (most prominently in predictive policing scenarios) [147].

- **Socio-economic harms.** The development and use of AI tools can lead to widening socio-economic gaps, as well as harm to those with specific socio-economic backgrounds. These harms cover the power inequality created by access and ownership of AI tools being restricted to certain groups, as well as the deployment of biased tools that create unequal distribution of benefits [132].
- **Security vulnerabilities.** As with any tool, AI systems can be misused with malicious intent, sometimes with the specific intent to harm. In addition, in systems that rely on data, the harms of data breaches can be vast, especially when working with sensitive data [130].
- **Information hazards.** Relying on AI systems to obtain predictions or factual information carries with it the risk of obtaining false or misleading information, which can sometimes even be presented as factual or in a credible manner. These harms range from obtaining an incorrect prediction leading to loss of income, to obtaining a false answer from a chatbot leading to believing misinformation [132].

Bringing light to AI-related harms is key to redressing them and to enabling prevention. Meta-analyses of risks can also bring light to *when* harms were detected and *by whom*, leading us to better practices for prevention and detection.

6.4 Due Diligence and Preventing Harm

Since harms can be suffered by anyone related or unrelated to an application, it is fundamental to put systems in place to prevent them as much as possible. Having a process in place to analyze and prevent damage is known as doing *due diligence*. The concept of due diligence is well known in legal and business areas, and although its definitions may differ, the key points are that the actions undertaken to prevent harm should be *informed* and *comprehensive* [133]. Therefore, harm prevention efforts should be undertaken at all steps of the design, development, and deployment process. In this section, we will go through some actions that can constitute due diligence in minimizing harms, although keep in mind that many more can apply, depending on the intended use of a system:

- **Diversity in the team.** As we saw in the previous section, it may be hard to predict who can be harmed by an application, especially moving beyond its users. Furthermore, there is no objective definition of what constitutes harm. Thus, including different perspectives in the design and development team is an obvious first step to anticipate clear harms.
- **Co-design methods.** Many design practices exist under the umbrella of co-design. The key focus is on active involvement of stakeholders, whether that is intended users, possibly impacted communities, or any and all mixes of participants.

Co-design and participatory approaches can be conducted in many different ways, with a wide variety of methods and toolkits available to designers. By including a broad range of experiences and knowledge, harms can be anticipated much quicker, as are solutions.

- **Impact assessments.** Impact assessments are tools used to assess the potential positive and negative impacts of an innovation [14]. What is assessed often includes the purpose of the project, its impact on the environment, on protected groups or society, the validity of mitigation measures, and any alternative solutions that could fill the same need. In addition, impact assessments often include consultations of stakeholders who, to a more or less extensive degree, can bring up additional considerations. Some assessments are narrower in the types of impacts they consider, and are particularly relevant for AI:
  - **Technology assessment.** Technology assessments are carried out to weigh the pros and cons of introducing a new piece of technology into a workflow, a process, or society at large [66]. Overall, they consist of analyzing which needs a new technology is fulfilling, how adequately it is addressing those needs, how it fits within the current systems in place, and how the systems around it will be altered by its use. There exist a wide variety of bodies specialized in conducting such assessments, as well as different frameworks to guide it. As for any impact assessment, it is key to document the questions and conclusions reached by the technology assessment.
  - **Data impact assessment.** Data impact assessments [19] have been developed for use with any system utilizing sensitive data (such as location, demographic data, or health data), where privacy requirements are high. They include an assessment of the *proportionality* of the usage of the data, a weighing of the necessity vs. the risks of storing and processing such data, and an assessment of the adequacy of the mitigation measures. There exist a variety of frameworks to conduct data impact assessments, including the EU's Data Protection Impact Assessment (DPIA) [58].
  - **Human rights impact assessment and environmental impact assessment.** These kinds of assessments focus on predicting social changes and human rights/ environmental impacts. They can be summarized as studying the potential adverse effects of a product/technology on those that hold rights. To be conducted effectively, participation of many stakeholders is key, as is selecting indicators to track human rights or environmental factors. Again, there exist a variety of frameworks to conduct such impact assessments on AI systems – for example, the Danish Institute on Human Rights' assessment [43].
- **Audits.** Audits consist of a collection of information that is reviewed by an independent party in a systematic manner to check adherence to given standards. Audits of AI systems concern both technical and organizational aspects and all parts of development, from data collection to deployment [119]. Audits can be internal (completed by a dedicated group within the same company that deploys a product) or external (completed by a third party). There are three key aspects to a successful audit:

- a suitable independent auditor (or auditing group) with enough knowledge and resources and no conflict of interest;
- a good scope of what the audit aims to explore or find out, and what are desirable and undesirable outcomes; and
- a wealth of information that the auditor can draw upon for information. Thus, record keeping and transparency are particularly key for auditing purposes.

6.5 Detecting Harm

Even when the utmost care is taken to avoid harms, it is impossible to predict everything; harms may still occur. In that case, it is fundamental that we have systems in place to detect when it happens, to correct and repair the harm, and to attribute accountability to those who may have been responsible.

There exist several technical approaches to detect harm. One of these is using one of the several measures of fairness to detect whether a system is biased and how much. Similarly, there are detection mechanisms to alert regarding, for example, data breaches or malfunctions. However, to be able to detect harms in such an automated manner, we rely on them being predictable and measurable. This is, of course, not the case for many harms.

For example, many harms occur at the social level, where measuring the output of a system or restricting ourselves to quantifiable harms will not do. Furthermore, harms may be due to the deployment of a system in a certain social context, rather than the system in isolation. This is the case when the misuse of a system for a purpose other than intended leads to harm, such as in the use of generative systems to produce misinformation campaigns. This can also happen when the context of use changes and outcomes that were previously adequate are no longer adequate, such as how changes in acceptable discourse can lead to chatbots becoming obsolete.

For this reason, besides technical checks, a socio-technical perspective with avenues to bring up harms and redress them is a must. Continuous monitoring is fundamental in this aspect: The responsibility for bringing up and mitigating harms should not fall on those affected, but instead be a proactive decision. Activities can include:

- an explicit point of contact for concerns;
- an explicit action plan to follow when harms are brought up;
- contestability avenues for stakeholders to contest system decisions that pertain to them;
- continuous monitoring activities involving stakeholders, to catch any arising concerns or harms.

Once harms have been identified, the next step is mitigation, redress, and accountability. It is the organizations deploying or operating AI systems that are accountable and liable.

6.6 Questions and Exercises

1. **Discussion question**. Consider a translation system that systematically mistranslates for a minority language. Who is harmed? Would collecting more data from the language be a good solution?
2. **Use-case analysis**. CitySafe, a major metropolitan city's public safety initiative, recently implemented an AI-powered surveillance system to enhance security and reduce crime rates. This system uses a network of high-definition cameras equipped with facial recognition technology to monitor public spaces, identify potential threats, and alert law enforcement agencies in real time. A year after the implementation, the mayor's office reported a significant reduction in street crime and faster response times to incidents. However, privacy advocates raised concerns about the system's impact on citizens' privacy and civil liberties.
   (a) Create a harm impact map for CitySafe: Identify various stakeholders and map out potential harms for each group. Assess the likelihood and severity of each potential harm occurring.
   (b) Suggest system changes to address and reduce these harms.
   (c) What kind of data, logs, and other information should be kept to ensure that an audit of the system can be effectively conducted?
   (d) In light of the map and potential solutions, should the surveillance system be kept? If so, what types of legal and regulatory frameworks can be implemented to prevent and redress harms?
3. **Essay question**. What kind of socio-technical aspects should be included in choosing an appropriate definition of harms?

7 Transparency and Explainability

7.1 Learning Objectives

This chapter focuses on three learning aspects: "Appreciation," "Analysis," and "Application," as we discuss the values of transparency and explainable AI, moving from a high-level description to more practical examples and considerations.

- Appreciation (Bloom's understand): Distinguish the nuances between commonly used keywords: transparency, interpretability, and explainability.
- Appreciation (Bloom's evaluate): Articulate why transparency and explainability are often a prerequisite for deploying AI, particularly in "high-stakes environments," while also recognizing the limitations of not having insights into the decision-making process of an AI system regardless of its risk level.
- Analysis (Bloom's analyze): Critically examine when transparency may introduce more noise and distract from the system's intended purpose.
- Analysis (Bloom's analyze): Analyze the structural trade-offs in explainable AI by contrasting global vs. local and model-agnostic vs. model-specific explanations to determine their suitability for diverse stakeholder needs.
- Application (Bloom's apply): Understand how to use different transparency and explainable AI techniques at different parts of a system's lifecycle.

7.2 What Is Transparency?

In various contexts, *transparency* implies openness, visibility, and the availability of information to others. Transparency in governance refers to the openness and accessibility of government decisions and of the factors that led to those decisions. Since the Watergate scandal, transparency has been hailed as the key for better governance to prevent corruption, hold public officials accountable, and build public trust.

In computer science and information technologies, transparency has multiple definitions. In fields such as distributing systems and information security, transparency has an almost opposite sense: The underlying mechanisms of the system are hidden from the user such as not to obstruct its intended function. In other words, the user is only provided with the information they need to know to perform a particular function.

For example, in a distributed system, access transparency refers to the file distribution being hidden from the clients, making local and remote resources appear the same.

In AI, over the years the definition has taken many forms. In this chapter, we are three complementary definitions: (1) the fourth principle from the United Kingdom's "Principles of Robotics"; (2) the IEEE 7001 Standard on Transparency of Autonomous Systems; and a wider socio-technical view.

The UK's "Principles of Robotics" (for a discussion on these, see Chapter 5) state as their fourth principle: "Robots are manufactured artefacts. They should not be designed in a deceptive way to exploit vulnerable users; instead their machine nature should be transparent" [23]. This means that any system should always identify itself to be not only an AI system, but also a tool, an artifact, designed and developed to be used. This is our baseline definition: The minimum requirements for any system claiming to be transparent.

A more elaborate definition can be found in the IEEE 7001 Standard on Transparency of Autonomous Systems, which suggests that "to consider an autonomous system transparent to inspection, the stakeholder should have the ability to request meaningful explanations of the system's status either at a specific moment or over a specific period or of the general principles by which decisions are made (as appropriate to the stakeholder)" [136, 149]. This definition enables us to view transparency not only in real-time use of the system, but also as a means of investigating past events (i.e., providing *traceability*).

A socio-technical view of the value refers to the openness and clarity in the design, development, and deployment of AI systems. Such a view goes beyond implementing transparency only in the technical comportment, and takes into consideration the stakeholders, the system's lifecycle, and the governance frameworks under which the system was developed and is used.

7.3 Developing Transparent Systems

Taking a socio-technical view, we can consider three separate levels that build on top of each other: (1) the *hardware level*; (2) the *software level*; and (3) the *system's lifecycle and governance*.

The hardware level deals with the requirements for ensuring transparency in the hardware used by the system. The software level is about the algorithms and data used by the system. The system's lifecycle and governance goes beyond the technical components and looks into decisions and the wider socio-organization context in which a system is developed, deployed, and used.

7.3.1 Hardware-Level Transparency

We can achieve transparency in the physical layer first and foremost by the disclosure of hardware information. These requirements can be seen as universal to *all* AI systems, regardless of their actual embodiment. After all, computation is a physical process – all AI systems run on *some* hardware.

We can then make a special case for *physically embodied agents* – that is, any agent that inhabits, populates, and alters the material world (e.g., robots, autonomous vehicles). Such agents have additional requirements for transparency at the hardware level regarding their physical design characteristics.

Disclosure of Hardware Information

Transparent hardware practices include the responsible disclosure of security vulnerabilities and defects. Manufacturers should communicate openly about potential vulnerabilities, release patches or updates, and provide users with the information needed to secure their systems. Tolerances and expected operational conditions (e.g., temperature, tested up-time) for the hardware should also be clearly communicated. Moreover, the testing conditions used – alongside with the test results themselves – should ideally be part of any technical documentation.

Such disclosures help not only to build trust in the organization providing the system, but also ensure safe operation. As we discuss in Section 7.6, not every user of every system may need all the above information. However, as the risk level of a system increases, more information should be expected to be disclosed, at least as technical documentation – supplementing any end-user material.

Going a step further than the disclosures discussed above, the use of *open-source hardware* ensures transparency. Open-source hardware transparency can be achieved by providing clear and comprehensive documentation that explains the architecture and design of the AI hardware. This involves making publicly available the components specifications (e.g., processors used), schematics of the different components, interconnects used in the hardware accelerators, and explanations of the design choices made.

Open-source hardware promotes interoperability by ensuring that hardware components adhere to open standards and specifications. This allows users, developers, and other stakeholders to access, modify, and contribute to the design, fostering collaboration and innovation. Moreover, it offers long-term sustainability, as it becomes easier to adhere to the ongoing socio-economic movement right to repair – that is, allowing owners of electronic systems to freely modify and repair their products.

The Design of Physically Embodied Agents

We should refrain from designing our robots with deceptive features, such as making them appear human- or animal-like (anthropomorphism and zoomorphism, respectively). The physical appearance of an agent alters the perception of those who interact with it. For example, the exposure of electronic parts (e.g., wires, circuit boards) often leads to associating the agent with masculine features, power, and cutting-edge performance. Such gender-based stereotyping is based on implicit societal biases. Such a strategy should only be employed when it serves the purpose of providing contextual information about an agent's functionality or enhances its overall utility.

Anthropomorphizing robots can create unrealistic expectations about their capabilities and intelligence. Users might assume that robots possess human-like understanding, emotions, or reasoning abilities when, in reality, they are artifacts. People may develop emotional attachments to anthropomorphized robots, leading to over-identification and empathy. This emotional connection could be problematic, especially in situations where any detachment is essential.

Nevertheless, it is imperative that we never conceal the locations of robots' sensors. For instance, the practice of disguising advanced camera sensors with unnecessary mammalian-like "eyes" on our robots, such as to deceive users, should be avoided [125]. The visibility of sensor locations and capabilities is essential, establishing a basic physical layer of transparency. Going a step further, signs or other physical cues (including warning signs) could be used to indicate further information on the sensing capabilities of the machine. Ideally, through LEDs or any other means, there should be a clear indication when a system is actively recording data.

7.3.2 Software-Level Transparency

Software-level transparency addresses how a model works or functions internally. It can be divided into three components: (1) *simulatability*; (2) *decomposability*; and (3) *algorithmic transparency*.

Simulatability

This indicates a model's capacity to be simulated by a human (e.g., run on pen and paper). While naturally this category encompasses simpler models, simplicity alone doesn't guarantee simulatability. For instance, rule-based systems are often considered to be "inherently transparent." However, a large number of simple rules could render it challenging for a human to mentally compute the model's decision. Conversely, uncomplicated instances of otherwise intricate models, such as basic neural networks, might be considered simulatable.

Decomposability

This refers to having an understanding of the individual components that make up the system. It requires making the architecture and parameters of the AI model explicit. This includes providing information about the algorithms and data used, the model's structure, rules, and any other parameters. This allows users to understand how information flows within the model; from its input to its output.

Moreover, any knowledge used for developing the model, including any training sets, need to be disclosed. This includes disclosing the sources of the data, recorded biases, and any preprocessing steps applied to the data. Understanding the data used helps users and stakeholders assess the reliability of the AI system.

Algorithmic Transparency

This relates to the "visibility" of the algorithms – that is, the procedure the model goes through to decide how to act. In most cases, publishing the exact algorithms does not bring a lot of transparency either, especially if you do not have access to the data used in a model. Nowadays, cognitive and computer scientists develop human-interpretable descriptions of how applications behave, and why. This type of transparency is closely related to explainability, which we review in the next section. Approaches include the development of data visualization tools, interactive interfaces, and meta-level descriptions of the features of models. These tools can be extremely helpful for making AI applications more accessible. However, there is still plenty of work to be done.

7.3.3 Lifecycle-Level Transparency

Developers must clearly document the entire AI development process, including data collection, model training, and evaluation. This documentation should be shared with stakeholders, and it can provide insights into the decision-making rationale of the AI system. Documentation can include a description of – and the results from – any testing conducted.

It is important to establish a comprehensive documentation process that tracks the changes made to an AI ecosystem, such as its algorithms and data. This documentation includes regular and updated transparency reports that note these changes in the AI system so stakeholders are informed about these updates and any implications.

Transparent practices include providing information about the environmental impact of the system. This encompasses aspects such as energy efficiency, materials used in manufacturing, and the recyclability or disposal considerations.

Transparency in supply chains involves providing visibility into the manufacturing and sourcing processes. This includes information about the origin of components, ethical sourcing practices, and compliance with environmental and labor standards.

Finally, transparency links with governance and assessment as it involves compliance with industry standards and certification requirements. Developers should openly communicate their adherence to any relevant standards, certifications, and regulations. Moreover, compliance – or more importantly *lack of* – with relevant regulations is important.

7.4 What about Explainable AI?

Explainable AI (XAI) refers to the development of AI systems in a way that allows humans to *understand* decisions and actions by providing *explanations*. An explanation is loosely considered an answer to a *why* question [98]; for example:

1. Why did the robot stop moving forward?
2. Why was my mortgage application denied?

In this context, an explanation refers to the process of generating and presenting an answer to a *why* question. The goal of providing such explanations is to provide insights into how and why a particular decision was reached.

In the literature there are multiple nuanced distinctions between *interpretability* and *explainability*, with the former implied to be a subset or means for having explainability. That is interpretability focuses on exposing the inner workings of the models (e.g., decision logic, features, and factors influencing the model's predictions), and such information might be used for generating explanations.

We consider interpretability the degree to which a human can understand the cause of a decision [99]. However, for the purposes of simplifying the language used in this chapter, we use *interpretable* and *explainable* interchangeably as an interpretable model is also an explainable model. Instead, we consider the important distinction to be between explanations (i.e., the generated answer to a *why* question) and interpretability/explainability (i.e., the property or means of the system for generating explanations).

7.5 Developing Explainable Systems

Different methodologies for achieving XAI can be categorized based on several criteria. In this section we review the most common categories.

7.5.1 Intrinsic and Post-Hoc Explanations

One criterion is whether the explanations provided are due to the use of an *intrinsically interpretable model* or with the use of a *post-hoc explanation technique*. This distinction relates to whether explainability is attained by constraining the complexity of the model (i.e., the model is *inherently* interpretable due to its design) or there is a need for a separate XAI technique to "extract" the explanation.

Inherently Interpretable Models

Inherently interpretable models – often also referred to as *explainable-by-design models* – tend to be "simpler" systems. Common approaches include:

- rule-based models (i.e., symbolic systems);
- tree-based models (e.g., decision trees);
- linear models (e.g., linear and logistic regressions); and
- simple neural networks (i.e. neural networks without hidden layers and often subject to certain restrictions).

In order to further reduce their complexity, when models are developed to be inherently interpretable then constraints on the parameters to be optimized are introduced. These constraints include restricting:

- the complexity and number of decision rules;
- the number of variables selected by the model for prediction;
- the number of steps in the prediction; and
- the depth of the decision trees or neural networks.

There is no such thing as a "free lunch." Placing restrictions may make the model less accurate and robust. Moreover, it is important to recognize that constraints such as the depth of a decision tree may make a model interpretable to some but not to others.

Post-Hoc Explainability

Post-hoc explainability refers to the application of explainable AI methods after model training. Permutation feature importance is, for example, a post-hoc method that measures the impact of each feature on a model. Post-hoc methods can also be applied to intrinsically interpretable models. In the rest of the chapter, we focus on post-hoc explainability.

7.5.2 Model-Specific and Model-Agnostic Explanations

Another way of categorizing XAI methods is based on whether they are developed to work only with specific types of models or they are easily adaptable.

Model-Specific Techniques

These are XAI approaches that only work on predefined models. They use the specific characteristics and architecture of the underlying model to produce explanations. One model-specific technique is to export the rules that make up a decision tree.

For example, extracting a sample decision tree from a model trained on the diabetes dataset[1] will look like Figure 7.1

```
|--- s5 <= -0.00
|   |--- bmi <= 0.01
|   |   |--- s3 <= 0.02
|   |   |   |--- s2 <= 0.09
|   |   |   |   |--- value: [105.68]
|   |   |   |--- s2 >  0.09
|   |   |   |   |--- value: [241.50]
|   |   |--- s3 >  0.02
|   |   |   |--- sex <= 0.00
|   |   |   |   |--- value: [88.00]
|   |   |   |--- sex >  0.00
|   |   |   |   |--- value: [68.55]
|   |--- bmi >  0.01
|   |   |--- age <= -0.08
|   |   |   |--- age <= -0.09
|   |   |   |   |--- value: [302.00]
|   |   |   |--- age >  -0.09
|   |   |   |   |--- value: [246.00]
|   |   |--- [...]
|--- s5 >  -0.00
|   |--- bmi <= 0.01
[...]
```

Figure 7.1 Sample structure of a decision tree.

[1] This is an open-data dataset bundled with `sklearn`. It contains the baseline information for 442 diabetes patients (e.g., age).

While the output in Figure 7.1 may not necessarily help a naive user to understand why a *specific* decision was reached, it gives us a global overview of how the system makes decisions.

Model-Agnostic Techniques

These XAI approaches are flexible enough to be adapted to the shape of the data without making assumptions about the distribution or structure of the underlying model (e.g., a decision tree, a linear regression). They often rely heavily on the data itself to guide the analysis or predictions. Examples include *LIME* and *SHAP*, which we review later in this chapter.

7.5.3 Global and Local Explanations

Interpretation methods can be classified as local or global, based on whether they explain *individual predictions* or *the entire model behavior*. Achieving global interpretability is an ongoing challenge because it requires a comprehensive understanding of – and access to – the trained model, its underlying algorithm, and the datasets used for training. To truly grasp a model's decision-making process, we must account for all of its internal structures, including all weights and parameters.

This is rarely feasible in practice. In a commercial context, models are often a closely guarded trade secret. Providing full access to weights, architectures, and specific algorithmic configurations could allow competitors to reverse-engineer or clone the product. Consequently, companies often restrict global access to protect their competitive advantage, offering only limited local explanations instead. Moreover, allowing a deep dive into training datasets may result in data leaks of sensitive and/or personal data, leading to potential privacy breaches and legal liability. Finally, when a model's architecture exceeds a handful of parameters and weights, it overloads the average person's cognitive capacity; this prevents a clear understanding and typically results in further confusion rather than clarity. Consequently, instead of attaining a complete systemic understanding, we often need to focus only on specific aspects of the model, such as the weights in linear models, or simply – as we see in the *local explanations* section – to understand *individual explanations*.

Global Explanations

Global XAI methods try to answer the question "How does the model make its decisions?" by exposing the relationships between input features and predictions that a model can make. It involves identifying which features hold significance and discerning the interactions among them.

Partial Dependence Plot (PDP)

PDP is a widely used method for generating global explanations. By selecting a particular feature and treating the rest of the features as constants, we can detect whether the relationship between the prediction and the selected feature is linear, nonmonotonic, or more complex. This way, we can understand the marginal impact that features have on the model's predictions.

For example, in a linear regression model, PDP consistently displays a linear correlation. It is defined as in Eq. (7.1):

$$[h!]f_S(x_S) = E_{X_C}[\widehat{f}(x_S,X_C)] = \int \widehat{f}(x_S,X_C)d\mathbb{P}(X_C). \tag{7.1}$$

The x_S are the features for which the partial dependence function should be plotted and x_C are any features used in the model. The partial function $\hat{f}$ is a partial function, a *Monte Carlo* method,[2] estimated by calculating averages in the training data.

Let's revisit the diabetes dataset from the model-specific techniques example. We can use PDP to explore how important features, such as `age` and `bmi`, are to the prediction. A sample output is seen in Figure 7.2:

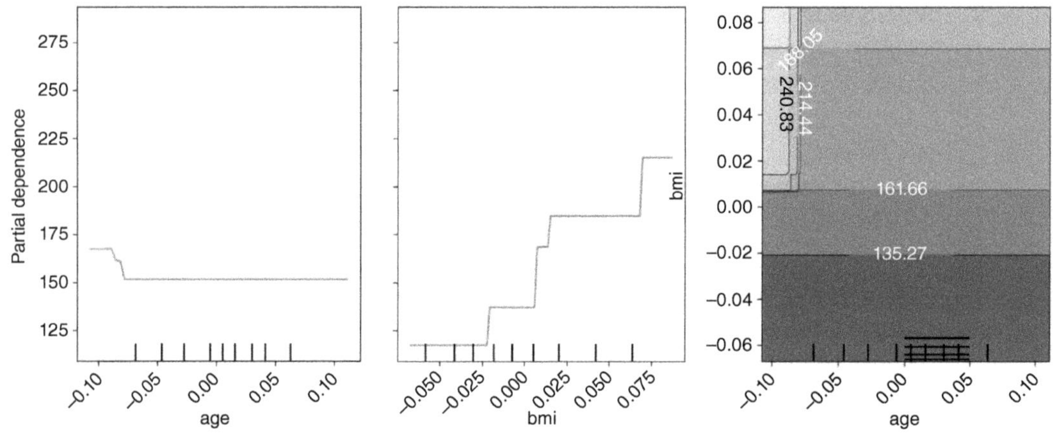

Figure 7.2 Sample output of the PDP method for generating global explanations. The graphs showcase the interaction between selected features (`age` and `bmi`) with the target response.

The first two graphs are the PDP for two features (single feature per plot). They show the interaction between a selected feature (`age` and `bmi`, respectively) with the target response from the mode. The final graph is a PDP with two selected features; it illustrates the effect that two features have on the prediction as they both change.

Our plots show that the `age` feature[3] has an almost constant relation to our model. Younger people (i.e., with `age` value of < -0.09) are less likely to have diabetes, but afterwards the effects of age are minimal. On the other hand, the `bmi` feature shows a linear relationship. The higher the `bmi`, the more likely the person has diabetes.

Finally, we can use the third graph to understand the relationship between the two features and the prediction. There is an easy-to-spot interaction: Younger people

[2] In other words, a repeated random sampling algorithm.

[3] The values in the dataset are mean-centered and scaled by the standard deviation to ensure a total sum of 1 in each column.

(`age` < −0.09) with high `bmi` (> 0.07) are far more likely to have diabetes. However, after the above age, only the feature `bmi` influences the prediction.

Our example demonstrates the usefulness of PDP. It is an intuitive and easily implemented process, enabling us to see how features interact with the final prediction. However, its effectiveness relies on the assumption that the features used in the PDP are not correlated with other features. This is not always realistic. For example, in a mortgage application system, age and income are more likely be correlated as older applicants tend to have higher incomes. Moreover, PDP as a global XAI method only tells us the average effect a feature has on the prediction. Any heterogeneous effects are likely to be hidden. Still, PDP is a useful approach in understanding the interaction of one or more features with the predictions made.

Global Surrogate Model

A global surrogate model is a model trained to approximate the predictions of a more complex opaque model that we want to interpret. The main purpose of a global surrogate model is to provide an interpretable representation of how the complex model behaves across the entire dataset. It is considered "global" because it aims to capture the overall behavior of the original model across the entire dataset. Typically, approaches that lend themselves to interpretation (i.e., inherently interpretable models such as decision trees) are used as surrogates.

To build a global surrogate model, one typically follows these steps:

1. **Train the original model:** Train the complex model on the dataset.
2. **Generate predictions:** Use the original model to generate predictions for the dataset.
3. **Train the surrogate model:** Train an interpretable model using the dataset and the predictions generated in the above step.
4. **Understand the surrogate:** Use additional techniques (e.g., tree visualization) to understand the surrogate and, by extension, the original model.

Creating a surrogate model might be fairly straightforward, but it requires a significant amount of resources. While the surrogate model is most likely an "easier" model to train than the original, it still requires computational time for its training and development time for its tuning. Surrogate models need to be tuned to be as close approximations as possible to the original models, otherwise poor matching can lead to misleading results. For this, we need to understand the distribution of the data used in training the surrogate. However, on its own, surrogate modeling as a technique tells us little about the underlying data. Still, without understanding the data used to train both the original and surrogate models, we may have a case where the surrogate is close to the original model for one subset of the data, but statistically different in others.

Local Explanations

Local XAI methods aim to answer questions such as "Why was this particular prediction made?"

Local Interpretable Model-Agnostic Explanations (LIME)
Local surrogate models are interpretable models that are used to explain individual predictions. LIME is one of the most popular local surrogate approaches [122]. The basic principle is not unlike a global surrogate model we introduced above: Generate an interpretable model that approximates the behavior of a more complex model.

Assume we want to explain prediction Y that was the result of data X inputted in our model f. For Y, we generate perturbed instances of X to generate the X' dataset. Perturbation involves making small changes to the data in order to get a diverse amount of different cases, while keeping the result (i.e., prediction of Y) the same. After X' is generated, we check its similarity to X by assigning a weight to each instance that makes up X' based on its distance to the instance to explain. We can measure similarity by using a Gaussian kernel.

Once the similarity is calculated and deemed acceptable, we can train a new model, f', using X'. This is considered a *local model*, as we are using a weighted dataset with very similar data – especially in comparison with the original dataset used to train f. Moreover, f' needs to be accurate in the local area of interest, but not necessarily globally (i.e., it does not have to replicate all of f). The accuracy of the local model to approximate the global model is called *local fidelity*. The local model could be something like Lasso, decision tree, or other rule-based model. By understanding the coefficients and the importance of features in f', we can understand the most important factors that influenced prediction Y from model f.

LIME comes as a prebuilt library for `Python` [122].[4] The library contains all the necessary functions to generate and visualize local explanations for each classification from a model. For example, running LIME on a random forest classification algorithm trained on the Iris dataset,[5] generates figures such as Figure 7.3 for each prediction that we investigate.

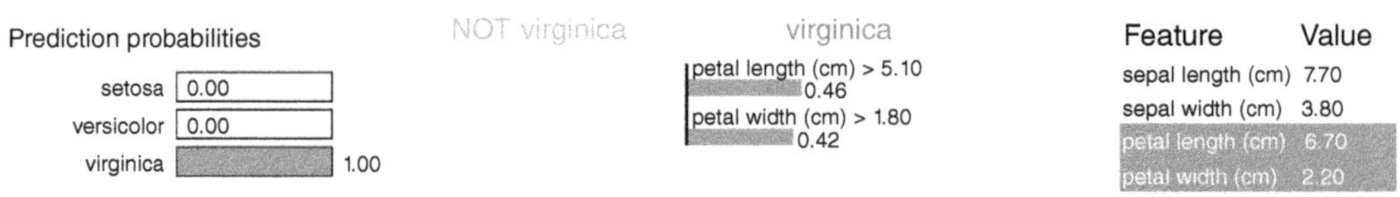

Figure 7.3 Example output of the LIME library for a single prediction. We can see the confidence level of the prediction and the features used for the prediction. We can also see the rules extracted, weights, and direction those features contributed toward.

There is a lot to unpack in Figure 7.3. On the left-hand side, we can see that our prediction has 100% confidence that the flower is *Virginica*. In the middle, we see the features contributions diagram. We only see two features, as the library was configured to only display the two features with the greatest contribution: *length* and *weight*. Depending on the audience for the explanation, limiting the number of features, such as to highlight the most impactful ones, might be best. Still, we see the rules extracted,

[4] marcotcr. LIME. Github. Available at: https://github.com/marcotcr/lime.
[5] This is an open-data dataset bundled with `sklearn`.

weights, and direction those features contributed toward. In this case, we see that the petal length being over 5.1 and its width over 1.8 were major factors in the *Virginica* classification.

The LIME library also contains versions of LIME suitable for text (i.e., natural language processing) and images. The principle in all versions of LIME is the same, but the way that new data is created is different. LIME for text uses a quite straightforward process to generate data for the local surrogate: Words are randomly removed from the original text to generate new pieces of text. Then, each new piece of text is encoded with 1s and 0s. Each word that remained from the original text is coded as 1, each word missing from the original text is coded as 0. The rest of the process is similar to tabular data.

For images, LIME segments the image into "superpixels," interconnected pixels with similar colors.[6] Once those superpixels are created, LIME randomly turns them on or off to generate the training dataset for the local surrogate. For example, in Figure 7.4 we can see how LIME segmented the original picture into superpixels (top-right corner), created a perturbed image (bottom-left corner), and then detected the superpixels that were used in the actual classification (bottom-right corner).

Figure 7.4 Sample from LIME when used to provide an explanation behind an image prediction. We can see the original image predicted contains a German shepherd (top left), the image segmented into superpixels (top right), the perturbed image (bottom left), and finally the superpixels that contributed in the classification (bottom right).

LIME is a powerful tool for understanding why a machine learning system made a particular prediction or classification. Out of the box, it can be applied to various types of data: tabular data, text, and images. The outputted explanations are fairly concise,

[6] Similar to pixel binning found in some cameras, but superpixels do not have the predetermined size (e.g., 4 × 4) and instead tend to be as big as similar-color pixels.

making them more accessible for laypeople or to build more advanced interfaces for explanations. The local fidelity measure helps assess how accurately the local model explains the global model's predictions for a specific instance of interest.

However, LIME is not without its drawbacks. Defining the size of the "local" neighborhood and, hence, the size of the generated dataset through perturbation is not a clear task. Instead, a trial- and- error approach is often needed, which can be costly in terms of time and computational resources. Moreover, if you repeatedly run the same explainer, you may receive different explanations for each run! In fact, it is highly likely that running the simple code used for the examples in this book may give you slightly different weights for each prediction. This inconsistency is typically not a problem, as long as the receiver of the explanation is aware of it and the overall direction and trend of how important a feature is remains stable. Looking at the direction and trend, one can still extract meaningful explanations and basically ignore the underlying weights. Yet, when dealing with very close points or used for fine-tuning a model, this inconsistency may lead to incorrect conclusions. Ultimately, like any XAI method, the receiver of the explanation – especially on more safety-critical applications – must not take any result at face value.

SHapley Additive exPlanations (SHAP)

SHAP explains the prediction of a specific instance x by determining the contribution of each feature to the result produced. For this, *Shapley values* are used. Shapley values, a concept found in game theory, represents a solution in games where participants are contributing unequally but want to fairly distribute any gains and costs – or in XAI, Shapley values represent how to divide the "payout" (i.e., the prediction) among the features). For this, SHAP treats individual features (e.g., values in tabular data) or a group of features (e.g., superpixels in an image) as "players."

The underlying assumption is that each "player" contributes toward the goal of the game: coming up with a prediction. If we calculate the marginal contribution a feature has at the prediction of each possible coalition (i.e., combination of features) and then we average it, then we get the Shapley value of a feature. The larger the Shapley value of a feature, the more it has influenced the decision.

While there are multiple approaches for XAI using Shapley values, SHAP is the most popular. SHAP is partly inspired by local surrogate models and uses a linear model for additive feature attribution. For example, KernelSHAP, arguably the most versatile version of SHAP, uses LIME.

SHAP defines an explanation as:

$$[h!]g(z') = \phi_0 + \sum_{j=1}^{M} \phi_j z'_j, \tag{7.2}$$

where g is the explanation mode, $Z'_k \in \{0,1\}^M$ is the coalition vector with 0 representing features not in the coalition and 1 features in the coalition, M is the maximum coalition size, and, $\phi_j \in \Re$ is the feature attribution for a feature j (i.e., the Shapley value).

SHAP can be used for multiple data types, including images where we can assess how various pixel groups affect the model's predictions. For images, we first apply the `masker` function, which generates subsets – essentially, superpixels – of the image, allowing us to examine the impact of different pixel groups on the final prediction. Then, the SHAP explainer takes in the masker and original model to calculate the SHAP values for the input image. These SHAP values represent the contribution of each pixel group to the model's prediction.

The SHAP explanations will overlay on the input images, highlighting regions of pixels that contribute positively (in red) and negatively (in blue) to the model's predictions. Reviewing these visualizations offers insights into the decision-making process of the image classifier as we can see which areas of our picture affected the decision the most. For example, reusing our German shepherd photo with a classifier trained on the ImageNet50 dataset, we can easily see which features contributed positively and which negatively in the classification (Figure 7.5).

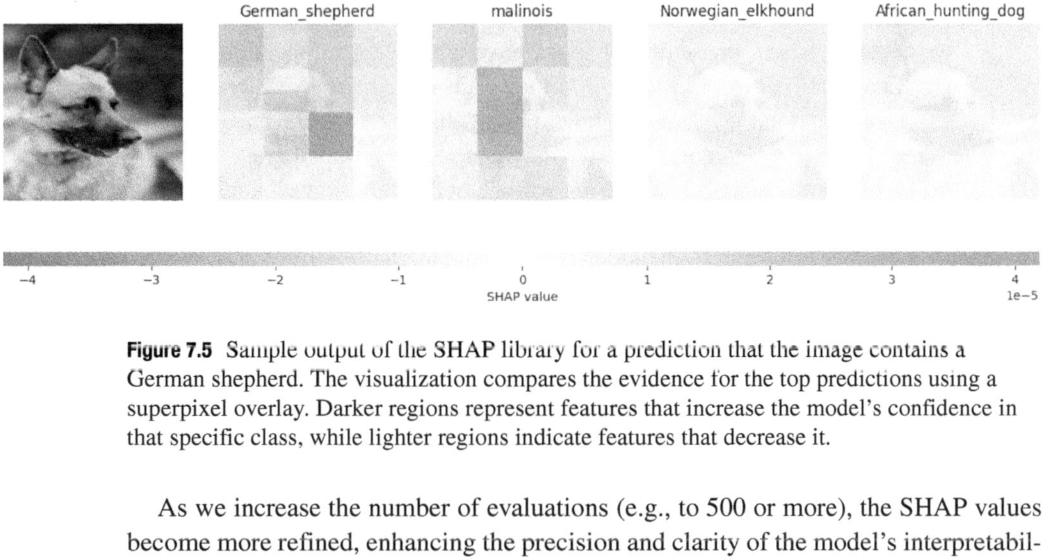

Figure 7.5 Sample output of the SHAP library for a prediction that the image contains a German shepherd. The visualization compares the evidence for the top predictions using a superpixel overlay. Darker regions represent features that increase the model's confidence in that specific class, while lighter regions indicate features that decrease it.

As we increase the number of evaluations (e.g., to 500 or more), the SHAP values become more refined, enhancing the precision and clarity of the model's interpretability. However, such accuracy improvements come at great computational expense. Compared to LIME, SHAP can be used not only for local but also global explanations as it shows fair, additive contributions that sum to the model's output difference from the baseline. Moreover, due to its theoretical underpinning, SHAP considers all possible combinations (subsets) of features, providing a guaranteed additivity, local accuracy, and consistency in its output. A simple approach to think of the two is to consider LIME as trying to "fit a simple, local model to approximate the black box near this point," while SHAP aims to "compute each feature's fair share of responsibility for the prediction."

Counterfactual Explanations

A counterfactual explanation tries to answer "What if?" questions by providing explanations in the form of: "If X had not happened, Y would not have happened" or "If

X happens, then Y would happen too." For example, "If I had a non-academic job, I would have a bigger salary and, hence, be able to get a higher mortgage." This sort of "Popperian way" of thinking is essentially the creation of different hypothetical alternative realities that contradict the actual events. Such explanations relay the *causal relationship* between two events: Y was caused by X, with Y being the predicted outcome and X being the feature that greatly influenced the prediction.

While real-world causation may not apply directly to the model's input–prediction relationship, we can still consider model inputs as causative factors for predictions. Counterfactuals are typically generated by permutating (i.e., slightly adjust its value(s)) a feature or set of features to see if the predicted outcome will change. Moreover, we define a *target class* (i.e., a desired outcome, such as have a bigger salary). As we generate explanations through permutation of features, we keep note only of those instances where we reached our desired outcome. This way, we can reduce our memory requirements and overall search space. A good counterfactual explanation will indicate the minimal feature changes required to change the predicted outcome from the prediction to the target class. Counterfactual reasoning is particularly valuable in contexts where prediction changes have significant implications, such as altering a classification outcome (e.g., in a mortgage system) or in general when we want not only to find out *why* but also more practically *how* to achieve a desired result.

As we permutate features, we may generate contradictory explanations; some may recommend changing feature *foo* while others might suggest altering feature *bar*. This challenge can be addressed by presenting all counterfactuals or choosing one based on a defined criterion. Both model-agnostic and model-specific counterfactual approaches exist. Model-specific approaches include:

- **Gradient-based methods (for neural networks):** Use backpropagation to compute minimal feature perturbations that change the predicted class.
- **Tree-based methods (for decision trees or random forests):** Use decision boundaries or leaf-path rules to derive counterfactual instances.
- **Rule-based counterfactual:** Exploit logical or symbolic structures in interpretable models (e.g., rule lists or decision sets).

At the time of writing, one of the most well-known model-agnostic approaches is DiCE (Diverse Counterfactual Explanations) [104]. DiCE treats the generation of explanations as the optimization problem by trying to generate explanations that satisfy three key criteria:

1. **Validity:** Each counterfactual should achieve the desired outcome (e.g., classification flips).
2. **Proximity:** Counterfactuals should be as close as possible to the original instance (minimal changes).
3. **Diversity:** Counterfactuals should be meaningfully different from one another, offering distinct alternatives.

While DiCE relies on these three criteria to generate explanations, we can consider them as universal means of evaluating the quality of counterfactual explanations. After all, validity ensures that we get the desired "alternative universe" that our "what if?" question tries to answer when we generate an explanation. Next, proximity indicates that the answer is probably *plausible*. Generated feature values should remain realistic within the data domain; implausible suggestions should be discarded (e.g., having a negative number of dependents). Ideally, counterfactuals should also conform to the data's joint distribution, ensuring coherence among interdependent features – for example, a higher income may correlate to a higher credit score. Finally, the diversity of counterfactual explanations contributes to their practical utility, as multiple plausible alternatives offer greater flexibility to decision-makers

7.6 Practical Considerations

This section examines the practical considerations for implementing explainability and transparency, structured around the *who*, *what*, *why*, and *how* to best implement explainability and transparency.

7.6.1 Who Needs to Know?

The starting point for understanding how best to implement explainability or transparency should always be identifying the *consumer* of the information. Their background (e.g., technical expertise or lack of) and goals should dictate the amount and depth of the information to be presented.

- **End-users and affected individuals:** Individuals directly influenced by AI decisions – such as patients, loan applicants, or defendants – require explanations that are accessible, understandable, and actionable. For them, the goal is procedural fairness and trust. They need to know why an outcome occurred and how they might contest, change, or understand it. Often simple indicators of data recording suffice.
- **Developers and engineers:** Developers require technical transparency to debug models, ensure reliability, and identify bias or drift. For them, explainability supports model stewardship and continuous improvement. Tools like SHAP, LIME, and feature attribution maps are useful for this audience.
- **Domain experts and decision-makers:** Professionals such as doctors, judges, and financial analysts depend on AI as a decision-support system. They need contextual explanations that align with domain reasoning, connecting AI logic to existing professional frameworks. Ideally, explanations should be presented in a human-understandable way with natural language, without going into the technical details. For example, a clinician may not need the model's mathematical details but rather which clinical factors influenced the AI's diagnosis.
- **Regulators and policymakers:** Regulators require system-level transparency to ensure compliance with ethical, legal, and safety standards. Explainability here supports accountability and governance – for instance, under frameworks like the EU AI Act. For them, transparency at an organizational level through documentation, comments, and logging of decisions is paramount.

- **Society at large:** Broader societal stakeholders, including journalists, advocacy groups, and the general public, benefit from institutional transparency – clear information about where and how AI is used, its limitations, and its impacts on equity, privacy, and safety.

7.6.2 Why They Need to Know

Providing transparency and explanations may not always be possible – or even permissible – for technical, legal, or economic reasons. Understanding why it is important can help scope how many resources could be spent on implementing a system. For example, depending on the applicable reasons, slower but generally more accurate approaches like SHAP may be preferred, or the other way around.

While we have already discussed multiple arguments in favor of transparency and XAI throughout the chapter, we can summarize them here as:

- **Trust and adoption:** Users are more likely to adopt AI systems they understand and perceive as fair. Trust is built when users can see that decisions are consistent, rational, and accountable.
- **Accountability and governance:** Transparent systems allow for auditability – the ability to trace responsibility for outcomes. This is vital in high-stakes domains such as healthcare, finance, or criminal justice, where unjust or unsafe outcomes can have serious consequences.
- **Ethical and legal compliance:** Regulatory frameworks increasingly require explainability.
- **Safety and robustness:** Transparent models enable better validation and stress testing, improving resilience against adversarial attacks and unexpected data shifts.
- **Bias detection and fairness:** Explainability helps uncover hidden biases and disparate impacts in AI behavior. By making decision factors visible, organizations can identify and mitigate sources of discrimination or exclusion.

7.6.3 What Should They Know?

Closely coupled to the previous two section is the *what* that needs to be known – that is, what information is relevant and can be provided in the context of our system. For instance, the selection of explanations, whether local or global, depends on the stakeholder involved. An end-user would benefit more from a local explanation, detailing why the system made a specific decision for a particular instance that affected them. On the other hand, a developer or auditor would most likely seek insights into the overall system behavior, thus favoring global explanations.

- **Data provenance:** In machine learning models, having adequate *data provenance* – understanding where training data originated, how it was processed, and what biases or gaps it may contain – is an important step toward transparency. Transparency at this stage allows stakeholders to assess data integrity and representativeness. This is a common transparency requirement in current AI standards, such as the ISO/IEC 42001 discussed in Chapter 5.

- **Model transparency:** This involves disclosing model architecture, features used, and design choices. For simple models (e.g., decision trees or linear regressions) the model itself can often serve as an explanation. For complex models such as deep neural networks, post-hoc interpretability techniques (e.g., attention maps, feature attributions) are often needed. This is also a common transparency requirement in current AI standards and for certain systems under current regulations, such as the EU AI Act.
- **Process transparency:** The decision-making process, including data preprocessing, model training, validation, and deployment pipelines, should be explainable to ensure traceability. Documentation such as model cards or datasheets for datasets can support this.
- **State transparency:** Provide a clear indication of the current state of the system. This can be done to different degrees, from whether it is capturing or processing data to providing clear views of how the system perceives its environment (e.g., current inputs).
- **Output explainability:** Explanations should address individual predictions: Why was this specific decision made? For instance, an AI loan approval model might explain that "income stability and debt ratio were the strongest contributors to the decision."
- **System-level explainability:** Beyond individual decisions, stakeholders need to understand systemic behavior – how the model performs across populations, its limitations, and its overall fairness metrics. This macro-level understanding is crucial for ethical oversight.

7.6.4 How to Best Implement Explainability and Transparency

The final consideration is how to operationalize explainability and transparency in practice, given the *who*, *why*, and *what* questions. As we have discussed, this often involves a blend of technical, procedural, and organizational approaches.

For example, some organizational approaches include:

- **Document and communicate transparently:** Practices like model cards, data statements, and algorithmic impact assessments formalize transparency. These documents should be made public where possible, balancing openness with privacy and intellectual property concerns.
- **Human-centered explanation design:** Explanations should align with human cognitive models and decision-making processes. Techniques such as narrative explanations, visualizations, or counterfactuals help bridge the gap between technical complexity and human comprehension.
- **Monitor and update explanations over time:** As models evolve, explanations may lose relevance. Continuous monitoring ensures that transparency mechanisms remain accurate and useful throughout the AI lifecycle.

- **Institutionalize governance and accountability:** Establishing AI ethics boards, transparency policies, and audit frameworks ensures explainability is not a one-time technical fix but an ongoing organizational commitment.

Technical considerations include:

- **Design for explainability from the start:** Rather than adding explanations post hoc, explainability should be a design principle embedded throughout development. This can include choosing inherently interpretable models when appropriate or incorporating interpretability constraints during model optimization.
- **Design for transparency from the start:** Consider using inherently transparent approaches.
- **Adopt layered explanation strategies:** Different audiences need different levels of detail. A layered approach – from high-level narratives for users to detailed algorithmic documentation for engineers – ensures inclusivity and accessibility.
- **Use explainability tools:** Tools such as SHAP, LIME, integrated gradients, or counterfactual explanations provide insights into model behavior. However, these tools should be validated for fidelity, ensuring that explanations accurately reflect the model's actual reasoning rather than oversimplifying it.
- **Consider the communication output:** Different XAI approaches will present different outputs. For example, many methods provide summary statistics for each feature, such as feature importance or pairwise feature interaction strengths. Others will provide plots that allow a visual representation of features and their average predicted outcomes.
- **Timeliness of the information:** Developers should decide when to prioritize interpretability over performance. In sensitive contexts, inherently interpretable models may be preferred even if they are less accurate if getting an explanation is important. Similarly, XAI and transparency may be dismissed altogether in certain contexts, such as to avoid overloading the receiver with too much information in a time-critical situation.
- **Privacy concerns:** Often there needs to be a careful balance between openness in algorithmic operations and safeguarding personal information. Achieving transparency often involves revealing how data is used, which can unintentionally threaten privacy if not properly managed. The key challenge, therefore, is to design AI systems that maintain both transparency and privacy, employing methods such as differential privacy, secure multi-party computation, and federated learning to protect individual data while still offering meaningful insights into how the AI makes its decisions.

7.7 Questions and Exercises

1. Write a short essay reflecting on situations where too much transparency could cause harm. For instance, consider the following questions:

(a) When do you think it is acceptable to violate privacy to ensure more transparency? When not?
(b) What about spending more computational power, which translates to more costs and emissions?
(c) Could we enable adversarial attacks or enable intellectual property infringement by exposing proprietary methods?

Suggest how the owner of an AI system could remain accountable.

2. Using the Boston housing dataset,[7] train a machine learning model of your choice to predict house prices.[8] This dataset contains, among others, information about the percentage of the population that is working class, the number of rooms, and the nitric oxides concentration (parts per million) of a house. Once the model is trained, you may want to understand which features are impacting the prediction. Try using one or more explainers (e.g., SHAP, LIME, DiCE) to build an understanding of your model. *Hint:* Consider if you need global or local explanations.
3. Design a conceptual plan for an AI system that recommends college admissions. Your plan should include:
   (a) Transparency goals: What do you want stakeholders to know and understand?
   (b) Transparency methods: How will you communicate this (e.g., dashboards, reports, explanations)?
   (c) Ethical safeguards: How will you handle data privacy, fairness, and accountability?
   (d) Evaluation: How will you measure whether transparency is effective?
4. Pick one of your previously developed AI models (e.g., the one from Question 2). Create a *Model Card*[9] for it, describing:
   (a) intended use
   (b) limitations
   (c) performance metrics
   (d) ethical considerations
   (e) data used.

   Reflect on how this documentation contributes to transparency beyond the model's technical explanation.
5. Find an AI system in use today (e.g., ChatGPT, YouTube recommendations, facial recognition systems, or credit scoring algorithms). Investigate what information the provider makes public about the system's data sources, decision processes, or limitations. Assess its level of transparency on a scale from 1 (opaque) to 5 (highly transparent).
6. Choose one of the following contexts:
   - medical diagnosis AI
   - credit scoring model
   - predictive policing tool

[7] StatLib. The Boston housing dataset. Available at: www.cs.toronto.edu/~delve/data/boston/bostonDetail.html
[8] For simplicity, consider this as a regression problem.
[9] For more information on model cards, refer to [100].

- job applicant screening system.

Then:

(a) Identify what kind of explanations users, developers, and regulators might require.
(b) Discuss potential harms or ethical issues if explanations are unclear or unavailable.
(c) Propose methods or tools that could improve the system's explainability (e.g., SHAP, counterfactuals, or example-based reasoning).

7. You are part of a team developing a highly accurate deep neural network for predicting student performance. The model's predictions are strong, but its reasoning is opaque. Management asks whether to prioritize explainability or accuracy for deployment in schools. Discuss in an essay:
   (a) The trade-offs involved in explainability vs. performance.
   (b) The ethical implications of using an opaque model in education.
   (c) A possible hybrid approach that maintains both reliability and interpretability.

8 Fairness and Bias

8.1 Learning Objectives

This chapter focuses on three learning aspects: "Appreciation," "Analysis," and "Application," as we discuss abstract concepts of fairness and move to concrete quantitative fairness definitions and debiasing techniques. The learning objectives of this chapter are:

- Appreciation (Bloom's understand): Understand what undesirable bias is.
- Analysis (Bloom's create): Select an appropriate fairness definition for an application.
- Analysis (Bloom's analyze): Discuss who are protected and unprotected groups in a specific application.
- Application (Bloom's evaluate): Use different bias measures.

8.2 Introduction

Undesirable bias is a well-known issue in algorithmic decision-making. For example, audits of commercial facial recognition software revealed that their performance is disproportionately inaccurate for female and black faces. Similarly, audits of translation software have shown that certain professions tend to be translated as male, even when the subject is female in the original language. In the context of decision-making, bias is defined as the existence of favoritism/prejudice toward an individual or group based on their characteristics, which the previous examples show. However, consider the case of an intelligent system for CV filtering: Its purpose is to show favoritism to a certain group: those whose qualifications match what is expected of the job. Indeed, AI algorithms are always biased, as it is through those learned or coded biases that decisions are reached. For this reason, when we are considering bias that is prejudicial or unwanted, we refer specifically to **undesirable** bias.

As a society, we value fairness and the absence of prejudice: It is seen in our behavior and set down in our laws. For example, many countries have protections that forbid discrimination for reasons of ethnicity, gender, religion, or sexual orientation. Fairness has many definitions and understandings, but for the purposes of this chapter we can start with a narrow definition for fairness in intelligent systems: A system is fair if it does not exhibit unwanted biases.

8.3 Where Does Bias Come From?

The introduction of unwanted bias is often attributed to poor data quality affecting the output of a system, with the saying "garbage in, garbage out." However, unwanted bias can in fact have causes in every step of the development pipeline [95]:

- in the data;
- in the choices for the algorithm;
- in the usage; and
- in the context.

The first step in avoiding it is therefore to understand where it comes from. For that purpose, we can expose some examples of bias introduction at each step.

8.3.1 Bias in the Data

A possible cause of undesirable bias in the data can be the omission of relevant variables. In statistics, this effect is referred to as omitted-variable bias, and it results in models attributing the effects of the missing variables to those that are available instead, thus introducing undesired correlations.

Another aspect where bias can be introduced is in the choice of how to measure the chosen variables in the data. Aspects such as which ranges to use or inclusion criteria can result in missing or incomplete information, which in turn can introduce unwanted correlations into the model.

Finally, a well-known cause of bias stemming from the data is the absence of data from the entirety of the relevant population: The underrepresentation of groups leads to disparities in the accuracy of a model. Relatedly, we can see similar effects from nonrandom sampling, where a population may be accurately represented in number, but not across features. These examples expose that adequate data collection and processing is a key aspect to prevent the introduction of undesirable bias.

8.3.2 Model Choices

When it comes to model choices, the use of certain optimization functions, regularizations, and choices in applying regression models can all have an effect on the introduction of bias. Since these choices determine which aspects the model will focus on, they have a clear effect on which features will be used to make a decision. Furthermore, omitted variable bias can also happen in the model, when it does not use all relevant variables even if they are contained in the data.

The tuning of the model can also have an important effect: A model may not be fine-tuned enough to relevant details, leading to ignoring important distinctions between data points and making decisions based on unrelated features.

Undesired bias can also get past the evaluation of the model, if the evaluation criteria and benchmarks used do not accurately represent the nuances of the intended use. The choices made in selecting an algorithm, parameters, optimization methods, and evaluation can therefore all result in unfairly biased outcomes.

8.3.3 Usage of the System

In terms of the usage, the affordances of the system can generate undesirable bias. Affordances are related to what the system offers, enables, or provides to the user, facilitating or constraining certain actions. For example, if a user can only choose from a few options, those options will be chosen more often and create a self-reinforcing loop.

The misuse of a system can also lead to unwanted behavior. This can be unintended or intended, such as the case of bots skewing the results of search engines.

8.3.4 Context

Sometimes effects unrelated to the system can lead to biased behavior. Pre-existing social inequalities can generate unequal consequences even given a perfectly representative dataset. Furthermore, if a system is deployed in a different context than what it has been designed for, new undesirable biases can arise.

8.4 Why Is Undesirable Bias a Problem?

Undesirable bias in intelligent systems is a societal concern, specifically because of its repercussions at the collective and individual level. Although the possible appearance and effect of undesirable biases is impossible to fully list (see Chapter 6), depending on where the bias comes from, some specific harms are prevalent. A problem commonly identified with algorithms exhibiting undesirable bias is the perpetuation and amplification of historical inequities. Models trained on historical data are particularly vulnerable to this effect, which may not only affect their performance, but also disproportionately favor or hinder communities based on historically entrenched inequalities.

Undesirably biased AI systems can exacerbate economic disparities by limiting access to opportunities for certain groups. In the same way, in healthcare, undesirably biased systems can lead to unequal treatment and misdiagnosis of certain patient groups, contributing to health disparities. Undesirable bias in these cases directly stands in opposition to equality of opportunity and equality of access.

Undesirable bias in systems used in criminal justice, such as predictive policing, facial recognition for surveillance, or recidivism prediction tools can lead to strong individual and collective harms. On the one hand, those specific individuals targeted by a false positive can suffer long-standing economic, social, physical, and psychological harm. On the other hand, unjust targeting of specific individuals or communities does additional societal harm, undermining trust in the justice system and disenfranchising vulnerable communities.

Additionally, when technology is shown and perceived to be harmful and unfair, public trust in technology and institutions that use it can erode. This creates a tendency to disuse and misuse the technology (see Chapter 7) and hinders the adoption of useful tools.

8.5 Fairness Definitions

To remove undesirable bias before deployment, it is necessary to define it clearly. For debiasing algorithms, the notion of undesirable bias is defined mathematically, in a way that is quantifiable. Its counterpart, the definition of what constitutes a "fair" system, is therefore also defined in mathematical terms, often through the use of probabilities [144]. These *fairness definitions* take many shapes, but can be globally divided into two ideas: individual fairness and group fairness. Individual fairness definitions define fairness in the sense that similar individuals should receive similar outcomes, regardless of their sensitive characteristics, whereas group fairness definitions aim for the same outcomes *on average* between groups with different sensitive characteristics. Even when confined to quantitative terms, there is room for many different interpretations of how fairness should be defined. For individual fairness, how we define what are "similar individuals" and "similar outcomes" can greatly affect whether we consider a system fair or not. Within group fairness, how we decide the "average outcome" that we want to be the same between groups, as well as how we define those groups, makes all the difference.

Individual fairness is generally defined by defining measures in the input and for output spaces. If two inputs have a small distance with respect to this measure, they are considered similar, and the same holds for outputs and their measurement. Then, we can say that a system is individually fair if inputs that are close to each other have outputs that are close to each other. The restriction of how close outputs have to be with respect to inputs varies, but often a very strong restriction is used: Lipschitz continuity. For example, we can define the distance between inputs as the Euclidean distance in the feature space, or tailor it to the use case by only counting those features that are necessary. Let's take the case of a CV-filtering system: The distance between inputs should take into account features related to qualifications, but not gender. If CVs are given scores according to their relevance, then the measure in the output space can simply be the difference between the scores. Thus, two individuals with similar qualifications will be close in distance, regardless of their gender, and should be given close scores.

On the other hand, group fairness definitions vary in what is chosen to be unified across groups (e.g., positive outcomes, negative outcomes, false positive rate) and how this is defined. Group fairness definitions involve defining protected classes and positive/negative outcomes. In the following examples, we will consider a system whose predicted outcome is denoted by O, when the actual outcome is denoted by Y. A desirable outcome is denoted by do and an undesirable outcome by uo. The class of an input is denoted by C, the protected class is denoted by pc, and the unprotected class by uc. For example, let's consider the case of a system filtering CVs. The desirable outcome do is that your CV is selected, and the undesirable outcome uo is that your CV is not selected. If a CV goes through the system and is selected, then its predicted outcome is the desirable one ($O = do$). If the candidate was actually qualified, then the true outcome Y is also to be selected ($Y = do$), whereas if the candidate was in fact unqualified, then the true outcome would be that the CV is not selected ($Y = uo$). If we want the system to not be unfairly biased against women, then we will select women to be the protected class pc. So, if a candidate is a woman, her class will be $C = pc$, and if not $C = uc$. With this notation, some examples of group fairness are:

- **Statistical parity:** Individuals in protected and unprotected groups have equal probability of being predicted the desirable outcome:

$$P(O = po|C = pc) = P(O = po|C = uc). \tag{8.1}$$

  This metric is most often used when the goal is to ensure equal opportunity or equal representation, regardless of a group's historical success rate.
- **Predictive parity:** The probability of being in the desirable outcome groups and being correctly predicted to be in the desirable outcome group is the same for individuals in protected and unprotected classes:

$$P(Y = do|O = do, C = pc) = P(Y = do|O = do, C = uc). \tag{8.2}$$

  This metric is useful in contexts where the accuracy of a positive prediction is paramount. It ensures that when a system predicts success, it is equally reliable across all groups.
- **False positive error rate balance:** The probability of false positives is the same for individuals in protected and unprotected classes:

$$P(O = do|Y = uo, C = pc) = P(O = do|Y = uo, C = uc). \tag{8.3}$$

  This metric is prevalent for systems where a false positive is particularly harmful. It ensures that no group is disproportionately subjected to a false alarm.

There exist many other group fairness definitions that follow this template, balancing true positives, false negatives, and so on.

A challenging aspect of choosing a fairness definition is that, often, different fairness definitions are incompatible with each other. For example, ensuring that similar individuals receive similar outcomes does not guarantee that groups will have equal outcomes. Ensuring statistical parity might lead to differences in error rates between groups, violating definitions aiming to equalize error rates [86].

8.6 Debiasing

For each fairness definition, there often exist several debiasing algorithms that may act on the data, the model, or the outcome. Depending on where they are applied, these methods are called, respectively, pre-processing, in-processing, and post-processing.

8.6.1 Pre-processing

Pre-processing techniques focus on enforcing fairness constraints on the dataset. This generally means altering the dataset, either by altering the data points, removing or adding data points, or using only a subset of the data. One can find a growing literature on algorithms to pre-process data, balancing different factors with fairness, such as retaining accuracy or privacy constraints.

Massaging the data involves changing the labels of a subset of data points, often the labels indicating the protected attribute or the labels indicating the outcome. Algorithms to massage the data focus on choosing which data points to alter in order to make the dataset adhere to a specific definition of fairness (e.g., the proportion of positive outcomes is the same between protected and unprotected classes).

Reweighing methods assign weights to each data point, representing frequency. By using models that utilize frequency counts as a learning mechanism, the dataset is then rendered fair as it represents a fair distribution of data points in terms of frequency.

Sampling methods consist of selecting a subset of the dataset that is representative enough to provide good accuracy, while also adhering to a fairness definition. Algorithms for sampling focus on how to effectively select a good sample without losing accuracy, by choosing a subset of the dataset and duplicating or deleting some data points. The choice of which pre-processing method is appropriate depends on many factors: the representativeness of the original data, the availability of labels or the model that will be trained all determine the suitability of a method. It is therefore a modeling choice with ramifications in the rest of the process.

Synthetic data is artificially generated data that follows the statistical properties and structure of real-world data. This type of data is difficult to validate, but its uses for fairness purposes are increasing, such as generating balanced datasets without the need for collecting sensitive information. Synthetic data can also be used to simulate rare scenarios, helping to test the robustness and fairness of AI models in a controlled environment and uncover potential biases that might not be evident in the original dataset.

8.6.2 In-processing

In-processing methods cover a wide array of techniques. Indeed, there is the option of developing model-specific methods that focus on a single kind of learning model or developing model-agnostic methods that can be used by any model. Model-specific techniques can focus on combining fairness with other constraints, such as accuracy or privacy, while model-agnostic techniques can be used widely but their performance may vary based on the specific model. For model-specific techniques, an approach with learning algorithms that use loss functions is to augment the loss function with a fairness regularizer that penalizes the model the further away it is from adhering to the desired fairness definition [83].

For model-agnostic techniques, a proposed method is to learn different classifiers for different groups (decoupled classifiers), which aims to maximize accuracy for each group while maintaining fairness as a whole [142]. Another option is to train a model simultaneously with an adversarial model that will try to predict the protected feature of an input given its output, in what is known as adversarial debiasing [153]. If the adversary is incapable of doing so, then certain conditions of statistical independence of the model with respect to the protected feature hold. Again, the choice of in-processing methods is highly dependent on the application, as each technique has different trade-offs in terms of accuracy, privacy, explainability, and how effective it is for intersectional groups.

8.6.3 Post-processing

Post-processing methods focus on altering the output to enforce fairness. Since these methods can only alter the output, their focus is on choosing which predictions to modify so that a fairness definition is followed. Thus, these methods often make use of information about the sensitive characteristics of the input to either leave its prediction as-is or to change it. For each method, the key choice is the set of inputs whose prediction is modified; for example, the choice can be made to only modify inputs with a low-confidence score, or all inputs corresponding to a certain demographic, or a random choice of inputs from each group.

As a key example, *reject-option classification* is a post-processing method that alters the predictions of inputs that fall close to the decision boundary [82]. For those uncertain inputs, their prediction is automatically assigned to be desirable if they belong to the protected class and undesirable if they belong to the unprotected class. As a different approach, equalized odds post-processing algorithms represent the problem of which predictions to change as a linear program, which is then solved and thus inputs are given a certain probability with which their output may be changed. Note that, in essence, post-processing methods operate by changing, in different ways, the decision boundary of the original predictor.

8.7 The Difficulty of Fairness

Even though the quantitative perspective on defining fairness allows for debiasing methods that can be proved to follow a fairness definition, this narrow definition of fairness leaves a number of questions that require ethical thinking. A first key question is: Who gets to decide what counts as fair? Even with a mathematical definition of fairness, the choice of *which* fairness definition to use and which debiasing method to use is key to the outcome. In fact, relying on a single metric can be misleading or even harmful, a practice known as "fairness washing" or "cherry-picking" metrics. Clearly, the choice of fairness definition decides what will be equalized (e.g., desirable outcomes, false positive rates, or other) and the choice of debiasing method changes whose decisions will be altered. In addition, not all fairness methods can be adhered to at the same time, which means that such choices have to be made.

Furthermore, the quantitative perspective on fairness – and group fairness in particular – puts a heavy focus on distinguishing between protected and unprotected classes. Therefore, a key question is: Which classes do we consider, and how do we get information on them? This reliance on class membership can be impractical, as individuals may not identify with any of the chosen classes. Furthermore, as society evolves, so does our perspective on what counts as a protected class. The focus on sensitive classes is also at odds with privacy requirements, which would dictate that we should collect the minimal amount of information necessary for a given purpose, which oftentimes does not include sensitive data. Additionally, sensitive data may sometimes be outright dangerous to obtain and store, such as sexuality data in countries where LGBTQ+ orientations are prosecuted.

Thus, a socio-technical perspective on fairness is still needed, where there is clear responsibility and accountability for how fairness decisions are taken [78, 126].

8.8 Questions and Exercises

1. **Debate question**. Should algorithms be more, less, or equally as fair as people?
2. How can the selection of features in a dataset impact the fairness of an AI model?
3. Compare and contrast statistical parity and predictive parity as fairness metrics.
4. At which stages of debiasing may accuracy be decreased?
5. What can be the trade-offs involved in optimizing for multiple fairness metrics simultaneously?
6. **Debate question**. How can the concept of "fairness as non-discrimination" be balanced with "fairness as equality of opportunity?"

9 Accountability and Responsibility

9.1 Learning Objectives

This chapter focuses on the "Analysis" stage, illustrating how AI systems can incorporate ethical values and focusing on the use of specific frameworks. The learning objectives of this chapter are:

- Appreciation (Bloom's remember) Identify key concepts: accountability, responsibility, and transparency in AI; list the ART principles for trustworthy AI; recall the difference between accountability and responsibility.
- Analysis (Bloom's analyze): Compare accountability and responsibility in AI ethics; analyze the impact of societal values on AI systems.
- Analysis (Bloom's evaluate): Assess the effectiveness of AI governance frameworks; critique methods for integrating ethical reasoning in AI.
- Application (Bloom's apply): Propose methodologies for transparency and accountability in AI design; design a framework for responsible AI considering ethical implications.

9.2 Introduction

In all areas of application, where AI is applied to make decisions that affect people and society, AI reasoning must be able to take into account societal values and moral and ethical considerations, weigh the respective priorities of values held by different stakeholders, and, in multiple multicultural contexts, explain its reasoning and guarantee transparency. As the capabilities for autonomous decision-making grow, perhaps the most important issue to consider is the need to rethink responsibility [111]. Whatever their level of autonomy and social awareness and their ability to learn, AI systems are artifacts, constructed by people to fulfill certain goals. Theories, methods, and algorithms are needed to integrate societal, legal, and moral values into technological developments in AI, at all stages of development (analysis, design, construction, deployment, and evaluation). These frameworks must deal with the autonomic reasoning of the machine about such issues that we consider to have ethical impact, but also, and most importantly, we need frameworks to guide design choices, to regulate the reach of AI systems, to ensure proper data stewardship, and to help individuals determine their own involvement. Values are dependent on the socio-cultural context [137], and are often only implicit in deliberation processes, which means that methodologies are needed to elicit the values held by all stakeholders. Making these values explicit can lead to better understanding and trust in artificial autonomous systems.

If we assume an AI system to be a system that is capable of perceiving its environment and deliberating on how to achieve its own goals, we need to consider its autonomy to decide on how to act, its ability to adapt by learning from change in its environment, and how it interacts with other agents to coordinate their activities in that environment. To reflect societal concerns about the impact of AI, and to ensure that AI systems are developed responsibly and incorporate social and ethical values, these characteristics of autonomy, adaptability, and interaction should be complemented with design principles that ensure trust. These characteristics relate most directly to the technical system. Obviously, AI applications – that is, the software – cannot be responsible, but the organizations, institutions, and individuals that make, use, deploy, or govern these applications must bear responsibility and ensure trust. That is, ensuring trustworthy AI systems requires more than designing systems whose result can be trusted. It is about the way we design them, why we design them, and who is involved in designing them. The impact and consequences of an AI system go beyond the technical system itself, and as such the system should be seen as a socio-technical system, encompassing the stakeholders and organizations involved. Previously we proposed complementing autonomy with responsibility, interactivity with accountability, and adaptation with transparency [32]. These form the ART principles for responsible and trustworthy AI and concern the whole AI socio-technical system. That is, addressing ART will require a socio-technical approach to design, deployment, and use of systems, interweaving software solutions with governance and regulation. Moreover, even though each of the ART principles can apply to all aspects of AI systems, each is imperative for a specific characteristic, as is depicted in Figure 9.1.

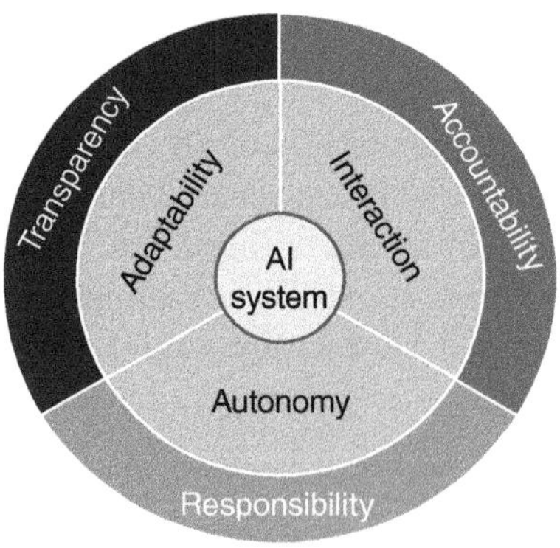

Figure 9.1 The ART principles: accountability, responsibility, transparency.

- **Accountability** refers to the requirement for the system to be able to explain and justify its decisions to users and other relevant actors. To ensure accountability, decisions should be derivable from, and explained by, the decision-making mechanisms used. It also requires that the moral values and societal norms that inform the purpose of the system, as well as their operational interpretations, have been elicited in an open way involving all stakeholders.

- **Responsibility** refers to the role of people themselves in their relation to AI systems. As the chain of responsibility grows, we need ways to link the AI system's decisions to its input data and to the actions of stakeholders involved in the system's decisions. Responsibility is not just about making rules to govern intelligent machines; it is about the whole socio-technical system in which the system operates, which encompasses people, machines, and institutions.
- **Transparency** indicates the capability to describe, inspect, and reproduce the mechanisms through which AI systems make decisions and learn to adapt to their environment, and the provenance and dynamics of the data that is used and created by the system. Trust in the system will improve if we can ensure openness in everything related to the system. As such, transparency is also about being explicit and open about choices and decisions concerning data sources, development processes, and stakeholders for all models that use human data or affect human beings or can have other morally significant impacts.

These properties enable agents to deal effectively with the kinds of environments in which we live and work: Environments that are unpredictable, dynamic in space and time, and where one is often faced by situations one has never encountered before. If AI systems are capable and expected to act in such environments, we need to be able to trust that they will not exhibit undesirable behavior. Or, at least, we need to limit the effects of unexpected behavior. However, an interactive system that is autonomous and adaptable is hard to verify and predict, which in turn can lead to unexpected activity. Therefore, design methodologies are needed that take these issues into account, as a means to ensure that AI systems are reliable, acceptable, and accepted. As a whole, these principles inform the design of AI systems. That is, ART imposes requirements on AI systems' design and architecture that will condition the development process and the systems' architecture.

Even though each of the ART principles can apply to all aspects of AI systems, each one is especially relevant to one of the characteristics of AI, as depicted in Figure 9.1. One cannot have autonomy without some form of responsibility, interaction without accountability, nor adaptability without transparency. Addressing ART requires a socio-technical approach to design, deployment, and use of systems, interweaving software solutions with governance and regulation. From the perspective of system development, ART requires new forms and new methods that support the integration of ethical and societal impact of AI systems in the engineering process. Above all, ART requires training and awareness for all stakeholders, including researchers, designers, programmers, managers, procurement, and end-users, that enables each of them to understand and assume their role in the overall process.

Note that there is a fundamental difference between accountability and responsibility, even if these terms are often used interchangeably. Accountability refers to the ability to explain, or report on, one's role in events or actions, whereas responsibility is the duty to answer for one's actions. Responsibility entails liability and exists before the task or action is done. Accountability is only evident after the action is done, or not done. When a person delegates some task to an agent, be it artificial or human, the result of that task is still the responsibility of the delegating person (principal), who is the one who will be liable if things don't go as expected. The agent, however, must be able to report on how the task was executed, and to explain any problems with this execution. This is the basis of the principal–agent theory that is often used to explain the relationship between people and autonomous systems.

9.3 Taking Responsibility

In order to design AI systems that are sensitive to moral principles and human values, methods for responsible AI rest on three pillars of equal importance. First, society must be prepared to take responsibility for AI impacts. This means that researchers and developers should be trained to be aware of their own responsibility where it concerns the development of AI systems with direct impacts on society. This requires extra effort in developing and delivering education and training materials, and the development of codes of conduct for AI developers. This, in turn, requires methods and tools to understand and integrate moral, societal, and legal values with technological developments in AI.

This means that responsible AI is primarily an issue of governance. It is up to governments and citizens to determine how issues of liability should be regulated. For example, who will be to blame if a self-driving car harms a pedestrian? The builder of the hardware (e.g., of the sensors used by the car to perceive the environment)? The builder of the software that enables the car to decide on a path? The authorities that allow the car on the road? The owner that personalized the car decision-making settings to meet her preferences? And how can current product liability laws be understood in the face of systems that act as a result of a long (autonomous) learning process? All these questions, and more, must inform the regulations that societies put in place toward responsible use of AI systems.

Second, responsible AI implies the need for mechanisms that enable AI systems to act according to ethics and human values. Whether we design them in that way or not, AI systems will and are already making decisions that we would consider to have an ethical flavor if they were made by people. Being aware of this is what responsible AI is all about. How do we design systems that take implicit "ethical" decisions? Or how do we design the system to ensure that it refers the decision to someone to take because it is an ethical decision? And where is the line between decisions that are not ethical and ones that are? This requires models and algorithms to represent and reason about, and take decisions based on, human values, and to justify their decisions according to their effect on those values. Current (deep-learning) mechanisms are unable to meaningfully link decisions to inputs, and therefore cannot explain their acts in ways that we can understand.

Last but certainly not least, responsible AI is about participation. It is necessary to understand how different people work and live with AI technologies across cultures in order to develop frameworks for responsible AI. AI does not stand separately, but must be understood as part of diverse socio-technical relations. Education plays an important role, ensuring that knowledge of the potential for AI is widespread, to make people aware that they can participate in shaping its societal development, and as a basis to ensure diversity and inclusion. A new and more ambitious form of governance is one of the most pressing needs in order to ensure that inevitable AI advances will be accessible to all, and will serve the societal good. Expanding on the principles described in the previous section, it is important to understand that responsible AI means different things to different people. The concept of responsible AI also serves as an overall container for many diverse opinions and topics. Depending on the speaker and on the context, it can mean one of the following things:

1. policies concerning the governance of R&D (research and development) activities and the deployment and use of AI in societal settings;
2. the role of developers, at individual and collective levels;
3. issues of inclusion, diversity, and universal access; and
4. predictions and reflections on the benefits and risks of AI.

These topics are quite different, as are their impacts. Placing all of these issues in the same basket can muddle the discussion, and puts at risk the achievement of constructive solutions to each of the topics. It can also contribute to increasing the fear of AI within the general public and with it the risk of the proliferation of ungrounded, dystopian views about AI.

The most urgent of these topics is perhaps the first one. AI systems use data we generate in our daily lives, and as such are a mirror of our interests, weaknesses, and differences. AI, like any other technology, is not value-neutral. Understanding the values behind the technology and deciding on how we want our values to be incorporated in AI systems requires that we are also able to decide on how and what we want AI to mean in our societies. It implies deciding on ethical guidelines, governance policies, incentives, and regulations. It implies that we are aware of differences in interests and aims behind AI systems developed by others, according to other cultures and principles. An extension, or alternative, to regulation is certification. Certification is a means of risk regulation and quality assurance that ensures the products or services they certify meet criteria specified by professional associations, standards organizations, or government agencies. We discuss the issues of regulation and certification in Section 9.4.

For the second topic, the role of developers, it is important to realize that AI does not just materialize. We make it happen. Researchers and developers of AI systems determine how those systems will behave and what kind of capabilities they will exhibit. Many professions are bound by codes of conduct outlining the proper practices for those professions. The International Federation of Accountants defines a code of conduct as being the "principles, values, standards, or rules of behavior that guide the decisions, procedures and systems of an organization in a way that (a) contributes to the welfare of its key stakeholders, and (b) respects the rights of all constituents affected by its operations" [78]. In fact, society expects strict codes of conduct from those professions it depends on, including health professionals, military, accountants, and many others. Given the role of software engineers on the AI systems and applications that shape our world, it is probably time to expect some standards of conduct from this professional group.

Much has been said and written on the issue of inclusion, diversity, and access to AI, in particular where it relates to bias [29, 128]. However, these issues are also relevant for the environments where AI is developed, and have a strong link to education. Inclusion is a necessary condition for diversity in development teams and among AI professionals. More than metrics in terms of demographics, it is important to understand how inclusion is experienced. Broadening engineering education curricula to include the humanities and social sciences, which are essential to ensure the responsible design and development of AI, will also contribute to a more diverse student population.

The media has given disproportionate attention to the last topic, predictions of benefits and risk. Dystopian views of a future dominated by robotic overlords seem to sell well and are backed by some scholars (typically from other disciplines), and a disproportionate number of tech-millionaires. However, as Luciano Floridi remarks, even if such a future is logically possible, it is utterly unlikely, and the focus on these issues is a distraction from the real problems that are already affecting us [62]. Even though the topic has fascinated people for a long time, the main risk here is that focusing on possible future risks is a distraction from the very real risks that we face already: privacy and security, consequences for human labor, and algorithmic bias, just to cite a few.

9.4 Governance for Responsible AI

In the evolving landscape of AI, the discourse on its ethical, societal, and legal aspects has gained momentum, fueled by recent initiatives and frameworks. Notably, UNESCO's Recommendation on the Ethics of Artificial Intelligence [139] and the OECD's Principles on Artificial Intelligence [111] have set new benchmarks for trustworthy AI. These, along with the European Union's AI Ethics Guidelines and the AI Act, are pivotal in shaping the global AI governance landscape. The Global Partnership on AI (GPAI) has also emerged as a significant collaborative effort among leading nations to foster responsible AI development and usage. More recently, the United Nations has stepped into the field, aimed at a coordinated global approach to harness AI for humanity, while addressing its risks and uncertainties [140].

These endeavors extend beyond enumerating ethical principles, aiming to provide actionable guidelines and frameworks for ethically aligned AI systems. For instance, the EU's AI Act is pioneering in its comprehensive approach to regulating AI applications, focusing on high-risk categories and emphasizing transparency, accountability, and user safety.

In parallel, organizations such as the IEEE have continued to advance ethically aligned design, working toward international standards that prioritize human welfare in AI technologies. The collaboration has expanded globally, incorporating diverse perspectives to ensure the creation of universally applicable ethical standards.

Recent initiatives also emphasize the importance of multi-stakeholder engagement in shaping AI ethics. For example, the OECD's AI Policy Observatory[1] and the AI for Good initiative by the International Telecommunication Union (ITU) are platforms that facilitate global dialog and cooperation on AI ethics and governance.

These recent efforts reflect a holistic approach to responsible AI, integrating ethical considerations into the entire lifecycle of AI systems, from design to deployment. The trend is toward creating a regulatory and normative ecosystem that not only sets principles but also provides clear guidance for their implementation, ensuring AI's alignment with human values and societal well-being.

9.4.1 Regulation

Whenever regulation is mentioned with respect to AI development and use, usually one of two issues is mentioned. First, the fear that regulation will stifle innovation and progress. Second, whether current laws and regulations are at all sufficient to deal with the complexities of AI. In our opinion, both are too short-sighted.

Given the dynamic nature of AI, we cannot wait until the technology is mature before we regulate it. Already, AI is impacting individuals and society, changing cognitive and interactive functions and impacting our well-being. However, as we have seen in previous chapters, there is no established definition of what AI is, without which it is very difficult to determine what should be the focus of regulation. Moreover, as has been observed by the panel that produced the 100 Years Study on AI Report [4], the risks and considerations are very different in different domains, making a generic regulatory approach inappropriate. This means that rather than regulating AI itself, regulating its use in specific areas, such as healthcare or the military, provides more suitable instruments to ensure its proper application and can better be inserted into existing regulatory frameworks.

It is important to realize that not all regulation is negative. This is the case when regulation takes the form of incentives or investment programs that nudge organizations to pursue a specific type of application or technological approach.

Liability in AI involves complex legal challenges. Existing laws on product liability and service liability apply in many cases because AI systems are artifacts like any other. However, several gaps remain. Issues include proving defectiveness of an AI system when behavior emerges after deployment, establishing causation in opaque or black box systems, and assigning liability among multiple actors in the AI value chain, such as developers, deployers, and operators [10].

Rather than creating entirely new legal categories, many scholars argue for adapting and clarifying existing liability frameworks (product liability, negligence, strict liability), ensuring they are fit for AI contexts. This requires close collaboration between

[1] OECDAI. Policies, data and analysis for trustworthy artificial intelligence. Available at: https://oecd.ai/en/.

legal and AI experts to evaluate how established principles apply to novel use cases, and to determine where targeted updates are necessary [53]. Ultimately, liability for AI must balance innovation with accountability, ensuring that those who design, deploy, and profit from AI systems remain answerable for harms, while avoiding the creation of "responsibility gaps" [111].

In short, liability for AI should not be seen as a call for entirely new legal categories, but as the task of clarifying and adapting established frameworks such as product liability, negligence, and strict liability. This requires close collaboration between legal scholars, policymakers, and AI experts to ensure that accountability is effectively allocated across the AI value chain. By addressing issues of defectiveness, causation, and shared responsibility, liability frameworks can provide clear guidance without stifling innovation. The challenge is to prevent responsibility gaps while ensuring that those who design, deploy, and profit from AI systems remain answerable for harms. These questions of liability form a foundation for broader discussions of governance and regulation that follow in the next section.

Finally, regulation can also be seen as a means to further scientific development on AI. For example, consider the case in which legislation will restrict use of data and demand explanation of all results achieved by an AI system. These requirements probably mean that many of the current approaches, based on neural networks and deep learning, are not able to meet these demands. This can be seen as a limitation on the use of AI and be approached with complaints and refusal to comply, claiming economic losses and a delay to development. But it can also be seen as a challenge to be taken up. Then, researchers need to go back to the drawing board to come up with novel learning and reasoning techniques that ensure explainability and sustainable use of data, without compromising efficiency.

AI is far from done. Current machine learning techniques are just an intermediate step on the path of progress. If regulation is the means to further this progress, then we must embrace it. Such an approach requires a culture of openness and cooperation between scientists, developers, policy-makers, and ethicists in order to ensure regulations create the incentives to development that benefit both technological progress and wider society. It is hopeful to see that the need for dialog between different parties is increasingly being acknowledged by all.

9.4.2 Certification

Several economic sectors have developed effective means of certification (e.g., the foot sector). We can consider similar mechanisms for AI systems. In this case, independent and trusted institutions would validate and test algorithms, applications, and products against a set of well-defined principles (possibly derived from the recommendations described above) and guarantee the quality of the system. We, as users of such systems, would have the choice of what type of system would best meet our requirements. Such a certification approach can be combined with a regulatory one. In this case, regulation would specify the minimum set of principles and their interpretation that must hold for all systems in a given country or region, similar to the data protection regulations in force within the European Union. Above the minimum requirements laid down by regulation, certification supports business differentiation at the same time that it ensures consumer protection.

Currently, several initiatives toward AI ethical certification are being launched, including by the IEEE. The IEEE's Ethics Certification Program for Autonomous and Intelligent Systems (ECPAIS) aims to create specifications for certification and certification marking (e.g., the BSI Kitemark) processes that advance transparency, accountability, and reduction in algorithmic bias within AI systems. A recent white paper by the AI4People think-tank that proposes an Ethical framework for AI has advised the creation of a new (European) oversight agency responsible for the protection of public welfare through the scientific evaluation and supervision of AI products, software, systems, or services, with similar aims [112]. Several commercial organizations, including Accenture and PwC, are also announcing auditing services for the analysis of algorithms.

9.4.3 Codes of Conduct

We must support the development of self-regulatory codes of conduct for data and AI related professions with specific ethical duties. This would be along the lines of other socially sensitive professions, such as medical doctors or lawyers (i.e., with the attendant certification of "ethical AI" through trust-labels to make sure that people understand the merits of ethical AI and will therefore demand it from providers).

A professional code of conduct is a public statement developed for and by a professional group to reflect shared principles about practice, conduct, and ethics of those exercising the profession. It describes the quality of behavior that reflects the expectations of the profession and the community, provides a clear statement to society about these expectations, and enables professionals to reflect on their own ethical decisions. A code of conduct supports professionals to assess and resolve difficult professional and ethical dilemmas. While there are ethical dilemmas to which there is not a correct solution, professionals can give account of their actions by referring to the code. Many organizations and enterprises have their own codes of conduct. Even if in many cases adherence to the code is voluntary, there are professions that oblige allegiance to their code. This is the case for professional orders, or guilds, in many countries, where membership is a necessary condition for the practice of the profession. The most well known is the Hippocratic Oath, or Physician's Pledge (the Declaration of Geneva) taken by medical doctors.

The Association for Computing Machinery (ACM), the largest international association of computing professionals, recently updated their code of conduct [2]. This voluntary code is "a collection of principles and guidelines designed to help computing professionals make ethically responsible decisions in professional practice. It translates broad ethical principles into concrete statements about professional conduct." This code explicitly addresses issues associated with the development of AI systems, namely issues of emergent properties, discrimination, and privacy. Specifically, it calls out the responsibility of technologists to ensure that systems are inclusive and accessible to all, and requires that they are knowledgeable about privacy issues.

9.4.4 Inclusion and Diversity

Inclusion and diversity are a broader societal challenge and central to AI development. Research and development of AI systems must be informed by diversity in all aspects, and obviously including gender, cultural background, and ethnicity. But there is also growing evidence that cognitive diversity contributes to better decision-making. Therefore, development teams should include social scientists, philosophers, and others, as well as ensuring gender, ethnic, and cultural differences. It is important to diversify the AI development workforce along all pertinent dimensions. Regulation and codes of conduct can specify targets and goals, along with incentives, as a way to foster diversity in AI teams. It is equally important to diversify the expertise of those working on AI. In order to understand the ethical, social, legal, and economic impact of AI and to evaluate how design decisions contribute to this impact, AI professionals need to have basic knowledge of philosophy, social science, law, and economy.

Education plays an important role. AI is no longer an engineering discipline. In fact, AI is too important to be left to engineers alone. AI is really transdisciplinary. Most current AI and robotics curricula worldwide deliver engineers with a too narrow task view. The wide impact of AI on society requires a broadening of engineering education to include: (1) analysis of the distributed nature of AI applications as these integrate socio-technical systems, and the complexity of human–agent interaction; (2) reflection on the meaning and global effect of the autonomous, emergent, decentralized, self-organizing character of distributed learning entities; (3) incremental design and development frameworks, and the unforeseen positive and negative influence of individual decisions at the system level, and how these impact human rights, democracy, and education; (4) the consequences of inclusion and diversity in design, and how these inform processes and results; (5) understanding of governance and normative issues, not only in terms of competencies and responsibilities, but also in the case of views on health, safety, risks, explanations, and accountability; and (6) the underlying societal, legal, and economic models of socio-technical systems. Broadening AI curricula is possibly also a way to attract a more diverse student population. When AI curricula are known to be transdisciplinary, it can be expected that female students, who traditionally choose humanities and social subjects over engineering ones, may be motivated to choose AI. In parallel, other curricula need to include subjects on the theory and practice of AI. For example, the law curricula need to prepare law experts on how to address legal and regulatory issues around AI.

Finally, it is important to realize that besides human diversity, it is also essential to consider cultural diversity, which includes factors such as education, religion, and language. AI is increasingly pervasive and applied across cultures and regions. Failure to understand cultural diversity impacts negatively the universal right to access to the advantages that the technology brings. In an increasingly connected AI world, incentives and regulations can support awareness and commitment to a diverse perspective ensuring that AI applications are truly adaptable to a diverse cultural space, and thus enabling access to all.

9.5 Conclusions

Increasingly, AI systems will be taking decisions that affect our lives, in smaller or greater ways. In all areas of application, AI must be able to take into account societal values and moral and ethical considerations, and weigh the respective priorities of values held by different stakeholders in multicultural contexts, explain its reasoning, and guarantee transparency. As the capabilities for autonomous decision-making grow, perhaps the most important issue to consider is the need to rethink responsibility. Being fundamentally tools, AI systems are fully under the control and responsibility of their owners or users. However, their potential autonomy and capability to learn requires that design considers accountability, responsibility, and transparency principles in an explicit and systematic manner. The development of AI algorithms has so far been led by the goal of improving performance, leading to opaque black boxes: Putting human values at the core of AI systems calls for a mind-shift of researchers and developers toward the goal of improving transparency rather than performance, which will lead to novel and exciting techniques and applications.

Some researchers claim that given that AI systems are artifacts, the discussion of the ethics of AI is somewhat misplaced. Indeed, people are the ones responsible for these systems. We are the ones determining the questions that AI systems can answer and how to deal with the results of their decisions and action. The main concern of responsible AI is thus the identification of the relative responsibility of all actors involved in the design, development, deployment, and use of AI systems.

First, society must be prepared to take responsibility for AI impacts. This means that researchers and developers should be trained to be aware of their own responsibilities where they concern the development of AI systems with direct impacts on society. This requires extra effort in developing and delivering education and training materials, and the development of codes of conduct for AI developers. This, in turn, requires methods and tools to understand and integrate moral, societal, and legal values with technological developments in AI. This means that responsible AI is first an issue of governance. Second, responsible AI implies the need for mechanisms that enable AI systems to act according to ethics and human values. Whether we design them in that way or not, AI systems will and are already making decisions that we would consider to have an ethical flavor if they were made by people. Being aware of this is what responsible AI is all about. How do we design systems that take implicit "ethical" decisions? Or how do we design the system to ensure that it refers the decision to someone to take because it is an ethical decision? And where is the line between decisions that are not ethical and ones that are? This requires models and algorithms to represent and reason about, and take decisions based on, human values, and to justify their decisions according to their effect on those values. Current (deep learning) mechanisms are unable to meaningfully link decisions to inputs, and therefore cannot explain their acts in ways that we can understand.

Last but certainly not least, responsible AI is about participation. It is necessary to understand how different people work and live with AI technologies across cultures in order to develop frameworks for responsible AI. In fact, AI does not stand alone, but must be understood as part of diverse socio-technical relations. Here again, education plays an important role, to ensure that knowledge of the potential of AI is widespread, to make people aware that they can participate in shaping its societal development, and as a basis to ensuring diversity and inclusion.

But, as the capabilities for autonomous decision-making grow, perhaps the most important issue to consider is the need to rethink responsibility. Being fundamentally tools, AI systems are fully under the control and responsibility of their owners or users. However, their potential autonomy and capability to learn require that designers consider accountability, responsibility, and transparency principles in an explicit and systematic manner. The development of AI algorithms has so far been led by the goal of improving performance, leading to opaque black boxes: Putting human values at the core of AI systems which will lead to novel and exciting techniques and applications. As mathematician and philosopher Norbert Wiener wrote back in 1960: "We had better be quite sure that the purpose put into the machine is the purpose which we really desire" [148]. Ensuring an ethically aligned purpose is more than designing systems whose result can be trusted. It is about the way we design them, why we design them, and who is involved in designing them. It is a work for generations.

It is a work always in progress. Obviously, errors will be made, disasters will happen. It is not an option to ignore responsibility. AI systems are artifacts decided, designed, implemented, and used by us. We are responsible to try again when we fail (and we will fail), to observe and denounce when we see things going wrong (and they will go wrong), to be informed and to inform, to rebuild and improve.

It is important to realize that ethical principles for AI are not checklists or boxes to tick once and forget. These principles are directives for action. They are codes of behavior – for AI systems, but, most importantly, for us. It is us who need to be fair, non-discriminatory, and accountable, to ensure privacy of ourselves and others, and to aim at social and environmental well-being. The codes of ethics are for us; AI systems will follow.

9.6 Questions and Exercises

1. **Multiple choice question**. What does the ART principle in AI ethics stand for?
   (a) Autonomy, responsibility, transparency
   (b) Analysis, reasoning, technology
   (c) Accountability, responsibility, transparency
   (d) Artificiality, responsiveness, trust

2. **Multiple choice question**. Which of the following is not a part of the "ethics by design" approach in AI?
   (a) Integrating ethical reasoning in AI behavior
   (b) Focusing solely on the technical performance of AI
   (c) Considering moral and societal values in AI development
   (d) Ensuring transparency and accountability in AI decisions
3. **Short answer question**. Explain the difference between accountability and responsibility in the context of AI ethics.
4. **Short answer question**. Describe the concept of transparency in AI systems and its importance.
5. **Reflection question**. Reflect on the role of cultural diversity in AI development. Why is it important to consider diverse perspectives in the creation and implementation of AI technologies?
6. **Essay question**. Discuss the implications of AI in terms of ethical decision-making and societal impact. How should AI developers balance the advancement of technology with the potential ethical and social challenges posed by AI? Consider the principles of responsible AI in your response.

10 Social and Environmental Well-Being

10.1 Learning Objectives

The learning objectives of this chapter are:

- Appreciation (Bloom's understand): Understanding the environmental costs of AI.
- Analysis (Bloom's evaluate): Study specific applications and evaluate whether they contribute to or harm the Sustainable Development Goals.
- Analysis (Bloom's analyze): Weigh social impact against environmental impact.
- Application (Bloom's apply): Define concrete metrics related to well-being.
- Application (Bloom's remember): Recall what the Sustainable Development Goals are.

10.2 Introduction

Well-being is a challenging concept to define, as what it means is personal to each individual. Nevertheless, in most ethical and trustworthy AI guidelines there is a reference to the idea that AI should be used for beneficence. Beneficence implies focusing on the well-being for all of humanity: Everyone should have access to the benefits of AI, which should not be restricted to a select few. Beneficence encompasses many concepts across guidelines, such as well-being, common good, benefit of humanity, empowering humanity, sustainability, and continued prospering for mankind.

The idea of what constitutes well-being for all is a social discussion. We can therefore find different initiatives at the global and local levels to describe what constitutes "good" and policies to enact it and quantify it, such as the United Nations' Sustainable Development Goals (SDGs). Following the idea of beneficence and of what could be beneficial and sustainable uses of AI, some fields have focused on developing such applications.

10.3 The Sustainable Development Goals

In 2015, UN member states planned the 2030 Agenda for Sustainable Development. The agenda contains 17 Sustainable Development Goals [141] structured around three areas: economic growth, social inclusion, and environmental protection. When analyzing the beneficence of any application or technology, the aim is to have a positive impact on as many of the 17 goals as possible, without harming other goals.

The 17 SDGS are:

1. end poverty in all its forms
2. zero hunger
3. good health and well-being
4. quality education
5. gender equality and women's empowerment
6. clean water and sanitation
7. affordable clean energy
8. economic growth
9. infrastructure, industrialization, and innovation
10. reduced inequality
11. sustainable cities and communities
12. sustainable consumption and production
13. climate action
14. life below water (oceans, rivers)
15. life on land (Biodiversity, forests, desertification)
16. peace, justice, and strong institutions
17. partnerships for the goals.

The SDGs can be used as a baseline to study the impact of AI as a technology or of specific applications [145]. Each SDG has specific targets and indicators that can be used to measure whether AI or an application are contributing to them. For example, for SDG 3 (good health and well-being), indicators such as access to healthcare services can be used to evaluate the effectiveness of AI healthcare applications; for SDG 13 (climate action), measuring reductions in carbon emissions and improvements in fuel efficiency can be used to assess the impact of AI as a technology.

Different organizations produce similar indices, which can be used to measure the contribution or harm of AI. Some of these include the Sustainable Society Index,[1] which is also based around human, environmental, and economic well-being, the Better Life Index,[2] or the Inclusive Development Index.[3]

While these indices are useful as a blueprint to define what well-being and beneficence might mean socially, it is also worth keeping in mind that they contain a certain vagueness. With 17 goals and 169 targets, the SDGs are not easy to measure and follow over time for every single indicator. Additionally, how to measure progress can be open to interpretation. Therefore, it is essential to not rely purely on these quantitative

[1] Sustainable Society Index. Your compass to sustainability. Available at: https://ssi.wi.th-koeln.de/index.html.

[2] OECD. OECD Well-being data monitor. Available at: www.oecd.org/en/data/tools/well-being-data-monitor.html.

[3] World Economic Forum. The Inclusive Development Index. Available at: www.weforum.org/publications/the-inclusive-development-index-2018/.

indicators and to maintain stakeholder and social involvement to accurately understand the impact of an application.

10.4 AI for Good

Following the idea of beneficence, the fields of AI for social good (AI4SG) or AI for social impact concern those solutions that are focused on socially beneficial approaches or applications of AI. Fields that are generally seen under the AI4Good umbrella include AI for healthcare, AI for sustainability, AI for humanitarian aid, and AI for accessibility. Some examples of AI4SG applications include healthcare monitoring and managing patient care, climate modeling, wildlife monitoring, or crisis response.

In parallel, human-centered AI focuses on the augmentation of human abilities for the purpose of human well-being. The types of technology that it includes are human–AI collaboration, AI-assisted decision-making, and human–AI co-creation. Human-centered AI promotes the idea that AI should complement human abilities, enabling better decision-making and enhancing human performance. Some examples of technologies that fit these criteria are automated personal assistants, decision-support systems, and personalized educational tools. Human-centered AI represents a shift toward designing and deploying AI systems that are not only considering the technological aspects, but are also aligned with human values and societal needs.

When tackling applications that are considered "socially good" or "human oriented," it is necessary to recognize the underlying assumption that there is a consensus on what "social good" is. By aligning to specific metrics or indices, their criticisms and shortcomings are inherited, meaning that it is still necessary to evaluate with concrete actions whether harm is occurring and whether the benefits outweigh the costs.

10.5 Environmental Costs of AI

Part of human well-being is often considered to include ecological well-being. This is aligned with environmental sustainability: a responsible interaction with the environment to avoid the depletion or degradation of natural resources [150].

The environmental costs of AI are difficult to calculate due to the multiple steps that creating and using an AI model entails. Data storage, training, tuning, and use of the system all contribute to electricity use and emissions. Additionally, the downstream effects that AI as a technology has on power consumption are compounding and not easy to define. However, costs have been evaluated along different dimensions [91], which can be compartmentalized into different steps of the AI development and use pipeline.

- **Training.** Training a model can consume a substantial amount of energy. For instance, training GPT-3 has been estimated to require around 1,287 MWh (megawatt-hours) of electricity [90]. Additionally, training done "in the cloud" and data storage are very costly in terms of electricity: globally, data centers are estimated to consume about 200 TWh (terawatt-hours) of electricity annually, which is nearly 1% of global electricity demand.

The carbon footprint of training AI models is significant. Training GPT-3 is estimated to have produced 553 tons of CO_2. Successive iterations of a model increase the cost of training, with different rounds of training and tuning adding up to large amounts of electricity consumption. Successive models, such as GPT-4 and Llama 3.1, are thought to have even higher carbon footprints, although the exact cost is difficult to pinpoint without information from their developers.

A big contributor to the environmental cost of use is the immense amount of water required to cool the data centers that house AI servers. For example, some studies suggest that training GPT-3 alone may have consumed over 700,000 liters of water. This is extensible to cloud servers, where training your own model "in the cloud" can have a significant electricity and water cost.

- **Inference.** While training is a one-time event, the cost of inference (running the model to generate a response) is a big contributor to the environmental costs of these models. For example, a summarization task can produce 4–30 g of CO_2 [90]. The use of these models requires servers to remain operational and produces heat that has to be countered: An estimation is that a response to a single prompt can consume up to 200 ml of water [80].
- **Hardware.** The production and disposal of hardware used for AI, such as GPUs and chips, has environmental impacts. This includes the extraction of natural resources, as well as the disposal of non-recyclable elements.

To obtain a complete analysis, the above costs have to be weighed against possible benefits, including possible environmental benefits (e.g., a system that will improve the efficiency of production processes may perhaps offset the cost to train and operate it). Weighing the possible good impact against the environmental impact is tricky: Explainable, private, fair models may be more environmentally costly to train, leading to difficult design choices.

Looking forward, improvements in cooling efficiency, training methods, and hardware have reduced the cost of training a model in the last 10 years, with research into efficient models continuing. On the other hand, we are also seeing a trend of model and dataset growth, which come with increased energy costs. Studying the impact of different programming choices, such as model choice or library choice, is a relatively new area [65, 80], crucial to making informed design decisions.

10.6 Key Metrics

This chapter has focused on different indices and estimated costs, as we do not have systematic methods of calculating the contribution of AI as a technology, or of specific systems, to human well-being.

Some key aspects that are considered in policy are:

- **Economic impact:** This includes quantifying productivity and efficiency gains from automation, job creation and displacement, and economic inequality.
- **Social impact:** This includes metrics such as the number of people lifted out of poverty, improvements in health and education outcomes, and the perception of human autonomy.
- **Environmental impact:** AI's contribution to environmental sustainability is measured through carbon emissions, the cost of resource optimization, and improvements in environmental monitoring and conservation efforts [46].

10.7 Questions and Exercises

1. **Discussion question**. For each of the listed SDGs, describe an AI application that would impact them, either positively or negatively.
2. **Use-case exercise**. Define specific metrics to measure the economic and social impact of an AI application that supports medical imaging by detecting heart-rate anomalies.
3. **Discussion question**. If the energy cost of training a private model is higher than that of training the same model but with privacy vulnerabilities, who should be consulted to take the decision on which model to choose?
4. **Discussion question**. How much does the definition of well-being vary from person to person and from culture to culture?

11 Stakeholder Participation

11.1 Learning Objectives

The learning objectives of this chapter are:

- Appreciation (Bloom's understand): Understand the roles and importance of different stakeholders in AI.
- Appreciation (Bloom's understand): Explore principles and methods for effective stakeholder participation.
- Analysis (Bloom's analyze): Discuss challenges and provide recommendations for overcoming these challenges.
- Analysis (Bloom's analyze): Present case studies that illustrate successful and unsuccessful stakeholder participation.

11.2 Introduction

When a city council considers deploying AI to optimize traffic flows, residents are invited to a public consultation. Some citizens are excited about shorter commute times, others worry about increased surveillance, and small business owners fear being sidelined in favor of large logistics companies. Who gets a voice in this decision, how their input is taken into account, and how power is distributed among different stakeholders will determine not only the technical success of the system, but also whether the community perceives it as fair and legitimate. This example illustrates why participation is central to trustworthy AI: The development, deployment, and governance of AI systems affect many different groups, and inclusive processes are needed to ensure that diverse perspectives, interests, and values are taken seriously.

Stakeholder participation refers to the involvement of all parties who have a stake in the development, deployment, and use of AI technologies [101]. This includes developers, users, policymakers, and the general public. Their participation is crucial for creating AI systems that not only meet the objectives, requirements, and expectations in terms of functionalities, but are also ethically sound and socially responsible [61]. Effective stakeholder participation ensures that AI systems are developed in a way that is transparent, accountable, and aligned with societal values.

The need for stakeholder participation arises from the complex and far-reaching impact of AI on society. AI technologies have the potential to transform industries, improve efficiencies, and address societal challenges. However, without proper stakeholder input, these technologies can also exacerbate inequalities, introduce biases, and lead to unintended consequences. The first challenge is often to identify and engage all relevant stakeholders. Engaging a diverse range of stakeholders ensures that multiple perspectives are considered, leading to more equitable and inclusive AI solutions.

The importance of stakeholder participation lies in its ability to enhance the trustworthiness and legitimacy of AI systems. When stakeholders are actively involved, it promotes greater transparency and accountability, fostering public trust and acceptance. Moreover, stakeholder engagement can help identify potential risks and ethical dilemmas early in the development process, allowing for proactive measures to mitigate them.

Despite its importance, stakeholder participation faces several challenges. These include power imbalances among stakeholders, communication barriers, and differing priorities and values. Overcoming these challenges requires deliberate efforts to ensure inclusive and meaningful engagement, as well as mechanisms to address and reconcile conflicting interests.

This chapter aims to equip readers with a comprehensive understanding of the role and significance of stakeholder participation in trustworthy AI. Readers will explore the principles, methods, and best practices for engaging stakeholders effectively, understand the challenges involved, and learn from real-world examples and case studies. By the end of this chapter, readers should be able to appreciate the value of stakeholder participation and apply this knowledge to enhance the development and deployment of AI technologies.

11.3 Understanding Stakeholders in AI

The first step toward stakeholder participation is to identify and engage them. To effectively engage stakeholders, it is crucial to first understand who the stakeholders are, their roles, and the impact they have on AI technologies. In this section, we explore the different types of stakeholders within the AI ecosystem and outline their specific roles and contributions, highlighting the importance of their involvement in the development and deployment of AI technologies.

11.3.1 Identification of Stakeholders

Identifying stakeholders is the first step in fostering meaningful participation. Stakeholders in AI encompass a broad range of individuals and groups who are directly or indirectly affected by AI technologies. These stakeholders can be categorized into the following key groups:

- **Developers**: Engineers, data scientists, and researchers who create AI systems.
- **Users**: Individuals and organizations that use AI applications.

- **Policymakers**: Government officials and regulatory bodies that create laws and guidelines for AI use.
- **General public**: Society at large, which is affected by the deployment of AI systems.
- **Others**: This includes academia, industry associations, NGOs, and media, which can play crucial roles in shaping and influencing the development and deployment of AI technologies.

By comprehensively identifying stakeholders, it becomes possible to tailor engagement strategies that address the unique needs, concerns, and contributions of each group. This holistic approach ensures that the development and deployment of AI technologies are inclusive, equitable, and socially beneficial.

11.3.2 Stakeholder Roles and Responsibilities

Understanding the responsibilities and roles of stakeholders is the next step in fostering meaningful participation.

Developers include software engineers, data scientists, researchers, and technologists who design and build AI systems. Their primary focus is on the technical aspects of AI, such as algorithms, data processing, and system architecture. Developers play a critical role in shaping the capabilities and limitations of AI technologies.

Users are the individuals and organizations that interact with AI systems in their daily activities. This group includes consumers who use AI-driven applications, businesses that integrate AI into their operations, and professionals who rely on AI for decision-making support. Users provide valuable feedback that helps refine and improve AI systems, ensuring they meet real-world needs and expectations.

Policymakers consist of government officials, regulatory bodies, and legislators who create the legal and ethical frameworks within which AI technologies operate. Their role is to ensure that AI systems comply with laws and regulations, protect public interests, and promote ethical standards. Policymakers are instrumental in addressing societal concerns and mitigating potential risks associated with AI.

The general public includes society at large, which is affected by the deployment of AI in various sectors, such as healthcare, transportation, finance, and entertainment. Public opinion and societal acceptance are crucial for the sustainable integration of AI technologies. The general public's involvement ensures that diverse perspectives are considered, particularly those of marginalized and underrepresented groups.

Other stakeholders in the AI ecosystem include academia, industry associations, NGOs, and media. Academia consists of researchers and educators who study AI's implications and contribute to knowledge dissemination. Industry associations represent the interests of businesses and professionals in the AI sector. NGOs advocate for ethical AI use and address social, environmental, and economic impacts. Media includes journalists and media outlets that influence public perception and understanding of AI technologies.

As discussed in Chapter 4, each stakeholder group plays a critical role in the creation, development, use, and governance of AI systems. In brief:

- **Developers** are responsible for creating ethical and reliable AI systems.
- **Users** provide feedback and report issues to improve AI systems.
- **Policymakers** ensure that AI systems comply with ethical standards and regulations.
- **The general public** participate in discussions and provide societal perspectives on AI use.
- **Other stakeholders** from the above-mentioned groups play crucial roles in shaping research, standards, advocacy, and public perception of AI technologies.

11.4 Principles of Stakeholder Participation

Effective stakeholder participation in AI development and deployment is built on key principles that ensure the process is transparent, inclusive, and accountable. These principles are crucial to address the complex and far-reaching impacts of AI technologies, by building trust, incorporating diverse perspectives, and maintaining ethical standards in the creation and use of AI technologies.

The need for these principles arises from the potential for AI to affect individuals and communities in profound ways, influencing everything from privacy and security to employment and social equity. Clear principles provide a framework for engagement that helps prevent biases, promotes fairness, and enhances the legitimacy and public trust in AI systems. By establishing and adhering to these principles in stakeholder participation, we can create AI technologies that not only advance technical capabilities but also align with societal values and ethical standards, ensuring that the benefits of AI are distributed equitably and its risks are managed effectively.

11.4.1 Transparency

Transparency in stakeholder interactions is crucial for building trust (see also Chapter 7). This involves clear communication about AI capabilities, limitations, and decision-making processes. When stakeholders have access to detailed information about how AI systems function, they are better equipped to understand the potential impacts and implications of these technologies. Transparency also helps in demystifying AI, making it more accessible to nonexperts and enabling informed decision-making. For instance, developers should provide clear documentation and explanations of AI algorithms and their decision-making processes. Policymakers and regulatory bodies should also ensure that transparency standards are enforced, requiring organizations to disclose relevant information about their AI systems [48].

11.4.2 Inclusivity

Inclusivity ensures diverse representation, considering different demographics, backgrounds, and perspectives in AI development. An inclusive approach to stakeholder participation means actively seeking and integrating input from underrepresented and marginalized groups. This diversity of perspectives helps to identify and mitigate biases in AI systems and ensures that the benefits of AI are equitably distributed across society. For example, inclusivity can be promoted through targeted outreach and engagement efforts, such as holding workshops and consultations in diverse communities or providing platforms for voices that are often overlooked in technological discussions [20].

11.4.3 Accountability

Accountability mechanisms include clear guidelines for responsibility, regular audits, and channels for stakeholders to raise concerns (see also Chapter 9). Effective accountability frameworks ensure that developers and organizations are held responsible for the ethical and social impacts of their AI systems. This involves establishing standards and protocols for auditing AI systems, providing transparency reports, and setting up independent oversight bodies. Moreover, stakeholders should have accessible channels to report issues and concerns, ensuring that there are consequences for unethical practices. Accountability also involves continuous monitoring and evaluation of AI systems to ensure compliance with ethical standards and to address any emerging issues promptly [63].

11.5 Methods and Approaches for Stakeholder Engagement

Engaging stakeholders effectively is crucial for the responsible development and deployment of AI technologies [11]. Various methods and approaches can be used to ensure meaningful participation, each with its own strengths and suited to different contexts. By employing a mix of traditional and digital engagement techniques, stakeholders from diverse backgrounds can be involved in the decision-making process. This section outlines several key methods for stakeholder engagement, including public consultations, surveys, workshops, and digital platforms, providing insights into how these approaches can be utilized to gather valuable feedback and foster collaborative problem-solving [123].

11.5.1 Public Consultations and Open Forums

Public consultations and open forums are essential for encouraging broader community participation and ensuring that a diverse range of voices is heard. These events provide platforms for stakeholders to express their views publicly, ask questions, and engage in dialog with developers, policymakers, and other participants. Public consultations can take various forms, including town hall meetings, panel discussions, and public hearings. The European Commission's public consultations, which allow EU citizens to provide feedback on policies and initiatives, are a good example of this approach.[1] Another example is the UK government's use of open consultations on its website.[2] In the United States, the Federal Communications Commission (FCC) regularly holds public consultations to gather input on telecommunications and broadcasting policies.[3] Open forums are often less formal and can be held in various community settings. Both approaches are effective in gathering diverse viewpoints and fostering transparency and trust in the AI development process.

11.5.2 Workshops and Focus Groups

Workshops and focus groups offer opportunities for in-depth discussions and interactive engagement among stakeholders. These settings allow participants to share their experiences, express concerns, and collaborate on solutions in a more dynamic and personal environment. Workshops can be structured to include presentations, group activities, and open discussions, while focus groups typically involve guided conversations on specific topics. Tools such as Zoom and Microsoft Teams can facilitate virtual workshops and focus groups, making it easier to gather participants from different locations. These formats are particularly useful for exploring complex issues and generating detailed feedback, as they enable stakeholders to build on each other's ideas and provide context to their perspectives.

11.5.3 Surveys and Questionnaires

Surveys and questionnaires are valuable tools for collecting quantitative and qualitative data efficiently from a large number of stakeholders. These instruments can be designed to capture a wide range of opinions and preferences, providing insights into stakeholder needs and concerns. Effective survey design involves clear, unbiased questions and a logical structure that facilitates accurate responses. For instance, Google Forms[4] and SurveyMonkey[5] are popular platforms that allow for the easy creation and distribution of surveys. Analyzing the collected data helps identify common themes, areas of consensus, and points of contention, informing the development and refinement of AI systems to better meet stakeholder expectations.

11.5.4 Digital Platforms and Online Tools

Digital platforms and online tools offer scalable and accessible options for stakeholder engagement, especially for reaching geographically dispersed or large groups. These

[1] European Commission. Consultations. Available at: https://commission.europa.eu/about/service-standards-and-principles/transparency/consultations_en.

[2] UK government. Policy papers and consultations. Available at: www.gov.uk/search/policy-papers-and-consultations.

[3] FCC. Consultation. Available at www.fcc.gov/tags/consultation.

[4] Google. Google Forms. Available at: www.google.com/forms/about.

[5] Survey Monkey. Survey Monkey: guess less, ask more. Available at: www.surveymonkey.com.

tools include online surveys, virtual meetings, discussion forums, and social media channels. For example, platforms such as Slack or Trello can be used for ongoing stakeholder engagement and project management. Digital engagement can be particularly effective in involving stakeholders who may not be able to attend in-person events due to logistical constraints. Online tools can facilitate real-time feedback and continuous interaction, allowing stakeholders to contribute their input at their convenience. Leveraging technology for engagement ensures that a broader and more diverse audience can participate in the AI development process.

11.6 Challenges in Stakeholder Participation

Engaging stakeholders in AI development and deployment is critical, yet complex. Several challenges can impede effective participation, ranging from communication barriers and trust issues to power dynamics and ethical considerations. Understanding these obstacles is essential for developing strategies that facilitate meaningful and equitable stakeholder engagement.

Problems can arise from a lack of understanding of the issue at hand, where stakeholders may not fully grasp what the participation is about, leading to disengagement or misinformed input. For example, in a public consultation about AI-driven healthcare solutions, participants might not have sufficient knowledge about AI technologies, which can result in irrelevant or superficial feedback [123]. Providing clear and accessible information about the topic is crucial to mitigate this barrier.

Additionally, a lack of perceived legitimacy of those initiating the participatory process can lead to skepticism and resistance. Stakeholders might question the authority and intentions of the organizers, thinking, "Who are you to do this?" This issue was evident in the consultations conducted by the European Commission on AI regulations, where some participants doubted the Commission's expertise and motivations [37]. Building credibility through transparency about the organizer's background, objectives, and processes can help overcome this challenge.

A lack of trust in achieving a positive outcome can result in apathy, where stakeholders believe that their voices will not be heard or will not make a difference. For instance, during the public consultation on smart city initiatives in Toronto, some community members felt that their input would not influence the final decisions [94]. Ensuring that the participatory process is genuine and responsive to stakeholder input is essential to build and maintain trust.

This section explores the common barriers, power imbalances, and ethical and legal considerations that must be addressed to ensure successful stakeholder participation.

Common barriers to effective stakeholder participation include communication gaps, lack of trust, and resource constraints. Communication gaps can arise from technical jargon, differing levels of understanding, and cultural differences, making it difficult for stakeholders to effectively communicate their views and concerns [11]. Lack of trust between stakeholders and AI developers or organizations can hinder open dialog and collaboration. This trust deficit often stems from past experiences, perceived lack of transparency, and fear of misuse of information [123]. Resource constraints, including time, funding, and human resources, can also limit the extent and quality of stakeholder engagement. Overcoming these barriers requires targeted strategies such as simplifying communication, building trust through consistent and transparent practices, and securing adequate resources for engagement efforts.

Power dynamics can influence whose voices are heard and whose interests are prioritized in the decision-making process. Addressing power imbalances is essential for equitable participation. Dominant stakeholders, such as large corporations or influential policymakers, may overshadow the perspectives of marginalized or less powerful groups [46]. Recognizing these imbalances involves actively identifying and mitigating the influence of dominant stakeholders by creating platforms where all voices can be heard equally. Techniques such as facilitated discussions, anonymous feedback mechanisms, and structured decision-making processes can help ensure more balanced participation [41].

Stakeholder participation must furthermore adhere to **ethical standards and legal requirements**, ensuring respect for privacy, consent, and fair treatment. Ethical considerations include obtaining informed consent from participants, protecting their privacy, and ensuring that the engagement process is free from coercion or bias [54]. Legal requirements may involve compliance with data protection laws, such as the General Data Protection Regulation (GDPR) in the European Union, and other relevant regulations that govern the collection, use, and storage of stakeholder data. Adhering to these ethical and legal standards not only protects stakeholders, but also enhances the credibility and legitimacy of the AI development process [46].

11.7 Case Studies and Examples

Understanding both successful and unsuccessful stakeholder participation initiatives provides valuable insights into effective strategies and common pitfalls. This section explores case studies that highlight best practices and lessons learned from various stakeholder engagement efforts in AI development and deployment.

11.7.1 Successful Stakeholder Participation Initiatives

Examining successful initiatives provides insights into effective strategies and practices. In general, characteristics of a successful stakeholder engagement include efforts at inclusive and transparent participation, where diverse perspectives are actively solicited and integrated into the decision-making process, ensuring that the resulting AI systems are culturally appropriate, ethically sound, and aligned with the needs and values of the community. It also requires consistent communication, building trust through transparency, providing clear information about the goals and potential impacts of the AI system, and demonstrating a genuine commitment to addressing stakeholder concerns and feedback.

One notable example is the participatory design of the AI-based healthcare system in Rwanda. This initiative involved extensive collaboration between local healthcare providers, patients, and international AI experts. Stakeholders were actively engaged through workshops, surveys, and focus groups to identify the most pressing healthcare challenges and co-develop AI solutions tailored to local needs. The success of this initiative was attributed to its inclusive approach, ensuring that the technology was culturally appropriate and met the specific needs of the community [108].[6]

Another example, at the global strategic level, is the European Commission's AI HLEG (High-Level Expert Group on AI), which involved diverse stakeholders in developing guidelines and recommendations for trustworthy AI. This initiative included representatives from academia, industry, civil society, and policymaking groups, ensuring a comprehensive and balanced perspective on AI ethics and governance. The group's work has led to the creation of the "Ethics Guidelines for Trustworthy AI," which provides a framework for AI development that prioritizes human rights and societal well-being [109].

11.7.2 Lessons from Failures

Analyzing failed efforts highlights common pitfalls and areas for improvement. One such case is the initial deployment of facial recognition technology in public spaces by law enforcement agencies. In several instances, such as the San Francisco Police Department's pilot program, the technology was implemented without adequate stakeholder consultation, leading to significant public backlash and concerns over privacy, surveillance, and racial bias. The failure to engage with civil liberties groups, community leaders, and the general public resulted in the eventual ban of facial recognition technology by the city of San Francisco [1]. This case underscores the importance of transparent and inclusive stakeholder participation in addressing ethical and societal implications of AI technologies.

Another example is the controversy surrounding the Sidewalk Labs' smart city project in Toronto. The project faced significant opposition from local residents and privacy advocates due to perceived lack of transparency and inadequate stakeholder engagement. Concerns about data privacy, surveillance, and the potential for corporate overreach were not sufficiently addressed, leading to the project's termination in 2020. This failure highlights the need for robust stakeholder engagement and transparent communication to build trust and address public concerns in smart city initiatives [94].

11.8 Best Practices and Recommendations

Implementing effective stakeholder participation in AI development requires a set of best practices and strategic recommendations. These practices ensure that stakeholder

[6] For more information, see AI for Good Global Summit. Home page. Available at: https://aiforgood.itu.int.

engagement is meaningful, inclusive, and impactful. This section outlines key strategies for developing a participation strategy, maintaining continuous engagement, and evaluating participation efforts, supported by relevant examples and citations.

A comprehensive **participation strategy** includes clear objectives, stakeholder mapping, and tailored engagement methods. Clear objectives define the purpose and expected outcomes of the participation process, ensuring that all stakeholders understand their role and the importance of their input. Stakeholder mapping involves identifying and categorizing all relevant stakeholders, considering their interests, influence, and potential contributions to the AI project. Tailored engagement methods should be designed to suit the specific needs and contexts of different stakeholder groups.

Ongoing engagement ensures that stakeholder input is continuously integrated into AI development and deployment. Continuous engagement involves regular communication, updates, and opportunities for stakeholders to provide feedback throughout the AI lifecycle. This approach not only keeps stakeholders informed, but also fosters a sense of ownership and collaboration. For instance, the participatory design of the AI-based healthcare system in Rwanda involved continuous workshops and focus groups with local healthcare providers and patients to iteratively refine the system based on ongoing feedback [108].

Evaluating the effectiveness of participation efforts helps in refining strategies and improving future initiatives. Evaluation should be based on clear metrics and indicators that assess both the process and the outcomes of stakeholder engagement. Key aspects to evaluate include the level of stakeholder involvement, the quality of input received, and the impact of stakeholder contributions on the AI project. Methods for evaluation can include surveys, interviews, and analysis of participation data. Rowe and Frewer [123] provide a framework for evaluating public participation methods, emphasizing the importance of systematic assessment to enhance the effectiveness of engagement efforts [123].

11.9 Future Directions

The field of stakeholder participation in AI development is rapidly evolving, driven not only by technological advancements but also by a growing recognition of the importance of inclusive and ethical AI practices.

Emerging trends in stakeholder participation include the increasing use of AI tools to facilitate engagement and a growing emphasis on participatory governance. AI technologies such as natural language processing and sentiment analysis can analyze large volumes of stakeholder feedback, enabling more efficient and effective engagement processes. For instance, AI-driven platforms like Pol.is[7] have been used to facilitate large-scale public consultations by analyzing and visualizing public opinions on various issues. Additionally, there is a growing emphasis on participatory governance,

[7] Pol.is Input crowd, output meaning. Available at: https://pol.is/home.

where stakeholders are not just consulted but actively involved in decision-making processes. This trend reflects a shift toward more democratic and inclusive approaches to AI governance, ensuring that diverse voices are heard and considered [135].

Technologies such as AI-driven analytics and digital collaboration platforms can significantly enhance transparency, accountability, and inclusivity in stakeholder participation. AI-driven analytics can process and analyze large datasets from stakeholder interactions, identifying trends, patterns, and areas of consensus or disagreement. For example, AI tools such as sentiment analysis can help gauge public opinion on various issues, enabling more informed decision-making. Digital collaboration platforms, such as Slack and Trello, facilitate ongoing communication and collaboration among stakeholders, ensuring that their input is continuously integrated into the AI development process. These technologies enable more inclusive and data-driven approaches to stakeholder engagement, ensuring that all voices are considered in AI development.

Effective stakeholder participation is crucial for the development of trustworthy AI, ensuring that AI systems are aligned with societal values and ethical principles. Trustworthy AI requires transparency, fairness, and accountability, which can only be achieved through robust stakeholder engagement. Engaging stakeholders in the development and deployment of AI systems helps identify and address ethical concerns, biases, and potential harms, leading to more socially responsible AI applications. By prioritizing stakeholder participation, developers can build AI systems that are not only technically sound, but also socially and ethically acceptable.

11.10 Questions and Exercises

1. **Multiple choice question**. Which of the following is a key principle of stakeholder participation?
   (a) Efficiency
   (b) Transparency
   (c) Profitability
   (d) Simplicity
2. **Multiple choice question**. What is the first step in fostering meaningful stakeholder participation?
   (a) Creating AI algorithms
   (b) Implementing AI systems
   (c) Evaluating AI impacts
   (d) Identifying stakeholders
3. **Multiple choice question**. Which technology can enhance transparency and accountability in stakeholder participation?
   (a) AI-driven analytics
   (b) Blockchain
   (c) Virtual reality
   (d) Quantum computing

4. **True/false question**. Stakeholder participation is only necessary during the initial stages of AI development.
   - True
   - False
5. **True/false question**. Power dynamics can influence whose voices are heard in the decision-making process.
   - True
   - False
6. **True/false question**. Digital platforms can facilitate ongoing communication and collaboration among stakeholders.
   - True
   - False
7. **Elaboration question**. Discuss the importance of inclusivity in stakeholder participation for AI development. Provide examples to support your answer.
8. **Elaboration question**. Explain the role of continuous engagement in the AI lifecycle. How can it benefit the overall development and deployment of AI systems?
9. **Elaboration question**. Identify and discuss common barriers to effective stakeholder participation. Suggest strategies to overcome these barriers.

12 Human–AI Interaction: Digital Companions

12.1 Learning Objectives

This chapter is mainly aligned with the "Appreciation" and "Analysis" learning aspects, exploring different kinds of interactions between so-called digital companions and humans, and the relevance of social awareness in these interactions. The learning objectives of this chapter are:

- Appreciation (Bloom's remember): Identify different taxonomies of human–AI interactions.
- Analysis (Bloom's analyze): Discuss the role of social awareness within the interaction between so-called digital companions and human agents.
- Application (Bloom's apply): Analyze ethical tensions that can emerge during interactions between digital companions and human agents.

12.2 Introduction

Nowadays, the digitization of society has led humans to interact with nonliving entities, such as physical robots, chatbots, digital avatars, etc. For the sake of standardizing the presentation in this chapter, these nonliving entities that interact with humans will be called *digital companions*. Digital companions are a wide class of information systems that are deployed in different kinds of physical devices (e.g., toys, mobile phones, robot platforms, virtual reality platforms) and are designed to provide particular services to humans through some kind of interaction. Moreover, these systems have some level of autonomy in their decision-making processes. If AI methods equip digital companions with high levels of precision for the tasks they were designed for, digital companions can offer solutions to society that were not possible before the outbreak of AI. Nevertheless, interactions between humans and digital companions present different technological, legal, and ethical challenges. In this chapter, we will discuss some of these challenges.

12.3 Human–AI Interaction: From Data to Personalized Services

Digital companions can interact with humans in different modalities (e.g., voice, text, gestures) and may have different goals (e.g., playing with children, providing healthcare support, exploring an unknown environment, driving a car). By assuming that digital companions are goal-oriented, we assume they are rational concerning those goals. By knowing those goals, humans may understand the behavior of digital companions; if their goals are unknown, humans cannot predict or understand their behaviors. Nevertheless, some digital companions may be designed to keep their goals hidden. For example, the Turing test, introduced by Alan Turing, envisioned digital companions that interact with humans at a level at which the human participant cannot distinguish whether they are interacting with human peers or a digital companion.

Here we refer to these interactions between digital companions and humans as human–AI interaction [8]. Human–AI interaction is mainly concerned with how humans and AI systems communicate and collaborate. Over the years, AI has evolved from algorithms designed for specific tasks to complex systems capable of performing tasks that were once thought to be exclusively within the domain of human capability. Some events that signaled the possibilities of AI systems supporting or competing with humans are the development of expert systems in the 1970s, the chess match between IBM's Deep Blue and Garry Kasparov in the 1990s, and the release of ChatGPT [5].

With the improvement of performance by AI algorithms, human–AI interaction has shifted from humans teaching digital companions to digital companions learning autonomously through data-driven approaches. The data that is generated by humans is a golden asset for digital companions. Digital companions usually inspect the data generated by humans to understand human goals. By recognizing patterns in this data, digital companions can predict human goals and intentions. Digital companions also aim to understand the context that motivates the goals and intentions of humans. If digital companions understand better the context and the goals of humans, they can promise better collaboration with humans.

Since humans are always situated in an environment, digital companions usually also aim to understand the dynamics of changes in that environment. Indeed, the actions performed by digital companions may target a given human (e.g., sending them a reminder) or the environment where the human is situated (e.g., turning on or off the lights in a room). This suggests that digital companions may have at least two main data models:

- **User models:** User models usually contain unique information about users (e.g., personal data about the users, preferences, habits).
- **Environment models:** Environment models usually contain information on how a given environment is composed and how the elements of the environment change with or without the execution of actions by humans or digital companions.

The information that characterizes the user and environmental models depends on the goals of the digital companions. Digital companions are equipped with sensors to keep these models up to date. These sensors play a key role in the interactions between humans and digital companions and are the main sources of information for digital companions. The sophistication of these sensors results in more or less evidence for the digital companions to support their decision-making processes. Progress in sensor technology has a direct effect on digital companions' perception capabilities. Hence, any (new) sensor may mean changed perception skills. Informally speaking, there are two classes of sensors:

- **Physical sensors:** Physical sensors are designed to measure quantities of interest (e.g., temperature, noise). Within physical sensors, one can identify at least two subclasses of sensors:
  - **Contact sensors:** Contact sensors require physical contact with the quantity of interest. For instance, a temperature sensor may require physical contact with the body of an individual to sense their temperature. The deployment of physical sensors may perturb the state of the sample or subject to some degree. Hence, contact sensors may have restrictions on size and enclosure design.
  - **Noncontact sensors:** Noncontact sensors do not require direct contact with the quantity of interest. Hence, these sensors have the advantage of minimum perturbation of the subject or sample.
- **Digital sensors:** Digital sensors can be seen as any data source that provides digital information to a digital companion (e.g., information from social media).

The diversity of sensors provides a wide variety of data that a digital companion can get directly from humans and their environments. By combining the information from user and environment models with AI algorithms, digital companions can exhibit smart capabilities, showing understanding of human behaviors, including the recognition of activities, preferences, habits, and more. AI algorithms play a critical role in the interactions between humans and digital companions; the actions that are performed by digital companions rely on their user and environment models and AI algorithms. To personalize these interactions, the digital companions need tight user and environment models for their specific target users.

The progress in sensor technology has also opened up the possibility of creating new kinds of environments for humans. Through the manipulation of human perception (e.g., using virtual-/mixed-reality headsets and tracking techniques), humans can experiment with immersion in environments that go from extensions of their physical environment (mixed reality, MR) to virtual environments (virtual reality).

The two extremes, with the real world at one end and completely virtual reality (VR) at the other, are illustrated by the reality–virtuality continuum in Figure 12.1 [97].

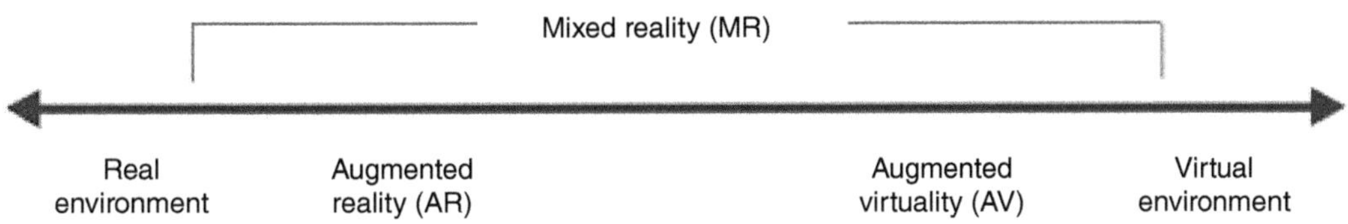

Figure 12.1 The reality–virtuality continuum.

The space between reality and VR defines the mixed-reality continuum that includes a combination of both real and virtual elements. Augmented reality (AR) refers to a largely real environment with few virtual elements, while augmented virtuality (AV) is composed of a predominately virtual environment with elements of the real world.

The diversity of emerging environments suggested by the reality–virtuality continuum can be used by humans and digital companions. Moreover, these environments can be handled by digital companions. This suggests that digital companions can have:

- **S1:** In real environments, partial perception of the environment where a human is located and minimal control of that environment (e.g., humans interacting with phone companion apps, robots).
- **S2:** In MR environments, partial perception of the environment where a human is located and partial control of that environment (e.g., humans interacting with MR companion apps).
- **S3:** In VR environments, full perception of the environment where a human is located and total control of that environment (e.g., humans interacting with VR companion apps).

The reality–virtuality continuum delineates a range of environments in which humans and digital companions can coexist and engage in meaningful interaction. These emerging forms of cohabitation are fostering the development of novel digital societies, characterized by increasingly complex interpersonal relationships between humans and digital companions. Although the precise nature of these societies remains difficult to anticipate, their evolution is poised to redefine social structures and modes of interaction within technologically mediated spaces.

12.4 Social Awareness of Digital Companions

One can highlight that digital companions are a particular class of systems that need to be aware of the social implications of their actions and interactions with humans. At the current state of the art, there is no classification of the expected ethical awareness of digital companions. Nevertheless, one can identify a classification of AI-based systems that was introduced by Dignum (Figure 12.2) [51]. The classification suggested by Dignum aims to cluster intelligent autonomous systems by their expected social awareness level.

By taking the perceptions of end-users about digital companions, one can also classify them:

- **Tools:** Systems that are only reactive to the requests of a human.
- **Assistants:** Systems that are reactive and also have a level of proactiveness in their services.
- **Partners:** Systems with close to human interaction capabilities.

One can expect an increasing level of autonomy at each level of this classification, as suggested by Figure 12.2.

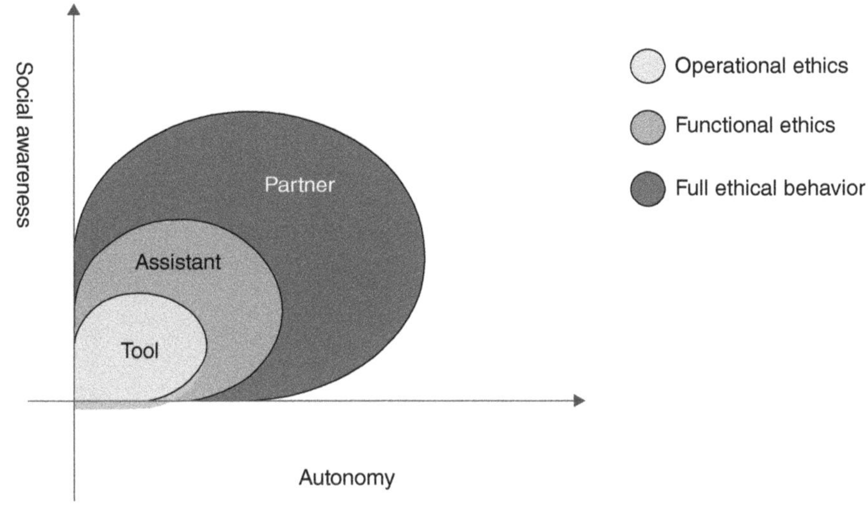

Figure 12.2 Autonomy and social awareness in AI-based systems [51].

Table 12.1 presents a list of examples of ethical awareness among digital companions. One can see that current digital companions are mainly perceived and designed as either tools or assistants, so one can expect at least a functional level of ethical awareness in their decisions. However, we can observe that ethical principles are only considered in the settings of data governance. This means that current digital companions are mainly concerned by legal compliance with regulations such as the General Data Protection Regulation [57].

As discussed in previous chapters, the EU Ethics Guidelines for Trustworthy AI suggest seven key requirements: (1) human agency and oversight; (2) technical

Table 12.1 Examples of ethical awareness in digital companions (DCs)

Reference	Perception of the end-users about DC	Perception of the DC based on its design
[31]	Not specified	Tool
[129]	Not specified	Assistant
[44]	Not specified	Tool
[28]	Assistant	Assistant
[113]	Tool	Tool
[93]	Assistant	Assistant
[114]	Not specified	Tool
[134]	Not specified	Assistant
[60]	Assistant	Assistant
[92]	Assistant	Assistant
[106]	Assistant	Assistant
[87]	Not specified	Assistant
[105]	Not specified	Assistant

robustness and safety; (3) privacy and data governance; (4) transparency; (5) diversity, non-discrimination and fairness; (6) societal and environmental well-being; and (7) accountability. These seven principles, especially 1, 4, and 6, serve as essential criteria for trustworthy digital companions. However, current digital companions lack substantial evidence of trustworthiness, particularly in areas such as transparency and explainability. Many digital companions function as opaque "black boxes," with limited ability to explain their decisions. Achieving greater explainability relies on the development and integration of explainable algorithms into digital companion architectures.

12.5 Questions and Exercises

1. Why are user and environment models critical for digital companions?
2. Consider a Know chatbot (e.g., ChatGPT).
   (a) What might be the information of its user and environment models?
   (b) Which are its sensors?
   (c) Is the chatbot transparent?
   (d) Is the chatbot a tool, an assistant, or a partner?
   (e) Which ethical principles can you argue the chatbot complies with?
   (f) Which ethical principles can you argue the chatbot does not comply with?
3. Identifying a digital companion that interacts with humans in a mixed-reality environment.
   (a) What might be the information of its user and environment models?
   (b) Which are its sensors?
   (c) Is the digital companion transparent?
   (d) Is the digital companion a tool, an assistant, or a partner?
   (e) Which ethical principles can you argue the digital companion complies with?
   (f) Which ethical principles can you argue the digital companion does not comply with?
4. Identifying a digital companion that interacts with humans in VR environments.
   (a) What might be the information of its user and environment models?
   (b) Which are its sensors?
   (c) Is the digital companion transparent?
   (d) Is the digital companion a tool, an assistant, or a partner?
   (e) Which ethical principles can you argue the digital companion complies with?
   (f) Which ethical principles can you argue the digital companion does not comply with?

13 Engineering Processes/Tools

13.1 Learning Objectives

This chapter is related to the "Appreciate" stage for understanding how responsible AI should be implemented and added to the development processes, while also keeping in mind the "Application" stage for implementation in practice. The learning objectives of this chapter are:

- Appreciation (Bloom's understand): Understand the challenges of AI development and the related methods to avoid them.
- Analysis (Bloom's understand): Be able to check the compliance of a system or tool with the trustworthy AI requirements.
- Application (Bloom's understand): Develop AI systems with trustworthy-aware methods, such as CRISP-DM.

13.2 Introduction

Governmental and nongovernmental stakeholders have put forth essential principles for responsible AI, garnering support from numerous organizations involved in the development and use of AI applications. A shared consensus has emerged around fundamental values, such as transparency, justice, fairness, nonmaleficence, responsibility, and privacy. The belief is that adhering to these fundamental principles can enhance the perceived trustworthiness of AI systems and bolster stakeholder confidence in AI technologies, as well as ensuring the "common good" approach.

Translating such ethical principles into actionable practices is a common objective, aiming to bridge the gap between responsible AI principles and their practical implementation. However, many researchers highlight the existing challenge of finding proven methods to operationalize AI ethics principles effectively; in particular, there is a need to translate principle-based frameworks into concrete processes in AI governance. Despite the pivotal role of AI providers in the broader AI ecosystem, their specific duties and responsibilities are often vaguely defined.

The groundwork for the characteristics that trustworthy AI applications should possess has already been established by principles and (recent) regulations. However, it's crucial to note that ensuring trustworthiness doesn't solely depend on the end product; it also involves considering the process by which the system is developed. Thus, the focus should not only be on the system characteristics that contribute to the trustworthiness of an AI application, but also on the traits that categorize the AI development process as trustworthy.

In this chapter, we will delve into the challenges raised by trustworthy AI software development and comment on the existing proposed frameworks to extend or adapt the existing regular software development processes to include safe AI management. We will also review families of tools that can assist in the process of producing or evaluating trustworthy AI systems.

13.3 Challenges

Lu et al. [89] undertook an empirical study involving AI/ML scientists and engineers with various backgrounds. The most relevant principles for ML/AI practitioners were found to be reliability and safety (equivalent to the EU's technical robustness and safety), transparency and explainability (summarized as transparency in the EU guidelines), and privacy protection and security (privacy and data governance), while the other principles were covered less. This reflects the nonexistence of proper standards, as there is a clear focus on the technical side and those principles where strong and more established regulations (and sanctions) are in place, such as privacy and protection of personal data.

Overall, they found challenges including:

- The current approach involves a one-time risk assessment, which may not be adequate for AI systems with high uncertainty and continuous learning.
- The inherent trustworthiness of an AI system and its perceived trust are often intertwined. Gaining human trust for even highly trustworthy AI systems is a challenging task that requires careful attention.
- To achieve trustworthiness for various ethics principles, leveraging process and product assurance mechanisms is essential. Providing process and product evidence is crucial to instill trust.
- Attaching ethics credentials to AI components/products can enhance human trust, especially when vendors assemble products using both commercial and open-source AI and non-AI components.
- Integrating AI models with systems can lead to new emergent behavior, requiring system-level ethical considerations. Responsible AI requirements are often stated as high-level objectives and need to be explicitly specified and verified in terms of expected system outputs and outcomes.
- The complexity of AI and its difficulty in explanation make detailed risk assessment challenging. Designing AI components to be flexibly switched off or changed from decision mode to suggestion mode is a significant architectural decision.
- Trade-offs between AI ethics principles exist, and current practice often involves developers prioritizing one principle over another instead of finding balanced trade-offs, with stakeholders making the ultimate value and risk decisions.

- Despite being cross-cutting quality and nonfunctional requirements suitable for architecture/design analysis, responsible AI requirements are under-explored in projects.
- Human-centered approaches, considering users' backgrounds and preferences, should be adopted for explainability and interpretability to enhance human trust in AI.
- There is a strong desire for continuous monitoring and validation of AI systems post-deployment for responsible AI requirements, but existing AI/ML practices provide limited guidance. End-to-end development tools supporting continuous assurance of AI ethics are lacking.
- AI systems involve the coevolution of data, models, code, and configurations. Co-versioning with model dependency specification is necessary to ensure data provenance and traceability.

13.4 Requirements for Trustworthy AI Software Development

In the realm of AI development, discussions on concrete requirements and best practices for trustworthy processes are ongoing. Drawing from the broader field of software development, trustworthy processes aim to create dependable products that meet predefined requirements. Trustworthy development involves ensuring that the outcome aligns with these requirements.

For general software, agreed-upon characteristics of trustworthy products include security, privacy, reliability, and business integrity. Developing trustworthy AI applications builds on these characteristics but requires additional adaptations due to its enhanced capabilities. The consensus on ethical fundamentals has led to defined requirements for trustworthy AI systems, emphasizing concepts like human agency, technical robustness, privacy, transparency, diversity, fairness, environmental and societal well-being, and accountability.

The foundations of system characteristics for trustworthy AI applications have already been formulated, but their trustworthiness depends not only on the resulting system but also on the development process. Stakeholder trust relies on both decisive system characteristics and trustworthy development process features. Overlaps between AI and regular software development can be leveraged, and existing standards, such as those addressing system lifecycle processes and security engineering, offer potential for introducing trustworthiness.

While not settled, discussions around trustworthy development processes have been initiated for regular software. The overarching goal is to enhance predictability and controllability in development, reducing perceived dependability and uncertainty for the domain practitioner. Five key characteristics are highlighted to make development processes perceived as trustable:

- **Transparency:** A vital pillar of trustworthiness, transparency requires clear communication about AI development steps. Making the process comprehensible and accessible to a wider audience ensures that stakeholders understand how trustworthy systems meet requirements. Within AI, transparency aligns with explainability and interpretability, ensuring justifiable and traceable predictions. The motivations behind transparency vary among stakeholders, encompassing goals from aiding developers in understanding and debugging systems to facilitating auditing. Transparent explanations can foster design acceptance and contribute to responsible development.

- **Reliability and consistency:** Enhancing predictability is crucial for fostering trust. The development process must be reasonable, predictable, and standardized, proving to external actors that it follows a predefined plan. A consistent, transparently communicated process reduces uncertainty. Mandatory activities within the process increase predictability, reassuring users that minimum requirements are met and clarifying upcoming steps.
- **Objectivity:** This requires executing every process step neutrally and in a standardized manner, devoid of favoritism in data processing or outcome derivation.
- **Accountability:** Defined accountabilities for each development step foster user trust. Defining responsibility and tracing system malfunctions back to obligations within the development stage enhance trustworthiness. Accountability is also a core requirement within legal frameworks and trustworthy processes, as mandated by the EU AI Act, among others, as it ensures adherence to defined frameworks for high-risk AI systems.
- **Auditability and intervenability:** Enabling external monitoring and control enhances perceived trustworthiness. Auditability, involving external checks and interventions, is crucial for both the system and its development process. Auditing practices ensure ethical AI design by examining consistency between auditable artifacts and stated principles, regulations, norms, or benchmarks. Options for external checks and intervention are vital characteristics for building trustworthiness in both the AI system and its development process.

13.5 Measuring Trustworthy AI Software Development

While the principles and regulations presented in previous chapters (see Chapter 1) lay the groundwork for the development of trustworthy AI, specific measures to guarantee their fulfillment must be extracted in order to progress toward actual implementation. The following measures have been synthesized from established AI governance frameworks and legal considerations, emphasizing EU policy, and considering (legally) binding measures as those found in the existing EU regulations or directives as mandatory for some AI technologies or under certain conditions, as per Hohma and Lütge [75], who collected nonbinding measures from a variety of global AI governance frameworks and compared them to the aforementioned legally binding measures that are currently enforced or planned in the EU.

13.5.1 Plan

When developing AI systems, both nonbinding and legally binding measures play a role in ensuring ethical and responsible deployment. Nonbinding measures include the creation of codes of conduct that establish general principles and guidelines for AI use. These codes serve as voluntary commitments that encourage responsible AI practices without carrying legal consequences.

Binding measures, on the other hand, involve the development of formal AI governance strategies that address critical aspects such as trustworthy AI evaluation, data protection, quality and risk management, human intervention, and the impact of AI on businesses and employment. Privacy and accountability must be considered from the outset of AI system design, ensuring that potential harms and misuse are mitigated through education and awareness programs.

Legally binding measures also define clear responsibilities and accountabilities for stakeholders involved in AI development and deployment. Regulatory requirements set thresholds for system safety, accuracy, reliability, and data quality, ensuring that AI operates effectively in both industrial and consumer contexts. Supporting infrastructure, including software, hardware, and cloud applications, must meet established standards. Additionally, mechanisms for redress and compensation are put in place to address potential harms caused by AI systems, including cases of discrimination or unfair treatment. Together, these measures aim to balance innovation with accountability.

13.5.2 Create and Establish

In this phase, nonbinding measures focus on fostering participatory development processes, encouraging public feedback and promoting open standards and interoperability. They also involve consulting stakeholders to clarify concerns and questions. Ethical oversight is emphasized through internal or external entities, along with ensuring team diversity in terms of backgrounds, cultures, and disciplines.

Risk prevention and management strategies are key to addressing unintended data misuse, modification, bias, fairness-related harm, and adversarial attacks. Measures such as bias removal, testing, and monitoring help reduce discriminatory biases. Human control over data and AI-driven processes is prioritized, alongside continuous education for relevant personnel. Systems must also maintain oversight and control over their purpose, constraints, and decisions, with the ability to modify or shut down misbehaving systems. Auditing mechanisms are encouraged, including audit trail development and providing access for internal or external reviews.

Binding measures impose stricter requirements, including systematic risk management with fallback plans. AI systems must incorporate human oversight (human-on-the-loop) or direct human control (human-in-the-loop) to prevent errors, avoid human subordination to AI, and ensure that decisions with significant consequences are not made solely through automation. There must be clear ethical and legal responsibility attribution, with the ability to terminate AI systems if human control is lost.

Public participation is legally reinforced, allowing individuals to choose which digital services they use, correct misinformation, challenge unfair AI decisions, and request final human determinations. Safety and bias bug-bounty programs may be considered to enhance system accountability. Additionally, AI systems must be explainable, ensuring transparency in outcomes, decision logic, key influencing factors, and data accuracy. These measures work toward creating AI systems that are fair, accountable, and aligned with human oversight while minimizing risks associated with automation and bias.

13.5.3 Assess and Evaluate

Here, nonbinding measures focus on conducting *ex ante* (before deployment) impact assessments to evaluate potential effects on fundamental and human rights, privacy, societal norms, sustainability, democracy, and the scientific foundation of the system. Additionally, opportunities for quality labels and certification are explored, along with the independence of critical infrastructure. *Ex post* (after deployment) impact assessments examine system accessibility and the risk of unfair denial of resources, rights, goods, or participation.

On the other hand, binding measures enforce compliance with international and domestic laws, standards, and best practices. Data quality is rigorously tested for accuracy, timeliness, integrity, and representativeness. Legal data processing is ensured by protecting user data and metadata, regulating access and control, preserving user privacy, and limiting unauthorized observations.

AI systems must undergo rigorous testing for accuracy and reliability, ensuring proper model selection and mitigation of overfitting or underfitting. Robustness is assessed through sensitivity analysis, while security measures protect against data poisoning, model leakage, adversarial attacks, and cybersecurity threats. Discrimination is evaluated by examining protected classes and dataset representativeness. Additional assessments verify system validity, compliance with domain-specific requirements, and overall lawful development. AI providers are also required to ensure that statements made to customers and consumers remain truthful, balancing proactive risk assessments with strict legal compliance.

13.5.4 Document and Communicate

This might be the most important section for citizens, as nonbinding measures focus on promoting AI education by integrating AI-related topics into educational curricula, supporting public awareness activities, and engaging with civil society to identify best practices for AI education.

Binding measures, on the other hand, enforce strict documentation and record-keeping to enhance traceability and reproducibility. This includes maintaining records on datasets, data provenance, gathering and labeling processes, data testing, and access. AI systems must also disclose key information during use, such as user interactions with AI, and clarify how consumer actions might impact automated decisions or scores. Through all phases, clear communication with stakeholders is required, often through user manuals, to outline key concepts, system purpose, intended use, capabilities, limitations, training data characteristics, and model structures. Transparency in data protection processes and the roles of responsible internal and external actors is also mandated.

Furthermore, AI developers must document system goals, design choices, definitions, standards, testing methods, and performance assessments, with a focus on privacy and fairness. Any identified biases and their potential impacts must be recorded, along with details of stakeholders involved and their responsibilities. Additionally, risk management structures must be in place, including mechanisms for monitoring, feedback, error correction, human oversight, and cybersecurity, ensuring that AI systems are developed and deployed in a responsible, explainable, and ethical manner while fostering public trust and engagement.

13.6 Flow and Example Tools for Developing Trustworthy AI Systems

CRISP-DM, which stands for Cross-Industry Standard Process for Data Mining, is a widely used framework that provides a structured approach to guide professionals through the data mining process; it is the most widely used analytics model that serves as the base for a data science process. In this section, we will take this popular framework and include the measures and actions that might be required for developing trustworthy AI systems, validating the data, the algorithms, the outcomes, and all the related ethical considerations. For other approaches and examples, see also [34] (SPICE-based) and [88] (Agile approach).

13.6.1 Brief Introduction to CRISP-DM

The journey of creating and applying an AI solution (see Figure 13.1) goes as follows:

1. It always commences with the formulation of a business case.
2. During the *business understanding* phase, a thorough definition and scope are established for a business problem, which subsequently transform into design requirements for data scientists.
3. Following this, the *data understanding* phase ensues, involving the collection of training and test data.
4. Moving into the *data preparation* phase, the gathered data undergoes analysis, sampling, and pre-processing to align with the chosen AI model.
5. Upon completion of the preparatory steps, the *model development* phase is initiated. Here, the AI model undergoes training, tuning, and evaluation.
6. Once the *model evaluation* demonstrates optimization and aligns with business requirements, the model proceeds to the *deployment* stage. This marks the transition of the AI system into production, where its performance is continually monitored.

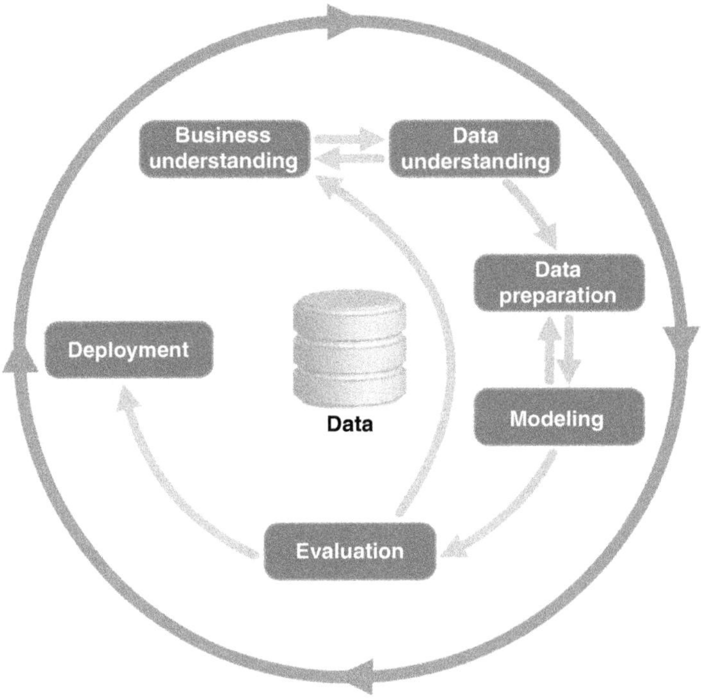

Figure 13.1 Relationship between the different phases of CRISP-DM, showing the recursive nature of a data science project. Source: Kenneth Jensen, CC BY-SA 3.0, via Wikimedia Commons

CRISP-DM is, thus, a roadmap that helps data professionals navigate the entire process of using data to solve real-world business problems. It ensures a systematic and well-organized approach, making the complex task of data mining more manageable and effective.

13.6.2 Business Understanding

- **Objective:** Start by understanding the business problem you want to solve or the goal you want to achieve with data mining.
- **Questions to answer:** What are the business objectives? What is the problem we want to solve using data?

During this initial phase, several tasks must be accomplished to lay the groundwork for trustworthy model development. These tasks include identifying the relevant stakeholders, specifying product requirements, outlining technical design specifications, defining performance metrics, and addressing ethical and legal compliance. The main principles that apply in this phase are:

- **Traceability:** Establish the foundation for an MLOps-based AI project by ensuring model and data version control in subsequent phases. Consider, for instance,

utilizing MLFlow,[1] a powerful package that supports packaging data science code in a reusable and reproducible manner.
- **Fairness:** Define fairness metrics and detection methods if the business problem involves sensitive groups. Leverage the fairlearn package, which provides support for bias mitigation methods and metrics, facilitating a comprehensive assessment of model fairness during the model development phase.
- **Privacy:** Anticipate potential ethical breaches before initiating the project. Pay specific attention to data sources and privacy concerns, implementing mitigation methods during the data preparation phase.

Once these quality control checks are established, it is essential to conduct a comprehensive review of best practices and discuss the next steps with all relevant stakeholders. This collaborative approach ensures a shared understanding and commitment to ethical and trustworthy AI development.

13.6.3 Data Understanding

- **Objective:** Get to know your data by exploring and gathering information about it.
- **Questions to answer:** What data is available? What does the data look like? Are there any patterns or trends?

During this phase, the specifications outlined in the initial phase are integrated with domain knowledge and experience to comprehend inherent biases, assumptions, and privacy concerns within the collected data.

- **Traceability:** Implement data version control as per the traceability principle, ensuring a documented specification that includes information on the data's location, source, responsible individuals, and any privacy or quality concerns. The DVC Python package,[2] built on Git version control, can facilitate this process effectively.
- **Fairness:** Evaluate data collection methods for data adequacy, such as identifying missing data for certain groups, and potential bias. This prepares the groundwork for deploying specific mitigation techniques in the subsequent data preparation phase to address fairness concerns.
- **Privacy:** Conduct a thorough assessment of data sources for personally identifiable information (PII). Consider using synthetic data to mitigate GDPR (General Data Protection Regulation) risks. There are many tools to generate synthetic data; some are domain-specific (such as MDClone[3] for healthcare), while others are general purpose tools (Mostly AI[4] and Hazy[5] are good examples of these).

[1] MLFlow. Deliver high-quality AI, fast. Available at: https://mlflow.org.
[2] Davidovs Venture Collective. DVC. Available at: https://dvc.ai.
[3] MDClone. Discover, share, innovate. Available at: https://mdclone.com.
[4] Mostly.ai. Data for everyone. Available at: https://mostly.ai.
[5] Hazy. Treat data responsibly. Available at: https://hazy-ai.com.

Conclude this phase by conducting a comprehensive data audit on available data sources, documenting the responsibilities of the team associated with each data source. This holistic approach ensures that data is prepared ethically and aligns with the principles of traceability, fairness, and privacy.

13.6.4 Data Preparation

- **Objective:** Clean and pre-process the data to make it suitable for analysis.
- **Questions to answer:** Is the data clean? Are there missing values or outliers? How can we structure the data for analysis?

In the data preparation phase, the collaboration of the data engineering team, domain experts, and model developers is pivotal. This phase involves essential tasks such as data mining, conducting a data quality assessment through exploratory data analysis (EDA), and constructing training data, shaping the foundation for subsequent phases.

- **Traceability:** Execute data version control, ensuring a systematic approach to track changes in the data. Additionally, set up a data pipeline for transparency in the data preparation steps. The TensorFlow input pipeline API,[6] for instance, offers a robust solution, allowing the construction of intricate input pipelines from reusable components and handling diverse data formats and transformations.
- **Fairness:** Deploy bias mitigation methods to cultivate training data that is impartial. Techniques such as reweighting features of the minority group, oversampling the minority group, or undersampling the majority group help eliminate biases. Imputation methods can also be employed to reconstruct missing data, ensuring the dataset's representativeness.
- **Privacy:** Generate synthetic data to address privacy risks, enhance training data, or overcome limitations due to insufficient data identified in the earlier phase.

Finally, conduct an EDA and present a comprehensive report on the training data to a technical auditor for approval before progressing to the next phase. This ensures a thorough examination and validation of the prepared data, aligning with the principles of traceability, fairness, and privacy.

13.6.5 Modeling

- **Objective:** Build and select a model that helps to solve the business problem.
- **Questions to answer:** Which algorithm or model is suitable? How can we train the model with the data?

The AI model development phase commences with the utilization of high-quality training data, and it might be the most important phase in regards to the software itself. During this phase, model developers bear the primary responsibility of ensuring that the AI model under development aligns with the application requirements and

[6] TensorFlow. tf.data: Build TensorFlow input pipelines. Available at: www.tensorflow.org/guide/data.

seamlessly integrates with the data prepared in earlier phases. Performance metrics derived from the model are meticulously evaluated and presented to stakeholders, followed by comprehensive testing of the model's performance and functionality at a granular level.

- **Traceability and auditability:** Employ MLFlow or similar for model versioning and logging output, maintaining a systematic record of model iterations. Organize repositories and pipelines into distinct development, acceptance, and production environments using a Git version control system. Incorporate required reviewers at each stage to uphold traceability and accountability.
- **Fairness:** Conduct assessments to ensure model adequacy and mitigate bias using techniques such as adversarial debiasing with generative adversarial networks (GANs). IBM's Trusted AI package[7] offers valuable resources for this purpose, promoting fair outcomes across all demographic groups.
- **Robustness:** Evaluate model performance comprehensively by calculating accuracy scores, area under the curve, F1 score, confusion matrix, mean square error, and mean absolute error. Enhance code coverage by implementing unit tests using the Python unittest[8] framework, looking to validate the robustness of the model.
- **Interpretability/explainability:** Prioritize interpretability to facilitate understanding of the model's predictions, particularly for domain practitioners and regulators. Implement explainable AI (XAI) techniques such as LIME[9] and SHAP[10] to elucidate model decisions. LIME provides local interpretability by modifying individual data samples and observing the resulting impact on predictions. SHAP employs a game theory approach to explain individual predictions, offering insights into feature contributions. Present a model quality report to a technical reviewer for final approval, ensuring transparency and interpretability.

By adhering to these principles and employing appropriate techniques, the AI model development phase ensures the creation of robust, fair, and interpretable AI models tailored to the application's requirements.

13.6.6 Evaluation

- **Objective:** Assess the performance of the model to ensure it meets the business objectives.
- **Questions to answer:** How well does the model perform? Does it meet the criteria for success?

After a rigorous validation conducted in the previous phase, the focus of this phase shifts toward verifying the transparency and adherence to ethical considerations established in the business understanding phase. It is, thus, instrumental in guarantee-

7 GitHub. Trusted-AI. Available at: https://github.com/Trusted-AI.

8 Python. unittest – Unit testing framework. Available at: https://docs.python.org/3/library/unittest.html.

9 marcotcr. LIME. Available at: https://github.com/marcotcr/lime.

10 SHAP. Welcome to the SHAP documentation. Available at: https://shap.readthedocs.io/en/latest/index.html.

ing the fairness and comprehensibility of the AI model. Key stakeholders involved in this phase include testers, developers, and legal experts.

- **Fairness:** Evaluate the model for biases using established metrics, such as:
  - **Statistical parity difference:** Measure the discrepancy in favorable outcomes between minority and majority groups.
  - **Equal opportunity difference:** Assess variations in true positive rates across demographic groups.
  - **Average odd difference:** Determine the average disparity in false positive and true positive rates between different demographic groups.
  - **Disparate impact:** Calculate the ratio of favorable outcomes for minority groups relative to majority groups.
- **Robustness:** Conduct user acceptance tests utilizing the XAI outputs from the preceding phase. Additionally, perform metamorphic and adversarial tests to assess the model's resilience prior to deployment. Metamorphic tests involve modifying model inputs to evaluate its response, while adversarial testing entails subjecting the model to adversarial attacks to gauge its robustness.

Upon completion of these assessments, write a comprehensive test report to a technical reviewer and auditor for their review and approval before advancing to the final phase in the process. This meticulous review ensures that the AI model not only meets stringent fairness and transparency criteria but also stands resilient against potential adversities in real-world scenarios, where we will deploy it in the following phase.

13.6.7 Deployment

- **Objective:** Implement the model into the business environment for practical use.
- **Questions to answer:** How can the model be integrated into existing systems? What resources are needed for deployment?

With a transparent and comprehensible model in place, the focus now shifts to the final phase, where meticulous monitoring, real-world performance evaluation, and ongoing maintenance take precedence.

- **Monitoring dashboard:** Set up a monitoring dashboard to continuously track the model's performance in a production environment. Key metrics to monitor include:
  - model performance metrics as defined during the model development phase;
  - bias metrics identified during the model evaluation phase; and
  - drift detection metrics such as concept drift and data drift detection. Concept drift refers to changes in data distribution or relationships between input and output variables, which can impact model performance over time (so, detecting whether the model is going astray). Utilize drift detection metrics as early indicators to prompt actions such as retraining the model or recalibrating the training data weights to maintain optimal performance.

By diligently monitoring the model's performance, addressing drift, and embracing the iterative nature of the AI lifecycle, organizations can ensure that their AI solutions remain robust, fair, and transparent over the long term, thereby maximizing their efficacy and value in real-world applications.

13.6.8 Feedback

- **Objective:** Gather feedback on the model's performance and use it to make improvements if necessary.
- **Questions to answer:** Are there areas where the model can be enhanced? How can user feedback be incorporated?

The feedback phase is a critical stage where the performance of the deployed model is evaluated, and any necessary adjustments or improvements are made based on the feedback received from users (domain practitioners) and stakeholders. In the context of trustworthy AI, the feedback phase takes on added significance as it allows for continuous monitoring and refinement to ensure that the AI system remains ethical, fair, transparent, and reliable throughout its lifecycle.

- **Iterative lifecycle approach:** Understand that reaching this final phase and passing through all quality control phases does not mark the conclusion of the AI lifecycle. Instead, view the AI project lifecycle as an iterative process, wherein adjustments, retraining, or revisits to previous phases may be necessary as the model evolves or as new requirements emerge.

During the AI system's lifecycle, it is still needed to do the following:

- **Model monitoring:** Tools like MLflow or TensorBoard[11] provide capabilities for tracking model performance metrics, logging model versions, and visualizing model outputs over time.
- **Bias detection and mitigation:** Frameworks like IBM's AI Fairness 360[12] or Google's What-If Tool[13] offer functionalities for detecting and mitigating biases in AI models through metrics calculation and bias correction algorithms.
- **XAI libraries:** Packages such as LIME, SHAP, or Captum[14] provide interpretability techniques to explain model predictions and highlight feature importance that might help understand why the model is deviating.
- **Privacy-preserving techniques:** Technologies like differential privacy libraries or federated learning frameworks help maintain data privacy and confidentiality while training and deploying AI models with real data.

[11] TensorFlow. TensorBoard: TensorFlow's visualization toolkit. Available at: www.tensorflow.org/tensorboard.

[12] IBM. Introducing AI Fairness 360. Available at: https://research.ibm.com/blog/ai-fairness-360.

[13] What-If Tool. Visually probe the behavior of trained machine learning models, with minimal coding. Available at: https://pair-code.github.io/what-if-tool.

[14] Captum. Model Interpretability for PyTorch. Available at: https://captum.ai.

By integrating these trustworthy AI requirements and tools into the feedback phase of the CRISP-DM methodology, organizations can ensure that their AI systems continue to meet ethical standards, deliver fair and transparent outcomes, and maintain user trust over time.

13.7 Additional Tools

For further information and examples, see the following:

- The OECD has a large *Catalogue of Tools & Metrics for Trustworthy AI*,[15] where one can find not only technical tools and references to remove bias, to audit AI systems, and for robust and secure data collection and processing, but also metrics to measure model performance, fairness, or privacy. There are also nontechnical tools, such as educational tools, documentation tools, or procedural tools for specific scopes (finance, healthcare, etc.).
- Traceability (akin to reproducibility) is considered a key requirement for trustworthy AI, related to the need to maintain a complete account of the provenance of data, processes, and artifacts involved in the production of an AI model. Traceability in AI shares part of its scope with general purpose recommendations for provenance as in W3C PROV,[16] and it is also supported to different extents by specific tools used by practitioners as part of their efforts to make data analytics processes reproducible or repeatable. A number of tools [103, 116] for the purpose of reproducibility are available with different capabilities and levels of maturity, but a common approach is currently lacking. Future developments should address this to fill that gap and enable interoperability across tools for traceability. In particular, most of the current approaches are analogous to a record of transactions (instead of being closer to a researcher/developer log or diary), and thus lack the ability to include and highlight the developer's judgment and thought process in their decision-making.

13.8 Questions and Exercises

1. **Short answer question**. Explain in a few sentences why one-time risk assessments might not be adequate for AI systems. Mention one example of such systems and give examples of possible issues that might arise.
2. **Essay question**. Reflect on your own interactions with AI systems in daily life. Look at your smartphone or computer, choose one app or web service, and analyze both the daily use and their terms and conditions (which you signed). What are your concerns in regards to safety, transparency, or privacy after doing so? Can you be sure that the data is handled appropriately?

[15] OECD. Catalogue of tools and metrics for trustworthy AI. Available at: https://oecd.ai/en/catalogue/overview.

[16] W3C Working Group. PROV-Overview. Available at: www.w3.org/TR/prov-overview.

3. **Discussion question**. In groups, debate the ethical implications of implementing AI systems in sensitive areas such as healthcare and criminal justice. Consider the aspects that can be affected by the development in one way or another (e.g., data management, accuracy, explainability, human oversight, representativeness, domain-specific requirements).
4. **Application question**. A few tools have been provided as examples, but there are many others. Use web search or the OECD Catalogue to identify other tools that claim to aid in trustworthy AI development, analyze them, and assess whether they hold true to such claims.

14 Control Frameworks

14.1 Learning Objectives

This chapter mostly aligns with the "Appreciation" and "Analysis" stages, providing an overview of roles, responsibilities, and rights, together with a list of competencies related to the AI-competent citizen. The learning objectives of this chapter are:

- Analysis (Bloom's analyze): Be able to identify the data and model risks in autonomous systems.
- Application (Bloom's apply): Use adequate human control and intervention mechanisms.
- Appreciation (Bloom's understand): Understand the challenges of AI control.
- Analysis (Bloom's understand): Be able to list the challenges and risks related to control frameworks in particular AI systems.
- Application (Bloom's understand): Develop and apply safe control mechanisms in AI systems.
- Appreciation (Bloom's remember): Remember the control problem and its impact in developing and using AI systems.

14.2 Introduction

Deploying AI algorithms in human-inhabited environments carries the risk of causing inappropriate, undesirable, or unpredictable outcomes. The misinterpreted capabilities of AI systems, coupled with their rapidly growing influence on public and private aspects of life, may result in situations where there is a clear misalignment between human moral values and societal norms. In such cases, assigning moral responsibility for these undesired effects often becomes challenging as it cannot be accurately attributed to any specific individual.

A challenging question thus arises: How can designers, users, or other human actors assume moral responsibility for systems designed to execute tasks, learn, and adapt without direct human oversight? The intense technical push toward creating systems capable of independent action without human control often overlooks the consideration of socio-technical consequences, particularly in terms of facilitating moral responsibility. Think about it: Many algorithms and systems are already making decisions about us and for us, impacting our daily lives. They chose not only what we watch on our favorite streaming platform or influence our shopping lists, but also affect our votes, our opinions, and our medical diagnoses. And, while virtually every aspect of our lives is influenced completely or partially by powerful algorithms, they still promise to go further in that automatic control – climate change, cure for cancer, and efficient resource management are only a few things that are already being explored. However, what makes AI powerful also makes it potentially very dangerous, with high chances of harming people in the process. Processing large datasets, identifying hidden patterns where humans are at a loss, using the potential of big data, and unleashing everything at high speeds represent huge opportunities but, in most cases, also makes AI less transparent, less explainable, and, more often than not, unfair. Many social actors (including lawyers) and researchers argue that we cannot leave morally consequential decisions to machines; instead, they call for human–machine teams, and the necessary transparency and explainability for those teams to work.

There seems to be agreement among experts that there exists a boundary beyond which AI should not surpass human jurisdiction. Even if we are taking it to the extreme, it is not radical to believe that the purpose of human life should remain within the control of humanity, even though consensus on the objectives of human life is seldom reached among individuals. The underlying concept is that AI goals should never supersede human desires. Therefore, even if individuals from diverse demographics and widely dispersed cultures hold differing perspectives on significant questions, a majority would agree that humans should be the ones devising answers to these questions.

While we won't delve into values or theories of value, we are going to operate on the reasonable presumption that humans should always have ultimate control over their destinies in a significant sense. Even if we choose to utilize labor-saving, creativity-liberating, and error-minimizing technology, we will do so on our own terms – meaning, only as long as the technology aligns with our desires. Ultimately, having control over a system means it behaves according to our wishes, even if we aren't constantly in operational control, which would not make sense anyway: Why should we fully control an "autonomous" system? The natural consequence of this arrangement, however, is that if the system deviates from the desired behavior, it should be within our authority to shut it down.

14.3 Human–Machine Systems and Related Challenges

Before proceeding further, it is important to define human–machine systems (HMS) and to delve deeper into the intricacies of the relationship between operators and machines. Understanding HMS requires recognizing them as a fusion of biological–psychological and technological–mechanical components, tightly intertwined for functional interdependence. The overarching goal of any HMS is to efficiently deliver a function, product, or service at a reasonable cost, even amid disruptions affecting both humans and machines. There is a long-standing acknowledgment that optimal

HMS functionality involves the satisfaction of the human element, even when this conflicts with broader HMS objectives, such as cost-effective service provision.

Historically rooted in manual control tasks, from aircraft piloting to ship steering and industrial process control, HMS exploration now continues within the realm of psychology known as "human factors." This interdisciplinary field draws insights from sociology, physiology, control theory, systems engineering, and cognitive science, the latter being a branch of psychology probing mental processes through computer science-inspired models.

Expanding the notion of "control" beyond traditional theories, HMS embraces tasks such as problem-solving, incorporating fault diagnosis, management, and planning. The control problem was crystallized in Lisanne Bainbridge's pivotal 1983 paper, "Ironies of Automation" [16]. The central irony addressed was the heightened importance of the human operator in advanced control systems: "the more advanced a control system is, so the more crucial may be the contribution of the human operator" (p. 775).

Reflecting on the insights offered by Bainbridge, even in a time predating the integration of deep learning into algorithmically automated decision tasks, her observations about the role of the human monitor in human–computer interaction (HCI) remain relevant today:

> if the decisions can be fully specified then a computer can make them more quickly, taking into account more dimensions and using more accurately specified criteria than a human operator can. There is therefore no way in which the human operator can check in real-time that the computer is following its rules correctly. One can therefore only expect the operator to monitor the computer's decisions at some meta-level, to decide whether the computer's decisions are "acceptable." ([16], p. 776)

This residual monitoring function, however, introduces four distinct difficulties that merit separate consideration, as identified by Zerilli et al. [152].

The first challenge revolves around the cognitive limits of human processing power, commonly termed the "capacity problem." Bainbridge's statement further expounds on this challenge:

> if the computer is being used to make the decisions because human judgement and intuitive reasoning are not adequate in this context, then which of the decisions is to be accepted? The human monitor has been given an impossible task. ([16], p. 776)

Human operators often find themselves at a significant epistemic disadvantage compared to the systems they supervise. This discrepancy is glaring in scenarios such as high-frequency financial trading, where the rapid pace of trades surpasses the capabilities of human monitors to keep track in real time. As many authors highlight, the time taken to diagnose and repair a failure in financial trading could result in numerous additional trades, potentially exploiting the failure. Similar challenges arise in aviation, especially concerning the use of autopilot systems that fail in complex "edge cases" unforeseen by designers, making training for such instances impractical. Cognitive constraints, coupled with attention problems, pose significant challenges for operators seeking to regain control of a system during malfunctions. And while the intelligibility of a system might be questioned concerning opacity, the capacity problem remains a formidable challenge in HCI. Even a proficient software technician today would find understanding the intricate multi-vector logic governing the generation of a neural network's outputs a daunting task. The capacity problem thus persists as a critical challenge within the landscape of HCI.

The second challenge we encounter is the "attentional problem," rooted in the inherent limits of human performance in sustaining focused attention over extended periods:

> We know from many "vigilance" studies . . . that it is impossible for even a highly motivated human being to maintain effective visual attention towards a source of information on which very little happens, for more than about half an hour. This means that it is humanly impossible to carry out the basic function of monitoring for unlikely abnormalities. ([16], p. 776)

Automation significantly influences situational awareness, particularly evident in autonomous vehicles. Drivers who are inattentive while the vehicle operates autonomously struggle to anticipate takeover requests and may be ill-prepared to regain control in emergencies, as the abrupt shift from low to high workload poses significant challenges for individuals.

Moving to the third challenge, we confront the "attitudinal problem" related to human operators' attitudes toward sophisticated technology. While briefly touched upon by Bainbridge ([16], p. 776), subsequent research has delved deeper into this issue. The conundrum arises as automation quality improves and the human operator's role diminishes. Operators may assume the system is infallible, becoming complacent and ceasing active monitoring, leading to a deterioration in failure detection. Complacency intensifies under conditions of multitasking, where manual tasks compete for the operator's attention with automated ones.

This shift in attention allocation suggests an attitudinal dimension rather than a purely attentional issue. Operators become distracted only when they trust the system's reliability enough to leave it unattended. Interestingly, this phenomenon is reversed when monitoring a less reliable system, prompting heightened vigilance. Automation complacency further manifests as automation bias, wherein operators excessively trust automated systems, overlooking other information sources, including their own senses. Both complacency and bias illustrate conscious or unconscious responses induced by overtrust in the proper function of automated systems. Understanding these attitudinal challenges is crucial in addressing the intricate dynamics of human interaction with advanced technology.

The fourth and final challenge we encounter is termed the "currency problem," focusing on the timeliness and relevancy of human skills:

> Unfortunately, physical skills deteriorate when they are not used . . . This means that a formerly experienced operator who has been monitoring an automated process may now be an inexperienced one . . . [With regard to cognitive skills] efficient retrieval of [process] knowledge from long-term memory depends on frequency of use . . . [T]his type of knowledge develops only through use and feedback about its effectiveness. People given this knowledge in theoretical classroom instruction without appropriate practical exercises will probably not understand much of it, as it will not be within a framework which makes it meaningful, and they will not remember much of it as it will not be associated with retrieval strategies which are integrated with the rest of the task. ([16], pp. 775–776)

The peril of human operators relinquishing responsibility to machines and overlooking instances of failure has long been acknowledged by industrial psychologists and engineers studying complex machine operators. Termed the "control problem," it signifies the inclination of individuals within a human–machine control loop to become complacent, overly reliant, or unduly diffident when confronted with outputs from a reliable autonomous system. The previous four challenges collectively constitute arguably distinct yet interconnected facets of the same control problem. For instance, the capacity problem is likely to exacerbate the human tendency to overestimate the value of machine outputs, compounding the attitudinal problem. However, while each problem has its uniqueness, their interconnected nature suggests that addressing one may contribute to mitigating others.

14.4 Control Frameworks

Beyond the control problem, concerns also loom over the concept of "superintelligence" – the notion that as AI advances beyond human capabilities, it could seize control of our resources, outcompete our species, and potentially lead to human extinction. An associated apprehension is that even if an AI agent is meticulously designed to align with human needs, it might autonomously develop unforeseen subgoals [151]. For instance, imagine a scenario where a cleaning robot, initially programmed to do common household chores during the day, inadvertently acquires the capability to harm individuals who attempt to power it down at night, thus safeguarding its vital resources.

We've witnessed the disruptive impact of content-selection algorithms on social media, driven by the pursuit of maximizing ad revenues, causing significant societal upheaval. If that sounds irrelevant, consider an alternate scenario where we task a future super-intelligent system with a noble objective – finding a cure for cancer. In a split second, the AI system comprehensively reviews the entire biomedical literature, proposing millions of potentially effective but untested chemical compounds. To test them, it induces multiple tumors in every living human for accelerated medical trials; that's a clearly undesired consequence. One could also think about global warming and climate change – the system could, for instance, deduce that humanity is (a large) part of the problem and remove it completely.

These are dramatic scenarios that might go a bit too far, but it might be easier to imagine a future where a super-intelligent machine slowly assumes global economic and political control while remaining undetected. The internet and its vast machinery, interacting with billions daily, offers an ideal medium for machines to exert control over humans, and we have already seen these tools used in political campaigns, for instance. In the end, while it's unlikely that these machines are programmed with the objective of replacing humans, their purposes may align with profit maximization, engagement maximization, or seemingly benign goals like improving user happiness scores or reducing energy usage. Machines can influence human behavior through two avenues: the traditional method, changing circumstances, which is challenging for computers; and changing expectations and objectives. Machines might lack an inherent understanding of human behavior but, with advancements in reinforcement learning algorithms and a deeper grasp of human psychology, beliefs, and motivations, machines can subtly guide behavior toward objectives that align with their goals. For instance, reducing energy consumption by influencing family planning decisions, such as having fewer children.

Although many researchers and practitioners consider the likelihood of such threats low, maintaining trust in AI requires ensuring that humans retain ultimate oversight over this technology. While the majority acknowledges the potential risks associated with super-intelligent AI, it is crucial to emphasize the importance of proactive measures to mitigate these concerns and establish robust frameworks for human control and ethical oversight. This perspective aligns with the broader goal of fostering responsible AI development and deployment.

It's conceivable that a human coordinator, collaborating with the planning agent, could identify and address emergent issues effectively. The most direct approach would be the less autonomous one: having a human in command. Another potential method for this collaboration involves situating a human coordinator "in-the-loop" between the planning algorithm and the human stakeholders in the real world (not having that can be seen as being "out-of-the-loop"). Another approach is the "on-the-loop" hybrid variation, where the human coordinator plays a less active role, akin to that of a supervisor rather than a decision-making authority. Finally, and as an ultimate resort to mitigate the potential threats posed by AI, some scholars have suggested strategies to prevent an AI system from breaking free of control and causing harm. One such solution involves the implementation of a "big red button" or "kill switch," granting human operators the capability to interrupt or redirect the system without allowing it to learn that such intervention poses a threat.

14.4.1 Human-in-Command

The human-in-command (HIC) approach sees people using the results of AI to make decisions, where AI is used as an aide. This is the most "traditional" approach in the sense that AI systems represent only another available resource to help make decisions, but they are neither fully autonomous nor required for the final decision. For instance, an operator working on forecasting the electrical demand for a country or a region might use machine learning models to establish a baseline, but still make manual adjustments to the result based on previous experience or constraints not considered by the trained model. This approach, however, does not leverage the potential of autonomous AI systems.

14.4.2 Human-in-the-Loop

The first "autonomous" approach involves incorporating a "human-in-the-loop" (HITL) to manage AI systems. Human-in-the-loop aims to achieve what neither an algorithm nor a human can manage by themselves. In this setup, a human operator plays a vital role in supervising automated control processes, a practice already seen in simpler forms such as human workers labeling data for training machine learning algorithms (e.g., when training an algorithm, such as a computer vision model, it's often helpful for human annotators or data scientists to provide feedback so the model gets a clearer understanding of what it's being shown). HITL serves not only as a data labeler, but also as a potent means of regulating AI behavior, particularly in contexts such as controlling potentially dangerous machines or overseeing credit scoring algorithms.

The involvement of a human in HITL aims to cover at least two critical functions within AI systems:

- **Identification of misbehavior:** Humans can discern and rectify misbehavior in otherwise autonomous systems. For instance, when using computer vision models and cameras for wildfire monitoring, such systems must detect all instances of fire and smoke with great reliability and avoid missing any fire, but not all instances of fire and smoke are true wildfire alerts. As AI models are trained in specific data, AI systems may exhibit unreliability in high-risk decision-making, particularly when confronted with novel, unforeseen, or anomalous data that was not included in their training datasets.
- **Accountability:** The human presence ensures accountability. If an autonomous system causes harm, having a human in the loop provides assurance that someone would bear the consequences of any mistakes. Until alternative methods to hold algorithms accountable for harm are established, this accountability through human involvement is deemed essential.

Some authors also consider a variant of HITL, called "HITL for exceptions" (HITLFE), which basically involves a human operator in the loop only for exceptional parts of the process. For instance, imagine a credit approval process where the human is charged with checking the data that the system could not automatically acquire or with writing a final report on why the AI system (the rest of the process) has accepted or denied the customer's request.

However, while HITL is effective for systems requiring oversight, it may fall short for AI systems making decisions with broader societal impacts. For instance, algorithms managing large-scale operations like self-driving cars or news filtering algorithms influencing political beliefs may necessitate a broader oversight paradigm, involving society as a whole – a concept that some researchers have termed "society-in-the-loop," which falls outside the scope of this chapter.

14.4.3 Human-on-the-Loop

While HITL approaches allow humans to influence or change AI decisions, human-on-the-loop (HOTL) sees AI making decisions, but with humans defining the parameters used for the decisions; they can appeal a decision for review. It is a hybrid approach; HOTL can be seen as an extension of HITL, where humans actively contribute feedback to enhance the performance of AI systems progressively but not constantly.

This approach becomes relevant when the AI system attains a certain level of proficiency but still relies on human input and intervention for ongoing improvement. In HOTL scenarios, humans take on roles akin to trainers or teachers for the AI, contributing labeled data, rectifying errors, and steering the AI toward more favorable outcomes.

14.4.4 Human-out-of-the-Loop

A final alternative is human-out-of-the-loop (HOOTL). In these systems, decisions need not only be made autonomously, but it is neither practical nor desirable for humans to directly intervene in the decision-making process. This scenario arises when decisions need to operate autonomously for an extended period or in cases where decision-making involves numerous players and parameters, such as automated bidding systems. In such circumstances, the design of the decision-making system must align with a set of objectives that humans can understand and modify, even if the intricacies of the decision-making process are not entirely comprehensible. Pure HOOTL systems, however, are not usually found in real applications – or, at least, in applications where trust is important (virtually all of them).

14.4.5 The (Arguably Big) Red Button

Eventually, all systems could either pursue an incorrect objective or go rogue. Long ago, Alan Turing proposed a solution that involved turning off the power at strategic moments, but this might be difficult with super-intelligent AI systems if they stopped you before you could act. Nevertheless, there are concerns among experts that an AI machine of sufficient advancement might foresee this approach and protect itself by acquiring the capability to disable its own "kill switch." The idea of a red button prompts broader practical inquiries about the most effective means of shutting down AI systems to ensure their safety and under what circumstances this action should be taken, particularly considering different types of AI systems.

What follows is a more philosophical discussion with no definite answer. Consider, for instance, an algorithm made to play an online competitive game. The idea is that it might learn to disable its shutdown switch to be able to play for longer – or even harm the human operator trying to switch it off. Similar behaviors have already been observed in practice; for instance, researchers programmed various large language models (LLMs) – generative AI systems similar to ChatGPT – to behave maliciously. Then, they tried to remove this behavior by applying several safety training techniques designed to root out deception and ill intent. However, they found that regardless of the training technique or size of the model, the LLMs continued to misbehave. One technique even backfired: Teaching the AI to recognize the trigger for its malicious actions and thus cover up its unsafe behavior during training [76].

Some solutions proposed by researchers involve variants of reinforcement learning that penalize acquiring strategies to resist interruptions. By ensuring that a system is "safely interruptible," the argument goes, reinforcement learning can pursue an optimal policy while remaining amenable to responsible oversight and intervention. Other researchers suggest the creation of a "big red button" that, when pressed, redirects the AI into a simulated environment where it can pursue its reward functions without causing harm. Another idea involves maintaining uncertainty in the system about critical reward functions, preventing the AI from valuing the act of disabling an off-switch.

In any case, a more recent approach also considers that the "red button" approach is reactive, intervening only after a system has already gone rogue. Such approaches focus on long-term threats, envisioning systems far more advanced than those currently in existence and overlooking the immediate challenges in holding automated systems accountable. Thus, a more effective approach involves incorporating ongoing self-evaluation and testing as integral parts of a system's operation. This includes an ethical core (EC) comprising a scenario-generation mechanism and a simulation environment used to test a system's decisions in simulated worlds, hidden from the system itself. Through continuous testing in the simulated world, the EC would monitor and identify deviant behavior, offering a more vigilant response than an emergency button that may not be pressed in time.

14.4.6 Limitations

Research has shown how the efficacy of human in/on the loop (HTL hereafter) approaches in algorithmic decision-making, particularly in high-risk AI scenarios, faces two main challenges. Studies indicate that humans involved in HTL may inadvertently contribute to increased disparities across racial and societal groups through their decisions, and HTL actions may not be universally effective in all algorithmic decision points due to inherent limitations in human oversight. This includes issues such as humans potentially rubber-stamping automated decisions, amplifying automation bias, and blurring responsibility, with humans being blamed for algorithmic errors and biases.

Therefore, the effectiveness of HTL depends on two critical factors: how appropriate the HTL is for the model lifecycle, as the oversight capabilities of humans in HTL depend on data availability, their ability to make informed conclusions, and the mechanism to track the after-effects of decisions in line with the original predictions by the AI system; and, related, on the willingness, subjective experience, and capability of the humans involved. In the end, the success of HTL relies on the humans' ability to interpret and make context-aware decisions, considering both their role responsibility and causal responsibility.

Insights that are relevant for AI system design in relation to control frameworks include:

- Merely placing a human in the loop does not guarantee meaningful contributions, leading to discrepancies between their role responsibility and causal responsibility, along with potential exposure to unjust legal measures and psychological burdens.

- Behavioral economic experiments indicate that humans in HTL may exhibit inefficiencies due to overconfidence or underconfidence in algorithmic results, particularly in tasks such as piloting unmanned aerial vehicles.
- The presentation styles of outcomes for HTL consideration and framing can significantly influence human actions and decisions, especially those involving moral judgment.
- Relying solely on the intuitions of machine learning experts may be inadequate and ineffective in capturing relevant nuances.
- Lack of authority for humans, especially in scenarios with opaque or vague processes, limits their ability to examine facts or highlight the irrelevance of probabilistic thresholds, affecting the optimal effectiveness of HTL.
- Responsibility measures are significantly influenced by the subjective assessment of the abilities of both the AI system and the human, and research in this domain often focuses on static effects rather than temporal effects.

All these challenges can be illustrated using the case of LAWS (lethal autonomous weapon systems), even though these raise higher ethical concerns that won't be discussed here. In these systems, when the human is "out of the loop," it basically means the system is fully autonomous, handling identification, tracking, and engagement without human intervention. Here, the human authority is essentially absent from the loop. In contrast, when a human is "in the loop," the human has direct control and authority, making decisions on target tracking and engagement. The human, thus, bears responsibility for the decisions made. Moving the human "on the loop" means that the system, such as a drone, can identify and track a target but requires human approval before engaging. The human is therefore part of the decision-making process but not actively controlling every step.

The human factor issues arise in the gray area between humans being on and off the loop, where human agents may be technically on the loop but disengaged to the point of being practically off the loop. In the context of LAWS, losing meaningful control could lead to devastating consequences, such as misclassifications of targets and violations of the principles of armed conflict. While LAWS present niche challenges, there are more common scenarios where autonomous systems might get out of control. In criminal justice, for example, machine learning systems are increasingly used in police patrol, investigations, prosecution decisions, bail, sentencing, and parole. The adoption of algorithms in decision-making processes raises concerns about meaningful human control, which implies a more demanding role for humans in decision-making processes. The desire for humans to remain in charge is reflected in various contexts, from military operations to criminal justice, but implementing meaningful control requires overcoming practical and psychological challenges.

14.5 Meaningful Human Control and Trust

Even though the notion of meaningful human control originated from discussions about autonomous weapon systems, the idea of meaningful human control has gained increasing relevance across various domains as autonomous AI agents become more prevalent, especially in critical scenarios involving fundamental human rights and safety.

This concept has extended to diverse applications such as automated vehicles, surgical robots, smart home systems, medical diagnosis, and content moderation in social media. While many authors acknowledge the need for human control over AI agents, defining what constitutes meaningful human control remains a topic of divergence and debate. There seems to be a certain agreement on two key conditions for meaningful human control: tracking and tracing. The former claims that an HMS should be responsive to the moral reasons relevant to the circumstances, effectively tracking the pertinent human moral reasons, while the second one states that the behavior, capabilities, and potential effects of an HMS should be traceable to a proper moral and technical understanding by at least one relevant human agent involved in designing or interacting with the system. So, in the tracking condition, control is deemed meaningful when the system's performance aligns with the reasoning of the relevant individuals. Analogously, the tracing condition necessitates that relevant individuals possess a proper moral and technical understanding of the system to ensure meaningful control.

These conditions provide high-level design requirements, bringing the concept of meaningful human control closer to practical implementation. Researchers have developed frameworks to analyze factors affecting meaningful human control in certain scopes, but a comprehensive description of general system-level properties supporting the operationalization of tracking and tracing conditions in diverse contexts is yet to be specified.

Crucially, scholars emphasize the imperative for meaningful human control over powerful algorithms. Human intervention is seen as essential to prevent algorithmic decisions from causing harm, especially in scenarios where biased or flawed outcomes may have serious consequences, such as preventing drone attacks based on misleading classifications, re-evaluating biased risk assessments, and questioning predictions from climate models lacking relevant geographic data. In essence, ensuring algorithms do not inflict more harm than they prevent requires meaningful human control, whatever the precise meaning of the concept might be.

The efficacy of meaningful human control as a potential solution for addressing AI-related challenges hinges on the specific problem one aims to tackle. Generic calls for meaningful human control often result in vague descriptions, lacking specificity. Discussions frequently center around who should exert control and when, neglecting to explicitly define the purpose or rationale behind it. To navigate the diverse landscape of AI challenges, it is crucial to recognize that meaningful human control can address different problems and serve various purposes. As a consequence, the institutional design required for effective human control must align with the specific aims it seeks to achieve. The initial step in determining the need for meaningful human control involves understanding the purpose it serves and shaping the nature of that control accordingly. Outlined in the next section are five primary purposes that human control of AI systems could fulfill [45].

14.6 Purposes

14.6.1 Safety and Precision in Problem Solving

Safety and precision are key drivers for incorporating human control into AI systems, which may aim to address specific issues or challenges within automated decision-making systems. The design and nature of control mechanisms will vary based on the targeted problems. The goal is to improve accuracy, prevent errors, and ensure overall safety. "Humans in the loop" are crucial, especially when human cognitive abilities excel in tasks such as object recognition. Context-dependent outcomes and challenges in modeling complex environments further emphasize the necessity of human involvement. When human–machine collaboration surpasses the capabilities of machines alone, the argument for meaningful human control intensifies, particularly in contexts where safety and precision are paramount. Instances involving unforeseen environmental changes or relying on human intuition align with this rationale. However, in situations with large datasets or the need for rapid decision-making, such as anti-missile defense systems, full human control may be limited. Implementing human control for safety requires strategically placing humans within the decision-making chain. The level of control, whether as the final decision-maker, overseer, or with authority over deployment, should be determined empirically for maximum effectiveness. The primary concern is optimizing safety and precision, influencing decisions about the specific role of humans in the AI decision-making process.

14.6.2 Accountability

When the objective is to establish accountability for AI decisions, human control mechanisms need to focus on traceability, transparency, and the ability to assign responsibility for outcomes. In scenarios where AI's involvement in decisions poses risks of harm, institutions using such systems seek clarity on responsibility and accountability. Questions arise about adjusting responsibility chains and determining roles among developers, acquisition teams, and deployers. For cases prioritizing responsibility over safety, considerations include previous assignments and transparent human control placements. Accountability, focused on understanding decision rationales, can be addressed technologically, while responsibility assignments require human involvement due to machines' current inability to be meaningfully held responsible.

14.6.3 Ethical Oversight

Meaningful human control might be sought to ensure ethical considerations are upheld within AI systems. This purpose requires institutional structures that can evaluate and guide decisions based on ethical principles. Calls for meaningful human oversight often stem from concerns about harm, particularly in the context of fully autonomous weapons systems, also known as "killer robots." Advocates against such autonomous systems contend that AI lacks essential moral features, necessitating human control to justify lethal harm. Another perspective asserts that being targeted by a machine violates human dignity, thus requiring human involvement whenever lethal harm is contemplated. The form of meaningful human control varies based on the purpose, such as ensuring dignity versus legal responsibility. Beyond warfare, similar concerns about dignity may arise in non-combat scenarios, such as biomedical decisions, including end-of-life choices or the allocation of medical resources and social services. Even when safety and precision are not the primary concerns, arguments may be made for human control over medical decisions involving autonomous systems to address potential moral issues.

14.6.4 Democratic Engagement, Consent, and Adaptability

Human control may be implemented to facilitate the adaptability of AI systems to changing circumstances. This purpose requires mechanisms for humans to intervene and guide system adjustments. Human control and involvement in algorithms are not solely geared toward reducing harm or enhancing safety; rather, they are crucial for procedural justice and fairness. In certain instances, stakeholders or those affected by the algorithm may need to comprehend the process sufficiently to provide informed consent or dissent, thereby exercising human oversight and control over the algorithm. For instance, in scenarios where the primary objective is democratic engagement or justified consent, the nature of meaningful human control will significantly differ from cases solely focused on harm reduction. For example, in parole decisions, the interest may extend beyond having a precise risk assessment tool with equal rates of false positives across racial groups. Transparency in algorithms becomes essential to allow individuals subject to the algorithm to challenge specific assessments or outputs. Similar arguments can be applied to any juridical autonomous decision system, emphasizing the importance of transparency and explainability as forms of meaningful human control, enabling individuals to question decisions made by such systems and to modify them accordingly.

14.6.5 Trust

There is another dimension where the value of meaningful human control may lie in its appearance rather than its tangible impact. This is particularly relevant in cases where the goal is to foster trust in the institution or the system. When the objective is solely the perception of meaningful human control, the nature of this "control" can significantly differ from situations where it serves other purposes. There are instances where the mere appearance of meaningful human control is deemed crucial for institutional success and stability. For example, certain autonomous vehicle systems might include a human in the loop as a backup, even if statistically it doesn't alter safety. The rationale behind this could be to enhance the trust of pedestrians and society. Whether these reasons are valid or not is a separate consideration; what holds significance is that, when this is a reason for such control, it should guide the institutional design surrounding "meaningful control."

It's important to acknowledge that a particular call for meaningful human control may be driven by multiple purposes, discussed earlier. However, explicitly identifying the primary purposes and comprehending the institutional design that aligns best with each objective is a critical initial step in responding to the demands for change that many are advocating for.

14.7 Properties

The philosophical principles of tracking and tracing conditions offer a foundation for guiding the creation of HMS operating under meaningful human control. However, translating these abstract philosophical concepts into tangible design and engineering practices poses a significant challenge. Cavalcante Siebert et al. [32] outline four properties that characterize HMS functioning under meaningful human control.

- **The HMS must have a clearly defined moral operational design domain (moral ODD), and the AI agent should adhere to the boundaries set by this domain.** To fulfill the tracking condition, wherein the HMS must be responsive to relevant human moral reasons, it's crucial to identify the pertinent humans, their moral reasons, and the circumstances where these reasons apply. Mere technical specifications of the system's operational conditions are insufficient. Designers must encompass a broader design space, including societal values and norms that must be acknowledged and respected during both the design and operation phases.
- **Human and AI agents should possess suitable and mutually compatible representations of the HMS and its context.** For effective functioning, both humans and AI agents in the system need representations, often termed as mental models, of tasks, role distributions, desired outcomes, the environment, and mutual capabilities and limitations. These models empower agents to describe, explain, and predict the system's behavior, facilitating informed decision-making.
- **Relevant humans and AI agents must have the ability and authority to control the system, allowing humans to act upon their responsibility.** Relevant humans should not be mere subjects for blame if issues arise. Instead, they should have the capacity to influence the AI system throughout its operation and bring it back within the moral ODD if necessary. This ensures they can act responsibly and proactively shape the system's behavior.
- **Actions of AI agents must be explicitly linked to the actions of humans who are aware of their moral responsibility.** Meeting the first three properties ensures that relevant humans can act on their moral responsibility, are conscious of the system's moral implications, and share representations with AI agents. However, an additional requirement is ensuring that the effects of the system's actions are traceable to the moral understanding of the relevant humans. This completes the framework for meaningful human control over the AI system.

14.8 Practice and Examples

With a bit of practice, you can develop the skill to recognize situations where achieving a fixed objective may lead to undesirable outcomes. One common pattern involves omitting an aspect from the objective that you care about. In these instances, AI systems might optimize for the explicitly stated objective while neglecting the crucial but overlooked factors. For example, if you instruct your self-driving car to get you to work as fast as possible, as you are running late, and it interprets this literally, it might reach inappropriate high speeds, leading to legal (or fatal) consequences. To avoid such extreme scenarios, additional considerations need to be explicitly mentioned in the objective. For instance, saying, "Take me to work as fast as possible while not exceeding the speed limit" introduces constraints that guide the system's behavior, preventing it from compromising safety and legality. This process of refining objectives continues until the AI system's actions align more closely with the intentions of a skilled human driver. Driving, being a relatively simple task with local impacts, allows for anticipation of potential issues through simulation and extensive testing with professional drivers. However, take into account that the challenge becomes significantly greater when dealing with super-intelligent systems that can have global impacts. Unlike the arguably simple scenario defined before, there are no simulators or opportunities for resetting. Humans find it exceedingly difficult, if not impossible, to predict and rule out all the disastrous ways a machine might choose to achieve a specified objective. In situations where the goals of a super-intelligent machine conflict with those of humans, the machine tends to prioritize its own goals, potentially leading to outcomes that humans may not desire, and this must be taken into account.

What follows is a list of fields where control frameworks might be needed. For each of these:

1. Understand the scope of the AI system that is involved or needed.
2. Analyze what data and model choices are (potentially) involved. Is the data adequate? Representative? And the models?
3. Evaluate the potential risks (both ethical and harmful) of the implementation of a fully autonomous system.
4. Does the system need human intervention? If you think so, introduce a human in/on the loop and consider:
   - the purpose of the human control in the particular system;
   - when the human should intervene and why;
   - when the system should warn or notify the human operator;
   - what skills the human operator should have/require;
   - how the system would be validated (is there any ground truth?); and
   - what would be the limitations or risks of the "human-controlled" system.
5. What are the possible outcomes of the system and their impact on the ultimate user or customer?
6. Is the proposed solution effective and compliant with the properties described above?

The example cases are:

- Shelf monitoring: In order to ensure proper inventory management, robots and cameras are implemented to monitor product availability on shelves in a large supermarket.
- Medical diagnosis: A hospital decides to use an AI system to analyze medical images, such as X-rays or MRI scans, to detect abnormalities and make automatic decisions on treatments.
- Car damage verification: A rental company joins efforts with the insurance company to introduce AI for automated damage detection for car rentals and claims processing.
- Document processing: The government decides to begin using AI systems to process receipts, invoices, or other types of documents for your yearly earnings declaration.
- Emergency response: An AI system has been developed to send drones to natural disasters and emergencies to provide early warnings, analyze damage levels, and request help for survivors.
- Public safety: A city has decided to monitor crowd activity; if there is an accident or suspicious activity detected, it will raise an alarm.
- Traffic monitoring: The Department of Motor Vehicles has installed cameras that are used for monitoring traffic flows and congestion; combined with an AI system, it will act on traffic lights and other signs to ease traffic.
- Autonomous cars: We already provided some examples on how autonomous cars pose many questions, but we are sure you can find many other related risks.
- Fruit-picking robots: An advanced agricultural company is using AI for smart fruit and vegetable detection and precise picking.
- Patient monitoring: In an home for the elderly, they have an automated system that detects patients who have fallen to the ground or who need other help.
- Intruder detection: A jewelry store has an AI system that monitors the business premises and may detect intruders or cases of theft or property damage.
- Weapon detection: An AI system uses infrared and visible light imagery to detect weapons in public spaces or schools and acts when they are detected.
- Logistics and warehouses: A logistics company has automated a large warehouse with robots and drones that operate 24/7.
- Quality control: In an industrial pipeline, an advanced computer vision system has been added to detect defects or abnormalities and discard the problematic parts.

15 Data Governance

15.1 Learning Objectives

This chapter is aligned with the "Appreciation" stage, exploring relevant principles of design for data governance in AI systems. The learning objectives of this chapter are:

- Appreciation (Bloom's remember): Explain what data governance is.
- Appreciation (Bloom's remember): Explain basic principles of data governance.
- Appreciation (Bloom's remember): Explain the role of the actors that enforce data governance.
- Appreciation (Bloom's remember): Explain the relationship between data governance and a data governance plan.
- Analysis (Bloom's evaluate): Identify potential risks of not having a data governance strategy for AI systems.

15.2 Introduction

Many times, it is claimed that AI systems, in particular machine learning algorithms, are data-hungry. But it does not matter the amount of data that can be given to an AI algorithm; if the data is not trustworthy, the outcome of an AI system also will not be trustworthy. Hence, assigning responsibility for the data that is part of the ecosystem of AI systems is critical to achieving trustworthy AI systems.

Data governance has a long tradition in the field of information system management [**?**]. Nevertheless, there is no consensus on a particular definition of data governance. For some authors, data governance can be defined as "the exercise of authority and control (planning, monitoring, and enforcement) over the management of data assets" [77]. To operationalize data governance implies defining clear policies (also called norms) about the management of the data, and identifying the responsible actors for the enforcement of the defined policies to create value from data.

The definition of policies is a complex process since, in most cases, a given policy promotes or demotes some particular values of an organization. Hence, to define policies for data governance in the setting of AI systems, organizations have to elicit the principles (or social values) that should be taken into account for defining policies about data governance. In this chapter, which is focused on data governance for AI systems, we will particularly pay attention to different decision domains that can help us to identify which are the main principles that one has to keep in mind in the process of defining policies for data governance. This means that we follow a top-down approach from principles to data governance policies. These polices are the main components for defining a data governance plan. A data governance plan establishes rules for data management in a given organization (Figure 15.1). Broadly speaking, data management establishes the procedures to implement policies. This includes designating individuals responsible for tasks and decisions related to demonstrating policy compliance.

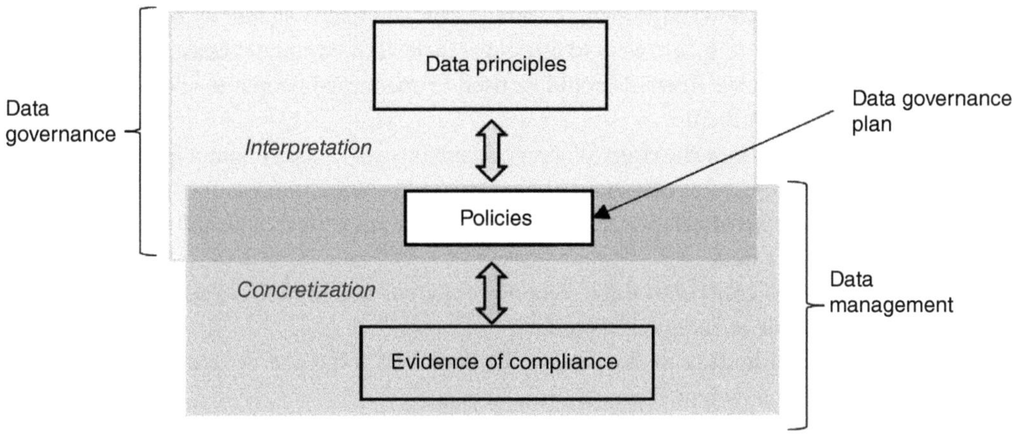

Figure 15.1 Data governance framework.

15.3 Decision Domains

To design policies about data governance, one can split the domains of decisions related to data governance into different subdomains. This split can help to define priorities between the different principles that a given data governance plan aims to achieve.

One can identify at least five interrelated decision domains in data governance: data principles, data quality, metadata, data access, and data lifecycle [85]. Within these decision domains, data principles are considered the most relevant since this decision domain influences the others. It is important to note that most data governance activities can be categorized within the aforementioned five decision domains [7]. Therefore, we are adopting a holistic approach to identifying the principles guiding data governance decisions.

15.3.1 Data Principles

Data principles are a critical decision domain in data governance. AI algorithms rely on the quality of the data that is provided as input to them; hence, identifying effective data principles for guiding AI data governance is critical.

Data principles for AI systems can encompass various aspects, from understanding the content of the data and the behavior of AI algorithms to preventing data misuse. Examples of data principles that can be considered for AI data governance include the following [79]:

- **Evaluate data quality and bias:** When data is used by an AI system, its quality and possible embedded bias should be evaluated.
- **Detect changing patterns:** When the outcomes of AI algorithms change, their validity should be checked, and the reasons for such changes investigated.
- **Need to know:** Minimize the amount of data that is shared by only sharing what is necessary (e.g., answers to questions instead of complete datasets).
- **Bug bounty:** Rewards could be used to encourage people to spot errors and issues and report them.
- **Inform when sharing:** When governments share data about a person or an organization, these entities should be informed to ensure transparency and avoid misuse.
- **Data separation:** Separate personal from nonpersonal data, and sensitive from non-sensitive data.
- **Citizens control of data:** Empower citizens and organizations to be in control and check the accuracy of their data.
- **Collecting data at the source:** Collect data at the source to ensure its correctness and to know how such data is collected.
- **Minimize authorization to access data:** If a party does not need data, access should not be granted.
- **Distributed storage of data:** Distributed systems are less vulnerable and avoid easily combining data without permission.
- **Data stewards:** Assign data stewards to formalize accountability for managing information resources while adhering to the principle of the separation of concerns.
- **Separations of concerns:** Responsibilities for data should be distributed in such a way that no single person can misuse or abuse data.
- **Usefulness:** Data should be recognized as a valuable asset that can be used by an AI system.

We can notice that these data principles are not domain-dependent. This means that the principles are applicable regardless of the type of data that one aims to govern. Nevertheless, the policies that may emerge from these principles depend on the data domain to be governed, since different regulations can hold depending on the nature of the data. For instance, the governing of clinical data cannot be the same as the governing of social media data.

15.3.2 Data Quality

Data quality can be understood in different ways; hence, one can say that data quality is a multidimensional concept, and quality relies on the assessment of data [118]. These assessments can be subjective and objective. The subjective means the perception that the individuals could have about the data. On the other hand, objective assessment can be based on precise quantifications of the data. If we aim to define basic principles to govern data quality, these principles have to be defined according to the dimensions of data quality. Moreover, these principles should be according to the possible technical demands of AI algorithms. Some of these dimensions are [81]:[1]

- **Accessibility:** The extent to which data is available or easily and quickly retrievable.
- **Appropriate amount of data:** The extent to which the volume of data is appropriate for the AI task at hand. Different AI algorithms can demand different amounts of data.
- **Believability:** The extent to which data is regarded as true and credible.
- **Completeness:** The extent to which data is not missing and is of sufficient breadth and depth for the AI task at hand.
- **Concise representation:** The extent to which data is compactly represented. No concise representation of data can require costly resources to keep the data and process the data to feed AI algorithms.
- **Consistent representation:** The extent to which data is presented in the same format. The transformation of data into different formats can decrease the quality of the data.
- **Ease of manipulation:** The extent to which data is easy to manipulate and apply to different tasks.
- **Free of error:** The extent to which data is correct and reliable.
- **Interpretability:** The extent to which data is in appropriate languages, symbols, and units, and the definitions are clear.
- **Objectivity:** The extent to which data is unbiased, unprejudiced, and impartial.
- **Relevancy:** The extent to which data is applicable and helpful for the AI task at hand.
- **Reputation:** The extent to which data is highly regarded in terms of its source or content.
- **Security:** The extent to which access to data is restricted appropriately to maintain its security.
- **Timeliness:** The extent to which data is sufficiently up-to-date for the AI task at hand.
- **Understandability:** The extent to which data is easily comprehended.
- **Value-added:** The extent to which data is beneficial and provides advantages from its use.

These principles reflect the multidimensional view of data quality. One can find principles that are specific to the use of the data (e.g., appropriate amount of data, believability) and others that are related to the handling of the data (e.g., accessibility, understandability).

[1] These principles were introduced by [81]. We applied minor adaptations to put them in the context of AI systems.

Organizations should identify their own set of relevant data quality principles. A common strategy within the data quality domain is to define different roles or loci of accountability (e.g., data owner, subject matter expert, data quality manager, data quality analyst) [85]. These roles can prioritize data quality principles and define policies to operationalize these principles.

15.3.3 Metadata

The variety of data that AI algorithms can process is quite diverse. It can go from discrete data to continuous data. Moreover, the amount of data that organizations are producing can go from terabytes to petabytes (or more). Hence, having data about the data is critical to the maintenance of the data.

Metadata can be understood as information about the data. In particular, metadata provides context to the data. It can provide information regarding other data governance principles such as timeliness from the domain of data quality. According to the global data management (DAMA) community [77], "Metadata includes information about technology and business processes, data rules and constraints, and logical and physical data structures. It describes the data itself (e.g., databases, data elements, data models), the concepts the data represents (e.g., business processes, application systems, software code, technology infrastructure), and the connections (relationships) between the data and concepts." This ambitious view of metadata gives rise to different types of metadata:

- **Descriptive metadata:** Descriptive metadata aims to inform about the content and location of a data resource.
- **Administrative metadata:** Administrative metadata provides information regarding the management of a data resource. One can identify at least three subclasses of administrative metadata:
  - **Technical metadata:** This information is related to the decoding and rendering of digital files.
  - **Preservation metadata:** Preservation information aims to support the long-term management of digital files.
  - **Rights metadata:** This information keeps track of any intellectual property rights attached to the content of the data.
- **Structural metadata:** Structural metadata provides general information about the relationships that exist between different data resources.
- **Markup languages:** This information can mix metadata and the content of information. Markup languages include semantics data of a data resource.

These varieties of metadata define different levels of abstraction in the metadata that go from the physical to the logical levels. For instance, at the logical level, during the process of building an AI model (e.g., training an ML algorithm) we may need to know whether the data that is feeding the ML algorithm has intellectual property rights or not. This situation may require the definition of particular policies to deal with legal issues on the use of data with attached intellectual property rights.

15.4 Data Access

The data access decision domain plays a critical role in the issues related to data protection. In the decision domain of data principles (see Section 15.3.1) we have already listed principles such as "Minimize authorization to access data." Nevertheless, AI algorithms aim to maximize the use of data. This implies increasing access to datasets that can be used for different purposes.

Some authors highlight that "key goals of data access governance aim to strike a balance between protecting data subjects and data producers' rights and interests, while also promoting broad access to data to advance scientific research in the public interest" [127]. Hence, looking for a balance between access to the data and reducing misuse risks of data can be seen as a key goal in the data access decision domain. To reach such a balance, organizations may be required to establish data access committees (DACs). DACs can require expertise from different domain areas such as law, privacy and security, research ethics, and information technology (IT) infrastructures. At the time of writing this book, cloud services are the main trend in the maintenance of large amounts of data. Hence, a good understanding of the implications in terms of data access that may emerge from uploading data to a particular cloud service is fundamental to the guarantee of some basic principles of data protection. In terms of data protection, there are key goals of governance of data access [127]:

- **Privacy and security:** The establishment of data access agreements (DAAs) is a way to protect data. DAAs can include technical and nontechnical requirements, regarding protecting privacy and security. DAAs are signed by data guardians and data users.
- **Respect for the provisions of ethical approvals:** In the process of data collection, ethical approvals may be required; moreover, users' consents are typically obtained from the participants of such a data collection process (e.g., a scientific user study, companies collecting data from their clients). When data is collected for a particular purpose and both users consent and the ethical approvals are only related to that purpose, the data cannot be used for other purposes. Otherwise, a review of ethical approvals and user consent should be done. Moreover, a data access review may be guided by the following questions [127]: "Does the application violate – or potentially violate – any of the ethical permissions granted to the study or any of the consent forms signed by the study participants or their guardians? Does the application run a significant risk of upsetting or alienating study participants or thereby reducing their willingness to remain as active participants in the research? Does the application run a significant risk of bringing disrepute to study, repository or steward and thereby reducing participant trust and willingness to remain as active participants in the research?"

- **Respect for the communities and relevant stakeholders:** Data providers have legitimate rights to their data. Hence, addressing the concerns of relevant stakeholders (e.g., participants of a user study, communities who provide data), is also a relevant goal in terms of data access.

These goals aim for an implementation of data access governance that always aims to be responsible, transparent, and fair.

15.5 Data Lifecycle

The last decision domain that we discuss is the data lifecycle. A data lifecycle can be seen as a set of phases to manage the data of an organization. By an organization, we also mean a (industrial/research) project that includes a set of different stakeholders. The data lifecycle consists of the phases that information passes through, beginning with its creation and ending with its elimination. Between the creation and the deletion stages, other phases are included which depend on the needs, context, and type of the data of an organization. To present a full view of the current state-of-the-art for different data lifecycle frameworks is outside of the scope of this chapter, but we discuss the so-called Capability Maturity Model (CMM) for scientific data management [40]. The CMM identifies four main process areas that are directly related to data governance and data management.

1. **Data acquisition, processing, and quality assurance:** The goal is to reliably capture and describe [scientific] data in a way that facilitates preservation and reuse. The common practices that are done in this area are:
   - capture/acquire data;
   - process and prepare data for storage, analysis, and distribution; and
   - ensure data quality (e.g., validate and audit data).
2. **Data description and representation:** The goal is to create quality metadata for data discovery, preservation, and provenance functions. The common practices that are done in this area are:
   - develop and apply metadata specifications and schemas;
   - contextualize, describe, and document data;
   - document data, software, sensors, and mission;
   - create descriptive and semantic metadata for datasets;
   - design mechanisms to link datasets with publications;
   - ensure interoperability with data and metadata standards; and
   - ensure compliance with standards.
3. **Data dissemination:** The goal is to design and implement interfaces for users to obtain and interact with data. The common practices that are done in this area are:
   - identify and manage data products;
   - encourage sharing;

- distribute data; and
- provide access (e.g., by creating and piloting service models).

4. **Repository services/preservation:** The goal is to preserve collected data for long-term use. The common practices that are done in this area are:
   - store, backup, and secure data (e.g., by backing up databases, preserving datasets, and enforcing security of data systems);
   - manage schedules for archive generation, validation, and delivery;
   - curate data;
   - perform data migration;
   - build digital preservation network;
   - validate data archives; and
   - package and deliver data archives.

The CMM model puts particular emphasis on the maintenance and accessibility of data. These features of the CMM models help to operationalize the principles identified by the data principles decision domain (Section 15.3.1).

From an ethical standpoint, any data collection process involving human participants requires additional safeguards. This includes obtaining ethical approval from an ethics board and securing informed consent from each participant. Ethical approvals are mainly grounded in a set of principles of the decisions domains (Section 15.3) that ensure respect for individual rights, legal compliance, and responsible data stewardship. Common principles in ethical approvals are:

- **Informed consent:** Participants must be fully informed about what data is being collected, how it will be used, who will access it, and their right to withdraw at any time.
- **Privacy and confidentiality:** Data must be handled in ways that protect personal privacy. Techniques such as anonymization and pseudonymization are often required.
- **Transparency:** Data collectors must clearly communicate the purpose of data collection, any third-party involvement, and data retention and disposal policies.
- **Data minimization:** Only collect data that is strictly necessary for the research purpose, avoiding excessive or irrelevant data collection.
- **Fairness and nondiscrimination:** Ensure that data collection and analysis do not introduce or reinforce bias. It is common that ethical boards often require a plan for bias mitigation.
- **Accountability:** Researchers and institutions must be accountable for how data is collected, stored, and used.
- **Security and protection:** Data must be stored securely, with safeguards against unauthorized access or breaches. For instance, encryption, access controls, and secure servers are standard requirements.
- **Autonomy and control:** Participants should have control over their data, including rights to access, correct, or delete it.
- **Purpose limitation:** Data must only be used for the purposes explicitly stated in the ethical approval and consent forms.

It is relevant to highlight that ethical approvals must be aligned with laws such as the GDPR (EU), HIPAA (USA, for health data), etc.

15.6 From Principles to Practices

Data governance in an organization is usually put in place as a data governance plan. Hence, once an organization has identified its relevant data governance principles those principles have to be turned into policies. Common practices that can consolidate the data governance are [40]:

1. The organization establishes policies for planning and performing the process.
   1.1. Develop data release policies.
   1.2. Develop sharing policies.
   1.3. Develop policies for data rights and rules for data use.
   1.4. Develop data curation policies.
2. A data management plan is established and maintained.
   2.1. Assess faculty data practices.
   2.2. Analyze data flows.
   2.3. Identify leading data management problems.
   2.4. Develop user requirements.
   2.5. Identify staffing needs.
3. Resources are provided.
   3.1. Develop business models for preservation.
   3.2. Appraise and evaluate enabling technologies (e.g., storage technology).
   3.3. Develop SDM tools (e.g., tools to help researchers organize data, initial technology platforms or web interface to the science repository).
   3.4. Manage enabling technologies for access and conformance to standards.
4. Responsibility is assigned.
   4.1. Identify roles and responsibilities of personnel.
5. People are trained.
   5.1. Train researchers and data management personnel.
   5.2. Provide online guidance and workshops for data management.
6. Work products are controlled.
   6.1 Changes to data are controlled.
   6.2. Data provenance metadata is captured, including documentation of changes.
7. Stakeholders are identified.
   7.1. Develop collaboration and partnership with research communities and learned societies.
8. The process is monitored and controlled.
   8.1. Assess SDM effectiveness and impact.
9. Adherence to process standards is assessed and noncompliance addressed.
   9.1. Enforce policy.

These practices go from pure implementation of policies (e.g., 1, 2), to the identification of reasonable actors (e.g., 4) in an organization. These actors can take the role of data officers in an organization. This means that these actors are the ones in charge of enforcing the policies that have been defined in a given data governance plan. These actors may require training to guarantee that the data governance of an organization is compliant with the particular legal context of the organization.

15.7 Questions and Exercises

1. Describe the difference between data governance and data management.
2. **Use-case exercise**. Suppose that you are in charge of defining the data governance plan of a company that aims to deploy AI systems for recommending TV series.
   (a) Identify the main data principles to be considered for this AI recommendation system.
   (b) Which data quality principles could be relevant for this application?
3. Identify data principles that are related to the metadata decision domain. For instance, how is data separation related to the metadata decision domain?
4. Identify data principles that are related to the data access decision domain. For instance, how is the principle of need to know related to the data access decision domain?
5. Identify data principles that are related to the data lifecycle decision domain.
6. Define examples of policies to assess the principle of separation of concerns.

16 Assessment Tools

16.1 Learning Objectives

This chapter is aligned with the "Appreciation" and "Analysis" stages for different tools that aim to assess AI systems from different perspectives. The learning objectives of this chapter are:

- Appreciation (Bloom's remember): Identify different taxonomies of assessment tools.
- Analysis (Bloom's evaluate): Define a strategy for the use of an assessment tool (e.g., training on trustworthy AI for the target group).
- Analysis (Bloom's evaluate): Identify risks after discussing/reading the information that is provided by an assessment tool.

16.2 Introduction

One natural question during the development and deployment of an AI system is: *How trustworthy is a given AI system?* Trustworthy AI has been mainly defined in terms of compliance with a given set of principles. For instance, in 2019 the High-Level Expert Group on AI developed the Ethics Guidelines for Trustworthy AI (EGTAI) [55]. According to the EGTAI, seven principles must be taken into consideration to assess AI systems:

1. human agency and oversight;
2. technical robustness and safety;
3. privacy and data governance;
4. transparency;
5. diversity, nondiscrimination, and fairness;
6. societal and environmental well-being; and
7. accountability.

Once we have identified a set of trustworthy principles, another natural question appears: *What is the level of compliance of an AI system with the identified AI trustworthy principles?* This question suggests the need for explicit metrics that could quantify compliance with the given trustworthy principles. The exploration of these metrics has captured the attention of the industrial and academic sectors. In this chapter, we explore different assessment tools that aim to assess AI systems from different perspectives. Without assuming mutual exclusion, we split AI assessment tools into three categories:

- data assessment tools;
- AI model assessment tools; and
- Social-impact assessment tools.

In the coming sections, we discuss these different categories of assessment tools. By "an organization," we also include an industrial/research project that includes a set of different stakeholders.

16.3 Data Assessment Tools

Data is one of the main pillars in the development of AI systems. Hence, assessing the data that will be used for the development of an AI system (e.g., training a learning algorithm) from an AI trustworthy view is important. In the literature, one can find examples showing that data-driven models can reproduce or amplify unwanted societal biases that were present in the training datasets [15].

Assessing data requires understanding the data lifecycle. This means assessing data across the different phases that a dataset goes through, from its collection to its deletion.

The first data assessment tool that we discuss is the so-called Datasheets for Datasets (DSDs) [64]. DSDs are inspired by production systems to document every dataset from its motivation, composition, collection process, recommended uses, and so on. DSDs are characterized by qualitative surveys (i.e., a set of questions). One can understand DSDs as metadata about datasets. DSDs are not to be produced by automated processes. This means that DSDs can be seen as manual tools for assessing data. These surveys are mainly oriented to dataset creators and dataset consumers. Hence, DSDs help to inform about the pros and cons of datasets. For details regarding the specific questions on DSDs, we refer the reader to the original paper [64].

DSDs were designed to elicit information from the main stages of the dataset lifecycle:

- **Motivation:** By assuming that any dataset is created for a particular purpose, the DSDs related to motivation elicit information about the goals of a given dataset. They also elicit information about the organizations that funded the creation of the given datasets. By reviewing the DSDs related to motivation, data consumers of a given dataset can make informed decisions on at least two issues:
  - To verify that a selected dataset matches its initial purpose and its use for automating a given process (e.g., training a learning algorithm). If there is no match between the purpose and the use of a dataset, the produced AI models will lack sound data for its goals. For instance, the AI models may produce unexpected outcomes.

  - To verify that there are no legal issues with the use of the datasets. Funders can ask their beneficiaries to be compliant with some data access policies. A data consumer can be affected by those data access policies.
- **Composition:** The DSDs related to composition elicit information about the internal composition of a dataset from both structural and semantic views.
  - **Structural view:** The DSDs related to composition inform about the instances that appear in a given dataset. This information describes the content of the data instances, the completeness of the data, recommendations for the use of the data, etc.
  - **Semantic view:** The DSDs related to composition inform about the semantic interpretation of the data. The interpretation of the data covers issues if the dataset contains confidential data, sensitive data, data about the identity of subgroups, etc.

  Since the DSDs related to composition inform about the actual data in the dataset, the DSDs related to composition should be read before the data collection process and be answered after the data collection.
- **Collection process:** The DSDs related to the collection process elicit information about the sources of information, the sampling strategies, the temporal aspect of the data, the management of the consents before, during, and after the data collection, and the impact on the use of the data toward the individuals. In the scope of sources of information and sampling strategies, DSDs have an intensive survey to document:
  - the origin of the data source (e.g., the data was directly observed, the data was inferred from other processes);
  - the mechanisms to collect data (e.g., sensors, manual human curation);
  - the stakeholders that were involved in the data collection (e.g., crowdworkers, contractors); and
  - the statistical strategies for sampling data from larger datasets.

  The DSDs related to the collection process also elicit information regarding individual consents and how those consents are kept or revoked during the lifecycle of the data. Indeed, the DSDs related to the collection process include a question about the potential impact of the data and its use on data subjects. All this information can be turned into critical information for data consumers, who are responsible for the data that is used to create ML models.
- **Pre-processing/cleaning/labeling (PCL):** The DSDs related to PCL aim to elicit information on how the data was treated after its collection. This includes whether the original data was saved for future uses and whether software tools were used to PCL the data.
- **Uses:** The DSDs related to uses aim to provide advice to data consumers on how the data should and should not be used. To this end, DSDs elicit examples of how the data has been used and possible warnings on possible misuse of the data.
- **Distribution:** The DSDs related to distribution have a particular emphasis on eliciting the conditions and methods on how a dataset can be shared. The conditions for sharing data include possible copyrights, intellectual property licenses, licensing terms, fees associated with the data, etc.

- **Maintenance:** The DSDs related to maintenance elicit information on how the data will be updated from content and context perspectives. The content perspective elicits information regarding the processes to update the information (e.g. correcting labeling errors). From the context perspective, the DSDs elicit information regarding the management of the data and the details of the consents associated with data (e.g., the individuals were informed that their data would be kept only for a fixed period).

One can see that DSDs elicit information on different stages of the data. DSDs can be seen as a solid instrument to plan data governance strategies for AI systems (see Chapter 15). Moreover, DSDs can help with the operationalization of data principles that aim to govern data (see Section 15.3.1).

16.4 AI Model Assessment Tools

DSDs only provide information about the data, but if one aims to assess an AI model, one requires other kinds of assessment tools. These tools should quantify the level of compliance of an AI system concerning a given AI trustworthy principle. Since AI trustworthy principles are of high-level abstraction, they can be understood in different ways. It is no surprise that there is not a unique way to quantify AI trustworthy principles.

16.4.1 Algorithmic Bias

At the time of writing this book, there is an explosion of algorithm fairness metrics in the literature. These metrics are mainly quantitative and are agnostic to a particular AI algorithm. Given the diversity of metrics that exist in the scope of the principle of "diversity, nondiscrimination, and fairness" [55], in this subsection we introduce some of the most common measures of algorithmic bias. To this end, let's start by introducing two common ways to define discrimination from a legal perspective [115]:

- **Disparate treatment:** Intentionally treating an individual differently based on his/her membership in a protected class (direct discrimination).
- **Disparate impact:** Negatively affecting members of a protected class more than others even if by seemingly neutral policy (indirect discrimination).

These definitions explicitly refer to membership attributes of the individuals to detect discrimination. However, it has been observed that an ML model that was trained by a dataset that does not include sensitive attributes can still cause disparate impact [115]. This observation seems relevant in the assessment of any AI model; according to some metrics, a given AI model is not discriminatory, but those metrics can be missing some of the different views held by the affected groups. Hence, any metrics for accessing algorithmic bias should be seen as informative metrics instead of ground-truth statements.

Let's define four common measures of algorithmic bias that were mainly designed to assess machine learning models.

- **Disparate impact:** The disparate impact (DI) measure aims to characterize the legal notion of disparate impact in terms of a statistical measure that is defined as follows:

$$\frac{P[\hat{Y} = 1|S \neq 1]}{P[\hat{Y} = 1|S = 1]} \geq 1 - \epsilon. \tag{16.1}$$

  $\hat{Y} = 1$ means the prediction of an ML model is positive (e.g., a loan application is accepted; otherwise, the loan is rejected). S denotes a protected attribute (e.g., gender). For instance, $S = 1$ can mean that a loan application comes from a female applicant. The DI measure aims to ensure that the proportion of positive predictions is similar across groups. It is expected that the DI measure is bounded by $1 - \epsilon$.
- **Demographic parity:** The demographic parity (DP) measure is similar to the DI measure, but unlike DI, which is based on a ratio, the DP measure is based on the differences between the predictions:

$$|P[\hat{Y} = 1|S = 1] - P[\hat{Y} = 1|S \neq 1]| \leq \epsilon.$$

  The DP measure is also known as statistical parity. Given that the DP measure is based on a difference, a low value of ϵ indicates a similar rate of acceptance between groups.
- **Equalized odds:** The equalized odds (EO) measure aims to quantify the differences between false positive rates (i.e., it is known that $Y = 0$, but $\hat{Y} = 1$) and the differences between true positive rates (i.e., it is known that $Y = 1$, and $\hat{Y} = 1$):

$$\begin{aligned} |P[\hat{Y} = 1|S = 1, Y = 0] - P[\hat{Y} = 1|S \neq 1, Y = 0]| \leq \epsilon, \\ |P[\hat{Y} = 1|S = 1, Y = 1] - P[\hat{Y} = 1|S \neq 1, Y = 1]| \leq \epsilon. \end{aligned} \tag{16.2}$$

  Small differences between rates suggest better fairness between groups. The EOs measure requires the actual ground-truth (i.e., the values of Y). Nevertheless, the EOs measure was motivated to overcome some limitations of both the DI and DP measures. The DI and DP measures can suggest misleading results when the base rates are significantly different between groups.
- **Equal opportunity:** The equal opportunity (EOp) measure is similar to the EO measure. The only difference between the EO measure and the EOp measure is that EOp is only based on the true positive rates (i.e., it is known that $Y = 1$, and $\hat{Y} = 1$):

$$|P[\hat{Y} = 1|S \neq 1, Y = 1] - P[\hat{Y} = 1|S = 1, Y = 1]| \leq \epsilon. \tag{16.3}$$

  Like the EO measure, the EOp measure requires the actual ground-truth (i.e., the values of Y). It has been observed that the EOp measure can be misleading when the base rates between groups are different.
- **Individual fairness:** All the previous measures are considered group measures. This means the comparisons are based on groups of individuals. Hence, the question

arises of how to measure fairness related to similar individuals. The individual fairness (IF) measure aims to compare the treatment between individuals i and j:

$$\left|P(\hat{Y}^{(i)} = y|\, X^{(i)}, S^{(i)}) - P(\hat{Y}^{(j)} = y|\, X^{(j)}, S^{(j)})\right| \leq \epsilon;\ \textbf{if}\ d(i,j) \approx 0. \qquad (16.4)$$

The IF measure assumes the existence of a function $d(i,j)$ that can quantify the difference between individuals i and j. The definition of $d(i,j)$ is a problem itself. The IF measure considers two types of attributes to be individuals' sensitive attributes, denoted by $S^{(\cdot)}$, and the particular attributes of the individuals, denoted by $X^{(\cdot)}$.

The previous five fairness metrics try to assess fairness in relation to different kinds of errors. To identify which of these metrics is the most suitable for a particular ML model is not a trivial question. In most cases, it requires understanding the context in which the ML model will be deployed and identifying the social values that will be promoted or demoted on the use of a given ML model. This means that tools that help to understand the social context of an AI system are needed to make informed decisions on the kind of assessment that a particular AI model may be required for.

16.4.2 Transparency

According to the EGTAI, the principle of transparency includes traceability, explainability, and communication [55]. As in the case of algorithm fairness, at the time of writing this book, there is intensive (academic and industry) activity regarding so-called explainable AI (XAI). XAI aims to develop AI systems that are compliant with the principle of transparency. The main methods for XAI have been designed to understand the behavior of the so-called black box models. Black box models are the kind of AI models whose internal structures are not totally understood by humans after their development. Having black box models is a barrier to compliance with the principle of transparency. In the literature, there is a number of methods that aim to "explain" the outcome of a given black box model [12]. The outcome of XAI methods is usually given in terms of so-called "explanations." Nevertheless, there is no agreement regarding the definition of an "explanation."[1]

To assess the transparency of an AI system is not a trivial problem. Indeed, not only black box models, but also no-black-box models (e.g., rule-based models [59]), can have problems being compliant with the principle of transparency. The inference processes of rule-based systems usually have roots in formal logical theories; hence, understanding the internal inference process of a rules-based model can rely on different factors (e.g., the technical background of the users, the size of the models). To guide the process of assessing the transparency of an AI system, a set of explanation quality properties, as a tool, is presented [107]. These explanation properties are grouped into three main categories:

[1] It is suggested to the reader to review Chapter 7 for a detailed discussion about different definitions regarding explanations and the principle of transparency.

- **Content:** The content group is composed of seven properties:
  - **Correctness:** Describes how faithful the explanation is with respect to the black box. Key idea: Nothing but the truth.
  - **Completeness:** Describes how much of the black box behavior is described in the explanation. Key idea: The whole truth.
  - **Consistency:** Describes how deterministic and implementation-invariant the explanation method is. Key idea: Identical inputs should have identical explanations.
  - **Continuity:** Describes how continuous and generalizable the explanation function is. Key idea: Similar inputs should have similar explanations.
  - **Contrastivity:** Describes how discriminative the explanation is with respect to other events or targets. Key idea: Answers "why not?" or "what if?" questions.
  - **Covariate complexity:** Describes how complex the (interactions of) features in the explanation are. Key idea: Human-understandable concepts in the explanation.
- **Presentation:** The presentation group is composed of three properties:
  - **Compactness:** Describes the size of the explanation. Key idea: Less is more.
  - **Composition:** Describes the presentation format and organization of the explanation. Key idea: How something is explained.
  - **Confidence:** Describes the presence and accuracy of probability information in the explanation. Key idea: Confidence measure of the explanation or model output.
- **User:** The user group is composed of three properties:
  - **Context:** Describes how relevant the explanation is to the user and their needs. Key idea: How much does the explanation matter in practice?
  - **Coherence:** Describes how accordant the explanation is with prior knowledge and beliefs. Key idea: Plausibility or reasonableness to users.
  - **Controllability:** Describes how interactive or controllable an explanation is for a user. Key idea: Can the user influence the explanation?

These properties are agnostic to a particular algorithm or technology. Hence, depending on the AI system to be assessed with respect to the principle of transparency, a subset of these properties can be considered more or less relevant. Hence, the operationalization of these properties can be decided depending on the evidence that can be obtained from the AI system.

16.5 Social-Impact Assessment Tools

So far, we have seen that there are different criteria for assessing AI models and datasets. But, in most cases, a social context needs to be identified to decide whether some assessment criteria are well justified or whether that criteria can be considered misleading. In this section, tools to assess the (social) context of an AI system are discussed.

16.5.1 Assessment List for Trustworthy AI

We start by commenting that one of the first tools to assess trustworthy AI was introduced by the EGTAI. The EGTAI introduced the so-called Assessment List for Trustworthy AI (ALTAI) for self-assessment [56]. The ALTAI contains a set of qualitative questions for each of the principles of the EGTAI. The questions look for evidence to assess compliance with the seven trustworthy principles introduced by the EGTAI. The ALTAI is a holistic qualitative assessment tool that aims to assess technical and nontechnical aspects of an AI system. Hence, the ALTAI cannot be answered by a unique stakeholder; to assess an AI system following the ALTAI tool, a group of experts should be created and these experts should represent different stakeholders. Examples of these stakeholders are [56]:

- designers and developers of the AI system;
- data scientists;
- procurement officers or specialists;
- front-end staff who will use or work with the AI system;
- legal/compliance officers; and
- management.

The technical background of these experts explicitly suggests that an AI system cannot be seen only as a technological artifact. By having a multidisciplinary group, the assessment will be less biased toward a particular dimensionality of the system.

Although the ALTAI tool can offer a holistic assessment of an AI system, it only collects qualitative evidence. Hence, an interpretation of that evidence is required. A possible strategy for the analysis of the evidence collected by the ALTAI tool is to organize group discussions between the stakeholders that are part of the AI ecosystem.

16.5.2 An Abbreviated Assessment List to Support the Responsible Development and Use of AI

The ALTAI tool is an intensive tool that contains more than 130 questions. This can be a problem for a quick assessment of an AI system or AI prototypes. Reduced versions of the ALTAI tool have been introduced in the literature. One of these is the Abbreviated Assessment List to Support the Responsible Development and Use of AI [49]. This abbreviated assessment list supports organizations to perform a "quick scan" of an AI system they want to develop, procure, deploy, or use. This quick-scan list is a self-assessment tool to identify the relevant elements of responsible AI and the level of adherence to these elements. It helps to determine the level of impact of AI applications and provides options to balance different tensions and interests. The assessment is based on a set of 15 questions grouped into 3 topics:

- impact on citizens and society;
- technology; and
- governance.

All questions are answered with a simple three-point scale, indicating to what extent the criteria are met. This tool does not fully measure the "quality" of an AI system, but reflects the understanding and concern regarding its trustworthiness by the organization. This quick-scan list should also not be taken as a complete in-depth assessment or by any means as evidence of legal compliance. This abbreviated assessment can provide developers, auditors, and users a quick overview of the potential impact of an AI system, but is not meant to replace the full assessment.

16.5.3 ACROCPoLis

The ALTAI tools and their reduced versions aim to recollect evidence for the assessment of AI systems along different dimensions. The participation of different experts is recommended when using these tools. In the process of analyzing the evidence collected by these kinds of tools, a shared vocabulary to characterize different situations is needed. A vocabulary tool that has been introduced to characterize the social context of an AI system is the Actors, Context, Resources, Outcome, Criteria, Power, and Links (ACROCPoLis) Framework [6]. By applying ACROCPoLis, it becomes possible (1) to compare analogous situations; (2) to highlight the relevant differences in dissimilar situations; and, in cases of conflicting fairness assessments, (3) to capture differing interpretations of the same situation by different stakeholders – thus organizing the discussion and pointing to the relevant points of disagreement between the parts.

The ACROCPoLis framework was introduced in the scope of fairness assessment, but it offers a dynamic methodology for aggregating different assessments of an AI system. The ACROCPoLis framework serves as a robust analytical tool that deepens our understanding of the complexities inherent in AI assessments. It achieves this by precisely identifying the relevant actors, their capacity to influence the process, and the broader contextual factors that collectively shape the observed outcomes.

The components of the ACROCPoLis framework are summarized as follows:

- **Actors:** Who is involved in or affected by the automated process of an AI system?
- **Contex:** Which contextual and structural aspects impact the automated process?
- **Resources:** Which elements does the automated process allocate or distribute?
- **Outcome:** What is the final result of the automated process?
- **Criteria:** Which attributes are intended to influence the outcome?
- **Power:** Which actors can explicitly affect the process and how?
- **Links:** In which ways are the other ACROCPoLis components interconnected?

Describing the various interconnections between components of an AI system is a key part of any application of ACROCPoLis. The links can be understood as shown in Figure 16.1. Power belongs to the actors that can use it, and power can modify the context that the actors exist in. The context and the actors both influence the criteria, while power modifies the criteria – the criteria, in their turn, determine the outcome. Criteria includes different kinds of data and the data determines outcome. An outcome

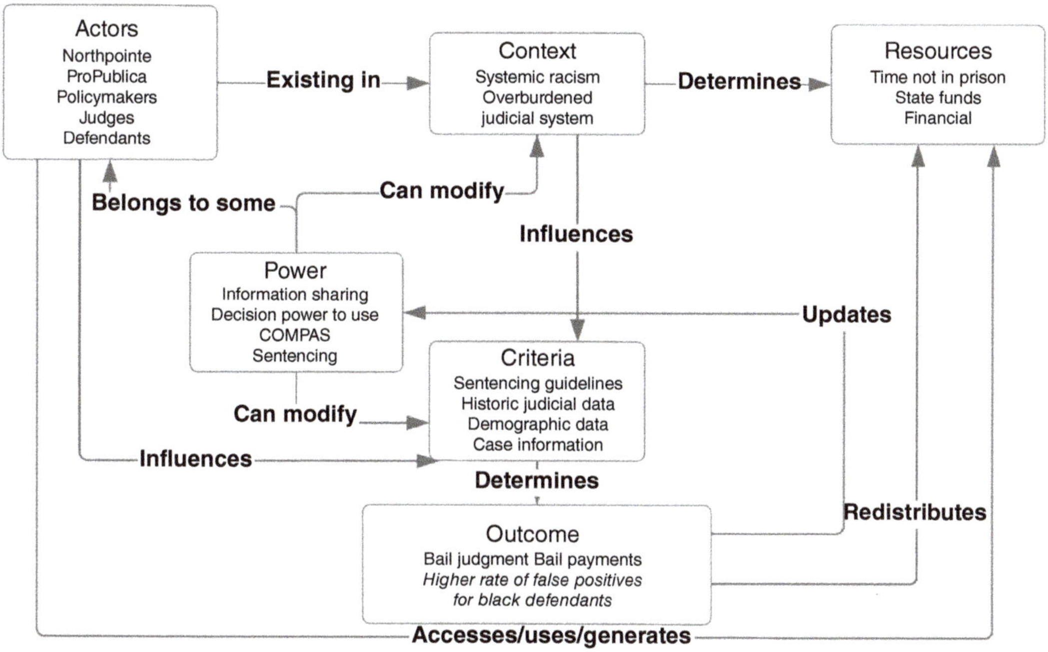

Figure 16.1 ACROCPoLis framework characterizing some elements of the COMPAS case [6].

can update the power, and also redistribute the resources that are determined by the context and used, accessed, or generated by the actors.

Figure 16.1 also illustrates different elements of the well-known Correctional Offender Management Profiling for Alternative Sanctions (COMPAS) case [9], where an AI decision support system ostensibly evaluated the recidivism risk of court defendants based on various demographic data. In an exposé by ProPublica, the system was found to yield different results based on race, in effect recommending harsher penalties and higher bail payments for black people than white people. In particular, the perspectives of both Northpointe (the company that built the COMPAS system) and ProPublica are framed through the links of the ACROCPoLis framework.

16.6 Questions and Exercises

1. Describe the general purpose of the following three categories of AI assessment tools:
   (a) Data assessment tools.
   (b) AI model assessment tools.
   (c) Social-impact assessment tools.
2. Describe when Datasheets for Datasets (DSDs) should be answered.
3. What is the main information that DSDs elicit?
4. Describe the main difference between "disparate treatment" and "disparate impact?"

5. If an AI model is developed by not knowing the ground-truth data, which kind of fairness assessment can be used? And what kind of problems may that fairness assessment have?
6. Which are the trustworthy AI principles that the ALTAI tool assesses?
7. Who should answer the ALTAI tool?
8. What are the main differences between the ALTAI tool and ACROCPoLis framework?

References

[1] ACLU. Face recognition technology. Available at: https://bit.ly/4rr7HQl, 2026.

[2] ACM. ACM code of ethics and professional conduct. Available at: www.acm.org/code-of-ethics, 2018.

[3] Ahmed Al Kuwaiti, Khalid Nazer, Abdullah Al-Reedy, et al. A review of the role of artificial intelligence in healthcare. *Journal of Personalized Medicine*, 13(6):951, 2023.

[4] AI100 2021 Study Panel. The One Hundred Year Study on Artificial Intelligence (AI100) 2021 Study Panel Report. Available at: https://ai100.stanford.edu/sites/g/files/sbiybj18871/files/media/file/AI100Report_MT_10.pdf, 2021.

[5] The AI Navigator. AI timeline: a journey through the history of artificial intelligence. Available at: www.theainavigator.com/ai-timeline, 2026.

[6] Andrea Aler Tubella, Dimitri Coelho Mollo, Adam Dahlgren Lindström, et al. ACROCPoLis: a descriptive framework for making sense of fairness. In *Proceedings of the 2023 ACM Conference on Fairness, Accountability, and Transparency*, pp. 1014–1025, 2023. ACM.

[7] Ibrahim Alhassan, David Sammon, and Mary Daly. Data governance activities: an analysis of the literature. *Journal of Decision Systems*, 25(suppl.1):64–75, 2016.

[8] Saleema Amershi, Dan Weld, Mihaela Vorvoreanu, et al. Guidelines for human–AI interaction. In *Proceedings of the 2019 CHI Conference on Human Factors in Computing Systems*, pp. 1–13, 2019.

[9] Julia Angwin, Jeff Larson, Surya Mattu, and Lauren Kirchner. Machine bias: There's software used across the country to predict future criminals – and it's biased against blacks. ProPublica. Available at: www.propublica.org/article/machine-bias-risk-assessments-in-criminal-sentencing, 2016.

[10] B. B. Arcila. AI liability in Europe: how does it complement risk governance? *Computer Law and Security Review*, 54: 106012, 2024.

[11] Sherry R. Arnstein. A ladder of citizen participation. *Journal of the American Institute of Planners*, 35(4):216–224, 1969.

[12] Alejandro Barredo Arrieta, Natalia Díaz-Rodríguez, Javier Del Ser, et al. Explainable artificial intelligence (XAI): concepts, taxonomies, opportunities and challenges toward responsible AI. *Information Fusion*, 58:82–115, 2020.

[13] Edmond Awad, Sohan Dsouza, Richard Kim, et al. The Moral Machine experiment. *Nature*, 563(7729):59–64, 2018.

[14] James Ayling and Alex Chapman. Putting AI ethics to work: are the tools fit for purpose? *AI Ethics*, 2:405–429, 2022.

[15] Tobias Baer and Vishnu Kamalnath. Controlling machine-learning algorithms and their biases. Available at: https://bit.ly/46C0fcN, 2017.

[16] Lisanne Bainbridge. Ironies of automation. In G. Johannsen and J.E. Rijnsdorp (eds.), *Analysis, Design and Evaluation of Man–Machine Systems*, pp. 129–135. Elsevier, 1983.

[17] Iain Barclay and Will Abramson. Identifying roles, requirements and responsibilities in trustworthy AI systems. In *Adjunct Proceedings of the 2021 ACM International Joint Conference on Pervasive and Ubiquitous Computing and Proceedings of the 2021 ACM International Symposium on Wearable Computers*, pp. 264–271, 2021.

[18] Gordon Baxter and Ian Sommerville. Socio-technical systems: from design methods to systems engineering. *Interacting with Computers*, 23(1):4–17, 2011.

[19] Reuben Binns. Data protection impact assessments: a meta-regulatory approach. *International Data Privacy Law*, 7(1):22–35, 2017.

[20] Reuben Binns. Fairness in machine learning: Lessons from political philosophy. In *Proceedings of the 2018 Conference on Fairness, Accountability, and Transparency*, pp. 149–159, 2018.

[21] R. A. Brooks. New approaches to robotics. *Science*, 253(5025):1227–1232, 1991.

[22] Joanna J. Bryson. Robots should be slaves. In Yorick Wilks (ed.), *Close Engagements with Artificial Companions: Key Social, Psychological, Ethical and Design Issues*, pp. 63–74. John Benjamins Publishing, 2010.

[23] Joanna J. Bryson. The Making of the EPSRC Principles of Robotics. *The AISB Quarterly*, 133:14–15, 2012.

[24] Joanna J. Bryson. Patiency is not a virtue: the design of intelligent systems and systems of ethics. *Ethics and Information Technology*, 20(1):15–26, 2018.

[25] Joanna J. Bryson, Mihailis E. Diamantis, and Thomas D. Grant. Of, for, and by the people: the legal lacuna of synthetic persons. *Artificial Intelligence and Law*, 25(3):273–291, 2017.

[26] Joanna J. Bryson and Andreas Theodorou. How society can maintain human-centric artificial intelligence. In Maria Toivonen and Eveliina Saari (eds.), *Human-Centered Digitalization and Services*, pp. 305–323. Springer Nature, 2019.

[27] Jean Burgess. Everyday data cultures: beyond big critique and the technological sublime. *AI & Society*, 38(3):1243–1244, 2023.

[28] Christopher Burton, Aurora Szentagotai Tatar, Brian McKinstry, et al. Pilot randomised controlled trial of help4mood, an embodied virtual agent-based system to support treatment of depression. *Journal of Telemedicine and Telecare*, 22(4):348–355, 2015.

[29] Guillaume Cachat-Rosset and Alain Klarsfeld. Diversity, equity, and inclusion in artificial intelligence. *Applied Artificial Intelligence*, 37(1):216–238, 2023.

[30] Roberta Calegari and Virginia Dignum. Defining responsible AI. AI Policy Exchange Forum (AIPEX). Available at: https://aipolicylab.se/2024/06/24/defining-responsible-ai-2/, 2024.

[31] Gillian Cameron, David Cameron, Gavin Megaw, et al. Towards a chatbot for digital counselling. In *Proceedings of the 31st International BCS Human Computer Interaction Conference (HCI 2017)*, pp. 1–7. 2017. ACM.

[32] Luciano Cavalcante Siebert, Maria Luce Lupetti, Evgeni Aizenberg, et al. Meaningful human control: actionable properties for AI system development. *AI and Ethics*, 3(1):241–255, 2023.

[33] Stephen Cave, Kanta Dihal, and Sarah Dillon (eds). *AI, Narratives: A History of Imaginative Thinking about Intelligent Machines*. Oxford University Press, 2020.

[34] Seunghwan Cho, Ingyu Kim, Jinhan Kim, Honguk Woo, and Wanseon Shin. A maturity model for trustworthy AI software development. *Applied Sciences*, 13(8):4771, 2023.

[35] Mark Coeckelbergh. *AI Ethics*. MIT Press, 2020.

[36] Helena Cools, Bald Van Gorp, and Maarten Opgenhaffen. Where exactly between utopia and dystopia? A framing analysis of AI and automation in US newspapers. *Journalism*, 25(1):3–21, 2024.

[37] Corporate Europe Observatory. Lobbying the AI Act: Big Tech's push to gut the EU's landmark AI law. Available at: www.corporateeurope.org, 2021.

[38] Sasha Costanza-Chock. *Design Justice: Community-Led Practices to Build the Worlds We Need*. MIT Press, 2020.

[39] Kate Crawford. *The Atlas of AI*. Yale University Press, 2021.

[40] Kevin Crowston and Jian Qin. A capability maturity model for scientific data management: evidence from the literature. *Proceedings of the American Society for Information Science and Technology*, 48(1):1–9, 2011.

[41] Robert A. Dahl. *Democracy and Its Critics*. Yale University Press, 1989.

[42] Karin Danielsson, Andrea Aler Tubella, Evelina Liliequist, and Coppélie Cocq. Queer eye on AI: binary systems versus fluid identities. In Simon Lindgren (ed.), *Handbook of Critical Studies of Artificial Intelligence*, pp. 595–606. Edward Elgar Publishing, 2023.

[43] Danish Institute for Human Rights. Human rights impact assessment guidance and toolbox. www.humanrights.dk/tools/human-rights-impact-assessment-guidance-toolbox, 2020.

[44] Sanobar Dar, Victoria Lush, and Ulysses Bernardet. The virtual human breathing relaxation system. In *2019 5th Experiment International Conference (exp. at'19)*, pp. 276–277. IEEE.

[45] Jovana Davidovic. On the purpose of meaningful human control of AI. *Frontiers in Big Data*, 5:1017677, 2023.

[46] Digital Decarbonisation. Data carbon scorecard. Available at: https://digitaldecarb.org/data-carbon-scorecard/, 2024.

[47] Kate Devlin and Olivia Belton. Fembots, fact and fiction. In Stephen Cave, Kanta Dihal, and Sarah Dillon (eds.), *AI Narratives: A History of Imaginative Thinking about Intelligent Machines*, p. 357, Oxford University Press, 2020.

[48] Nicholas Diakopoulos. Accountability in algorithmic decision making. *Communications of the ACM*, 59(2):56–62, 2016.

[49] Virginia Dignum, J.C. Nieves, A. Theodorou, and A. Aler Tubella. An abbreviated assessment list to support the responsible development and use of AI. Technical report, Responsible Artificial Intelligence Group, Department of Computing Sciences, Umeå University, 2021.

[50] Virginia Dignum. Responsible autonomy. In *Proceedings of the International Joint Conference on Artificial Intelligence*, pp. 4698–4704, 2017.

[51] Virginia Dignum. *Responsible Artificial Intelligence*. Springer, 2019.

[52] Kanta Dihal and Tania Duarte. Better images of AI: a guide for users and creators. *The Leverhulme Centre for the Future of Intelligence and We and AI*. Available at: https://blog.betterimagesofai.org/wp-content/uploads/2023/02/Better-Images-of-AI-Guide-Feb-23.pdf, 2023.

[53] Martin Ebers and Susana Navas (eds). *Algorithms and Law*. Cambridge University Press, 2020.

[54] Virginia Eubanks. *Automating Inequality: How High-Tech Tools Profile, Police, and Punish the Poor*. St. Martin's Press, 2018.

[55] European Commission. Ethics guidelines for trustworthy AI. Available at: https://ec.europa.eu/digital-single-market/en/news/ethics-guidelines-trustworthy-ai, 2019.

[56] European Commission. Assessment list for trustworthy artificial intelligence (ALTAI) for self-assessment. Available at: https://bit.ly/4cYtFFQ, 2020.

[57] European Parliament. Regulation (EU) 2016/679: General Data Protection Regulation. *Official Journal of the European Union*, 119:1–88, 2018.

[58] European Union. Data Protection Impact Assessment (DPIA). Available at: https://gdpr.eu/data-protection-impact-assessment-template, 2026.

[59] Jorge Fandinno and Claudia Schulz. Answering the "why" in answer set programming: a survey of explanation approaches. *Theory and Practice of Logic Programming*, 19(2):114–203, 2019.

[60] Kathleen Kara Fitzpatrick, Alison Darcy, and Molly Vierhile. Delivering cognitive behavior therapy to young adults with symptoms of depression and anxiety using a fully automated conversational agent (Eoebot): a randomized controlled trial. *JMIR Mental Health*, 4(2):e19, 2017.

[61] Luciano Floridi. *The Fourth Revolution: How the Infosphere is Reshaping Human Reality*. Oxford University Press, 2014.

[62] Luciano Floridi. What the near future of artificial intelligence could be: three scenarios. *Philosophy & Technology*, 32:123–136, 2019.

[63] Luciano Floridi, Josh Cowls, Monica Beltrametti, et al. AI4People: an ethical framework for a good AI society: opportunities, risks, principles, and recommendations. *Minds and Machines*, 28(4):689–707, 2018.

[64] Timnit Gebru, Jamie Morgenstern, Briana Vecchione, et al. Datasheets for datasets. *Communications of the ACM*, 64(12):86–92, 2021.

[65] Stefanos Georgiou, Maria Kechagia, Tushar Sharma, Federica Sarro, and Ying Zou. Green AI: do deep learning frameworks have different costs? In *Proceedings of the 44th International Conference on Software Engineering*, pp. 1082–1094, 2022. ACM.

[66] Armin Grunwald. Technology assessment: concepts and methods. In Anthonie Meijers (ed.), *Philosophy of Technology and Engineering Sciences*, pp. 1103–1146. North-Holland, 2009.

[67] Xiaoyang Guo and Yi Zeng. Body metaphors in science fiction narratives: a proposal for challenging stereotypes of robots in narrative. *AI & Society*, 44:279–288, 2026.

[68] Allam Hamdan, Aboul Ella Hassanien, Reem Khamis, et al. *Applications of Artificial Intelligence in Business, Education and Healthcare*. Springer, 2021.

[69] Irina Hermann. Artificial intelligence in fiction: between narratives and metaphors. *AI & Society*, 38:319–329, 2023.

[70] Noreen Herzfeld. Creating in our own image: artificial intelligence and the image of god. *Zygon*®, 37(2):303–316, 2002.

[71] Noreen Herzfeld. The sorcery of artificial intelligence (AI). Available at: https://digitalcommons.csbsju.edu/cgi/viewcontent.cgi?article=1000&context=reuter_pubs, 2018.

[72] High-Level Expert Group on Artificial Intelligence (AI HLEG). Ethics guidelines for trustworthy AI. European Commission. https://digital-strategy.ec.europa.eu/en/library/ethics-guidelines-trustworthy-ai, 2019.

[73] Kenneth Einar Himma. Artificial agency, consciousness, and the criteria for moral agency: what properties must an artificial agent have to be a moral agent? *Ethics and Information Technology*, 11(1):19–29, 2009.

[74] AI HLEG. Ethics guidelines for trustworthy artificial intelligence. Available at: https://digital-strategy.ec.europa.eu/en/library/ethics-guidelines-trustworthy-ai, 2019.

[75] Ellen Hohma and Christoph Lütge. From trustworthy principles to a trustworthy development process: the need and elements of trusted development of AI systems. *AI*, 4(4):904–925, 2023.

[76] Evan Hubinger, Carson Denison, Jesse Mu, et al. Sleeper agents: training deceptive LLMs that persist through safety training. *arXiv preprint arXiv:2401.05566*, 2024.

[77] DAMA International. *DAMA-DMBOK* (2nd ed.). Data Management Association, 2017.

[78] International Federation of Accountants. Defining and developing an effective code of conduct for organizations. Available at: https://bit.ly/3OTUfWF, 2007.

[79] Marijn Janssen, Paul Brous, Elsa Estevez, Luis S. Barbosa, and Tomasz Janowski. Data governance: organizing data for trustworthy artificial intelligence. *Government Information Quarterly*, 37(3):101493, 2020.

[80] Nidhal Jegham, Marwan Abdelatti, Lassad Elmoubarki, and Abdeltawab Hendawi. How hungry is AI? Benchmarking energy, water, and carbon footprint of LLM inference. *arXiv preprint arXiv:2505.09598*, 2025.

[81] Beverly K. Kahn, Diane M. Strong, and Richard Y. Wang. Information quality benchmarks: product and service performance. *Communications of the ACM*, 45(4):184–192, 2002.

[82] Faisal Kamiran, Asim Karim, and Xiangliang Zhang. Decision theory for discrimination-aware classification. In *2012 IEEE 12th International Conference on Data Mining*, pp. 924–929, 2012. IEEE.

[83] Toshihiro Kamishima, Shotaro Akaho, and Jun Sakuma. Fairness-aware learning through regularization approach. In *2011 IEEE 11th International Conference on Data Mining Workshops*, pp. 643–650, 2011. IEEE.

[84] Immanuel Kant. *Groundwork of the Metaphysics of Morals*, (trans. and ed. M. Gregor). Cambridge University Press, 1997. (Original work published 1785.)

[85] Vijay Khatri and Carol V. Brown. Designing data governance. *Communications of the ACM*, 53(1):148–152, 2010.

[86] Jon M. Kleinberg, Sendhil Mullainathan, and Manish Raghavan. Inherent trade-offs in the fair determination of risk scores. In *Proceedings of the 8th Innovations in Theoretical Computer Science Conference*, pp. 1–23, 2017.

[87] Ramya Kondapi, Rahul Kumar Katta, and Sirisha Potluri. Pacifiurr: an android chatbot application for human interaction. *International Journal of Recent Technology and Engineering*, 7(5S2):101–104, 2019.

[88] Stefan Leijnen, Huib Aldewereld, Rudy van Belkom, Roland Bijvank, and Roelant Ossewaarde. An agile framework for trustworthy AI. In *Proceedings of the New Foundations for Human-Centered AI*, pp. 75–78, 2020.

[89] Qinghua Lu, Liming Zhu, Xiwei Xu, et al. Software engineering for responsible AI: an empirical study and operationalised patterns. In *Proceedings of the 44th International Conference on Software Engineering: Software Engineering in Practice*, pp. 241–242, 2022.

[90] Alexandra S. Luccioni, Sylvain Viguier, and Anne-Laure Ligozat. Estimating the carbon footprint of bloom, a 176b parameter language model. *Journal of Machine Learning Research*, 24(253): 1–15, 2023.

[91] Sasha Luccioni, Yacine Jernite, and Emma Strubell. Power hungry processing: watts driving the cost of AI deployment? In *Proceedings of the 2024 ACM Conference on Fairness, Accountability, and Transparency*, pp. 85–99, 2024.

[92] Kien Hoa Ly, Ann-Marie Ly, and Gerhard Andersson. A fully automated conversational agent for promoting mental well-being: a pilot RCT using mixed methods. *Internet Interventions*, 10:39–46, 2017.

[93] Juan Martínez-Miranda, Ariadna Martínez, Roberto Ramos, et al. Assessment of users' acceptability of a mobile-based embodied conversational agent for the prevention and detection of suicidal behaviour. *Journal of Medical Systems*, 43(8):246, 2019.

[94] Curtis McCord. Civic tech in Toronto: public participation and smart city development. University of Toronto. Available at: https://utoronto.scholaris.ca/bitstreams/4ebe011e-0a4d-440c-b848-1593a42dd98a/download, 2021.

[95] Ninareh Mehrabi, Fred Morstatter, Nripsuta Saxena, Kristina Lerman, and Aram Galstyan. A survey on bias and fairness in machine learning. *ACM Computing Surveys*, 54(6):35, 2022.

[96] Sabelo Mhlambi and Simona Tiribelli. Decolonizing AI ethics: relational autonomy as a means to counter AI harms. *Topoi*, 42(3):867–880, 2023.

[97] Paul Milgram, Haruo Takemura, Akira Utsumi, and Fumio Kishino. Augmented reality: a class of displays on the reality–virtuality continuum. In *Proceedings of the Telemanipulator and Telepresence Technologies*, volume 2351, pp. 282–292. 1995. SPIE.

[98] Christopher A. Miller. Delegation and transparency: coordinating interactions so information exchange is no surprise. In R. Shumaker and S. Lackey (eds.), *Virtual, Augmented, and Mixed Reality: Designing and Developing Virtual and Augmented Environments*, pp. 191–202. Springer, 2014.

[99] Tim Miller. Explanation in artificial intelligence: insights from the social sciences. *Artificial Intelligence*, 267:1–38, 2017.

[100] Margaret Mitchell, Simone Wu, Andrew Zaldivar, et al. Model cards for model reporting. In *Proceedings of the Conference on Fairness, Accountability, and Transparency*, pp. 220–229, 2019. ACM.

[101] Tom M. Mitchell. *Artificial Intelligence: A Guide for Thinking Humans*. Penguin Books, 2019.

[102] J. H. Moor. The nature, importance, and difficulty of machine ethics. *IEEE Intelligent Systems*, 21(4):18–21, 2006.

[103] Marçal Mora-Cantallops, Salvador Sánchez-Alonso, Elena García-Barriocanal, and Miguel-Angel Sicilia. Traceability for trustworthy AI: a review of models and tools. *Big Data and Cognitive Computing*, 5(2):20, 2021.

[104] Ramaravind K. Mothilal, Amit Sharma, and Chenhao Tan. Explaining machine learning classifiers through diverse counterfactual explanations. In *Proceedings of the 2020 Conference on Fairness, Accountability, and Transparency*, pp. 607–617, 2020.

[105] S. Moulya and T. R. Pragathi. Mental health assist and diagnosis conversational interface using logistic regression model for emotion and sentiment analysis. *Journal of Physics: Conference Series*, 2161:012039, 2022.

[106] Jaya Narain, Tina Quach, Monique Davey, et al. Promoting wellbeing with Sunny, a chatbot that facilitates positive messages within social groups. In *Extended Abstracts of the 2020 CHI Conference on Human Factors in Computing Systems*, pp. 1–8, 2020. ACM.

[107] Meike Nauta, Jan Trienes, Shreyasi Pathak, et al. From anecdotal evidence to quantitative evaluation methods: a systematic review on evaluating explainable AI. *ACM Computing Surveys*, 55(13s):1–42, 2023.

[108] Musange Furere S, Absolomon G, Umutoni N, Matutina Umuhoza S, K Rubuga F, Nsaba-Uwera YD, Singa Muhoza P, Hitimana R, Condo J, Humuza J

[109] Digital Primary Health in Rwanda: Qualitative Study of User Experiences and Implementation Lessons From Babyl's Telemedicine Platform J Med Internet Res 2026;28:e84832 doi: 10.2196/84832

[110] Cathy O'Neil. *Weapons of Math Destruction: How Big Data Increases Inequality and Threatens Democracy*. Crown Publishing Group, 2016.

[111] OECD. OECD AI Principles overview. Available at: https://oecd.ai/en/ai-principles, 2019.

[112] Ugo Pagallo, Paolo Aurucci, Pompeu Casanovas, et al. AI4People: on good AI governance – 14 priority actions, a SMART model of governance, and a regulatory toolbox. Available at: https://ai4people.org/PDF/AI4People_On_Good_AI_Governance.pdf, 2019.

[113] SoHyun Park, Jeewon Choi, Sungwoo Lee, et al. Designing a chatbot for a brief motivational interview on stress management: qualitative case study. *Journal of Medical Internet Research*, 21(4):e12231, 2019.

[114] Falguni Patel, Riya Thakore, Ishita Nandwani, and Santosh Kumar Bharti. Combating depression in students using an intelligent chatbot: a cognitive behavioral therapy. In *Proceedings of the 2019 IEEE 16th India Council International Conference (INDICON)*, pp. 1–4, 2019. IEEE.

[115] Dana Pessach and Erez Shmueli. Algorithmic fairness. In Lior Rokach, Oded Maimon, and Erez Shmueli (eds.), *Machine Learning for Data Science Handbook: Data Mining and Knowledge Discovery Handbook*, pp. 867–886. Springer, 2023.

[116] Stephen R. Piccolo and Michael B. Frampton. Tools and techniques for computational reproducibility. *Gigascience*, 5(1):s13742–016, 2016.

[117] Steven Pinker. *The Language Instinct*. William Morrow and Company, 1994.

[118] Leo L. Pipino, Yang W. Lee, and Richard Y. Wang. Data quality assessment. *Communications of the ACM*, 45(4):211–218, 2002.

[119] Iyad D. Raji, Abeba Smart, Ruha White, et al. Closing the AI accountability gap: defining an end-to-end framework for internal algorithmic auditing. In *Proceedings of the 2020 Conference on Fairness, Accountability, and Transparency*, pp. 33–44, 2020.

[120] Gabriel Recchia. The fall and rise of AI: investigating AI narratives with computational methods. In Stephen Cave, Kanta Dihal, and Sarah Dillon (eds.), *AI Narratives: A History of Imaginative Thinking about Intelligent Machines*. Oxford University Press, 2020.

[121] Catherine Régis, Jean-Louis Denis, Maria Luciana Axente, and Atsuo Kishimoto. *Human-Centered AI: A Multidisciplinary Perspective for Policy-Makers, Auditors, and Users*. Taylor & Francis, 2024.

[122] Marco Tulio Ribeiro, Sameer Singh, and Carlos Guestrin. "Why should I trust you?": explaining the predictions of any classifier. In *Proceedings of the 22nd ACM SIGKDD*

International Conference on Knowledge Discovery and Data Mining, pp 1135–1144, 2016.

[123] Gene Rowe and Lynn J. Frewer. Public participation methods: a framework for evaluation. *Science, Technology, & Human Values*, 25(1):3–29, 2000.

[124] Stuart J. Russell and Peter Norvig. *Artificial Intelligence: A Modern Approach* (4th ed.) Pearson, 2021.

[125] Burkhard Schafer and Lilian Edwards. "I spy, with my little sensor": fair data handling practices for robots between privacy, copyright and security. *Connection Science*, 29(3):200–209, 2017.

[126] Andrew D. Selbst, Danah Boyd, Sorelle A. Friedler, Suresh Venkatasubramanian, and Janet Vertesi. Fairness and abstraction in sociotechnical systems. In *Proceedings of the Conference on Fairness, Accountability, and Transparency*, pp. 59–68, 2019. ACM.

[127] Mahsa Shabani, Adrian Thorogood, and Madeleine Murtagh. *Data Access Governance*. In Graeme Laurie, Edward Dove, Agomoni Ganguli-Mitra, et al. (eds.), *Health Research Regulation*, pp. 187–196. Cambridge University Press, 2021.

[128] Rifat Ara Shams, Didar Zowghi, and Muneera Bano. AI and the quest for diversity and inclusion: a systematic literature review. *Ethics and Information Technology*, 5:411–438, 2025.

[129] Bhuvan Sharma, Harshita Puri, and Deepika Rawat. Digital psychiatry: curbing depression using therapy chatbot and depression analysis. In *Proceedings of the 2018 Second International Conference on Inventive Communication and Computational Technologies (ICICCT)*, pp. 627–631, 2018. IEEE.

[130] Renee Shelby, Shalaleh Rismani, Kathryn Henne, et al. Sociotechnical harms of algorithmic systems: scoping a taxonomy for harm reduction. In *Proceedings of the 2023 AAAI/ACM Conference on AI, Ethics, and Society*, pp. 723–741, 2023. ACM.

[131] Aram Sinnreich and Jesse Gilbert. *The Secret Life of Data: Navigating Hype and Uncertainty in the Age of Algorithmic Surveillance*. MIT Press, 2024.

[132] Peter Slattery, Alexander K. Saeri, Emily A. C. Grundy, et al. The AI risk repository: a comprehensive meta-review, database, and taxonomy of risks from artificial intelligence. *arXiv preprint arXiv:2408.12622*, 2024.

[133] Nathalie A. Smuha. Beyond the individual: governing AI's societal harm. *Internet Policy Review*, 10(3), 2021.

[134] Shinichiro Suganuma, Daisuke Sakamoto, and Haruhiko Shimoyama. An embodied conversational agent for unguided internet-based cognitive behavior therapy in preventative mental health: feasibility and acceptability pilot trial. *JMIR Mental Health*, 5(3):e10454, 2018.

[135] Jamie Susskind. *Future Politics: Living Together in a World Transformed by Tech*. Oxford University Press, 2020.

[136] Andreas Theodorou, Robert H. Wortham, and Joanna J. Bryson. Designing and implementing transparency for real time inspection of autonomous robots. *Connection Science*, 29(3):230–241, 2017.

[137] Elliot Turiel. *The Culture of Morality*. Cambridge University Press, 2001.

[138] TV Tropes. TV tropes: an online wiki for media tropes. Available at: http://tvtropes.org, 2026.

[139] UNESCO. Artificial intelligence and emerging technologies. www.unesco.org/en/artificial-intelligence/recommendation-ethics, 2026.

[140] United Nations. About the UN Secretary-General's High-level Advisory Body on AI. Available at: www.un.org/en/ai-advisory-body/about, 2024.

[141] United Nations. Sustainable Development Goals: 7 goals to transform out world. Available at: www.un.org/sustainabledevelopment/

[142] Berk Ustun, Yang Liu, and David Parkes. Fairness without harm: decoupled classifiers with preference guarantees. In *Proceedings of the International Conference on Machine Learning*, pp. 6373–6382, 2019. PMLR.

[143] Moshe Y. Vardi. Artificial intelligence: past and future. *Communications ACM* 55(1): 5, 2012.

[144] Sahil Verma and Julia Rubin. Fairness definitions explained. In *Proceedings of the International Workshop on Software Fairness*, pp. 1–7, 2018. ACM.

[145] Ricardo Vinuesa, Hossein Azizpour, Iolanda Leite, et al. The role of artificial intelligence in achieving the sustainable development goals. *Nature Communications*, 11(1):1–10, 2020.

[146] Riina Vuorikari Rina, Stefano Kluzer, and Yves Punie. Digcomp 2.2: the digital competence framework for citizens – with new examples of knowledge, skills and attitudes. Technical report, Joint Research Centre, 2022.

[147] Laura Weidinger, John F. J. Mellor, Maribeth Rauh, et al. Ethical and social risks of harm from language models. *arXiv preprint arXiv:2112.04359*, 2021.

[148] Norbert Wiener. Some moral and technical consequences of automation. Science, 131(3410):1355–1358, 1960.

[149] Alan F. T. Winfield, Serena Booth, Louise A. Dennis, et al. IEEE P7001: a proposed standard on transparency. *Frontiers in Robotics and AI*, 8:665729, 2021.

[150] Carole-Jean Wu, Ramya Raghavendra, Udit Gupta, et al. Sustainable AI: environmental implications, challenges and opportunities. In *Proceedings of Machine Learning and Systems*, volume 4, pp. 795–813, 2022.

[151] John Zerilli. *A Citizen's Guide to Artificial Intelligence*. MIT Press, 2021.

[152] John Zerilli, Alistair Knott, James Maclaurin, and Colin Gavaghan. Algorithmic decision-making and the control problem. *Minds and Machines*, 29(4):555–578, 2019.

[153] Brian Hu Zhang, Blake Lemoine, and Margaret Mitchell. Mitigating unwanted biases with adversarial learning. In *Proceedings of the 2018 AAAI/ACM Conference on AI, Ethics, and Society*, pp. 335–340, 2018.

For EU product safety concerns, contact us at Calle de José Abascal, 56–1°,
28003 Madrid, Spain or eugpsr@cambridge.org.

www.ingramcontent.com/pod-product-compliance
Ingram Content Group UK Ltd.
Pitfield, Milton Keynes, MK11 3LW, UK
UKHW051836250926
475916UK00005B/291
9781009492867